Jack Toffey's War

Jack Toffey's War

A Son's Memoir

JOHN J. TOFFEY IV

FORDHAM UNIVERSITY PRESS

New York : 2008

Fordham University Press has no responsibility for the persistence or accuracy of URLs for
external or third-party internet websites referred to in this publication and does not
guarantee that any content on such websites is, or will remain, accurate or appropriate.

Library of Congress Cataloging-in-Publication Data

Toffey, John J., 1931–
    Jack Toffey's war : a son's memoir / John J. Toffey IV.—1st ed.
        p.   cm.—(World War II : the global, human, and ethical dimension)
    Includes bibliographical references and index.
    ISBN 978–0-8232–2979–6 (cloth : alk. paper)
    1. Toffey, John James, 1907–1944.   2. World War, 1939–1945—
Campaigns—Mediterranean Region.   3. World War, 1939–1945—Campaigns—
Africa, North.   4. World War, 1939–1945—Campaigns—Italy.   5. United States.
Army—Biography.   6. Soldiers—United States—Biography. I. Title.
D766.T64   2008
940.54′1273092—dc22
[B]

                                                                    2008026059

                    Printed in the United States of America
                          10 09 08   5 4 3 2 1
                                First edition

With love I dedicate this book
to my late wife,
Irene Tobin Toffey,
and to the grandchildren and great-grandchildren of
Lt. Col. John J. Toffey Jr., who never got to know him.

CONTENTS

Preface   ix

Acknowledgments   xv

Chapter 1. The First Letter   1

Chapter 2. Young Jack   11

Chapter 3. Fort Dix and the Forty-fourth Division   22

Chapter 4. Coast to Coast, 1942   39

Chapter 5. French Morocco   56

Chapter 6. Tunisia   73

Chapter 7. Algerian Interlude   86

Chapter 8. Sicily   99

Chapter 9. Summer Interludes   116

Chapter 10. Southern Italy   129

Chapter 11. Italian Interlude   149

Chapter 12. Anzio: The Can-Dos   161

Chapter 13. Anzio: The Willing and Ables   181

Chapter 14. The Roads to Rome   197

Chapter 15. The Paths of Glory   210

Epilogue   229

Notes   235

Sources   253

Index   261

On Memorial Day 2004, our bus followed its escort of local police through the main gate of the Sicily–Rome American Cemetery at Nettuno, Italy. The hum of conversation that had filled the bus since we left our hotel suddenly ceased as we began our slow progress beside the symmetrical rows of white crosses. At the rear of the marble memorial building, the bus parked in the shade of some umbrella pines, and we followed our guide to reserved seats under a white canopy in front of the building. Lawns, gardens, paths, and gravestones had been made to look their best under the Mediterranean sun. It was a beautiful morning in a lovely and serene place. In a less troubled world, the snipers atop the memorial building would have seemed out of place.

My sister, my wife, our granddaughter, and I were part of a tour put together by veterans of the Italian campaign who were returning to commemorate the sixtieth anniversary of the Anzio beachhead and the liberation of Rome. My father had fought his way from French Morocco through Tunisia, Sicily, southern Italy, and the beachhead before he was killed just outside Rome. He is one of the 7,861 Americans buried in the place in which we were gathered for the Memorial Day ceremony. Anne, my sister, had been to the cemetery once fifty years ago; I had come twenty-two years ago. Irene, my wife, and Molly, my granddaughter, never had. The veterans, many of whom had family with them, were there because they had made it through the war. Anne, Irene, Molly, and I were there because my father hadn't.

Though I had begun to work on this book several years earlier, I hadn't really understood until that day in the cemetery why I had undertaken to write it. It was for the same reason that we were at the cemetery: because Dad hadn't come home from the war. Those who did had found admiring audiences for their stories. Men and women with literary credentials or aspirations published accounts of their experiences. As spokesmen for "the greatest generation," others talked to Tom Brokaw or to Stephen Ambrose or were interviewed on the History Channel. Perhaps others addressed their local historical societies or spoke to respectful townspeople at Veterans Day ceremonies. Still others found it sufficient to confide in their immediate families. Dad got to do none of these.

A couple of years earlier, a Ninth Division veteran asked why I had waited so long. I think he meant that because so many veterans were dying—a thousand a day, I read somewhere—I had missed the chance to talk to many of the men who had served with Dad. He was right. I often found myself wishing that I had had the chance to interview the general or lieutenant colonel or corporal or Red Cross worker I was writing about at the moment. During and just after the war, several men who had served with Dad had come to visit my mother, sister, and me, bringing news or anecdotes. Their visits were special because they had seen him more recently than we had. But they did all the talking, and I didn't know what questions to ask them.

Why did I wait so long? I had not considered writing about my father until I came into possession of Dad's letters as well as letters about him after my mother died in 1996. As I read them, I realized how little I knew beyond the basic details of his military service. I wanted to find out a great deal more about battles in which he had fought, his hospitalization after having been wounded, his return to combat, his transfer from the Ninth Division to the Third Division, and the circumstances surrounding his death.

As a boy and the son of a soldier, I thought I knew a lot about the war we were in. By the time Dad went overseas, I knew the difference between the light and heavy .30-caliber machine guns, the 105mm howitzer and the 155 "Long Tom," the P-47 and P-51, the B-25 and B-26. As the baseball players who had been my peacetime heroes went to war, generals replaced them in my personal pantheon. Some names I knew already. Marshall, MacArthur, and McNair had served with my grandfather in the Philippines or on the Mexican border, at Fort Benning or Schofield Barracks. The new commanders, too—Allen, Clark, Eddy, Eisenhower, Patton, and Truscott—seemed larger than life. So did Medal of Honor winners like Lieutenant Colonel Jimmy Doolittle and Private Rodger Young. The newspapers kept us in heroes.

But what we really wanted from the newspapers was news of Dad. My mother, sister, and I filled a scrapbook with stories of Dad's doings filed by various war correspondents. Then George Biddle published his *Artist at War*, in which the artist devotes seventy-two pages to the month he spent in Italy with Dad's battalion. In the years right after the war, the regiments and divisions in which Dad had served published their histories. For a high-school term-paper topic, I had chosen the Anzio beachhead. Those were the sources of what I knew about my father's service in the war, and that was a long time ago.

In 1998 I found Dad's name in Edwin P. Hoyt's *The GI's War: American Soldiers in Europe During World War II*. If Hoyt mentioned my father, might others have done so as well? I decided to learn a lot more about World War II, or at least the part of it in which my father had fought. As I began to read, one book led to another, one reference suggested another. The unpublished material—manuscripts, diaries, memorials, and other collected papers in various libraries and archives, too—might have something about my father that had not been of interest to the writer whose citation first called them to my attention. I would have to see for myself.

Nearly all the men my father's age or older who had been field-grade and general officers in the war were dead, but other veterans, of company grade or in the enlisted ranks in the war, were still around. Through the "alumni associations" of the Third and Ninth Infantry Divisions, I contacted several of them, and they were invariably willing to give me their recollections of my father. In person or by phone, letter, or email, I had wonderful conversations with these men. Talking with them brought back what I had felt a half-century earlier.

To learn more about my father's experiences in World War II, however, is not necessarily to write a book about them. I could have investigated to my satisfaction and then gone on about whatever else I was doing. But the accumulated material seemed to have a potential worth beyond answering my questions about what my father had done in the war. All the reading and rummaging had yielded hundreds of pages of notes. With the application of proper punctuation and appropriate transitional elements, these notes could become acceptable sentences, even prose.

My father's correspondence sometimes required explication. Some of it embellished images contained in the family folklore—nouns from my childhood. In reviewing remembrances of these things past, my sister and I could usually reach a consensus of two. Other references in the correspondence were to people and places of whom or which I had no current knowledge or recall. With Mother gone, her generation offered no authoritative spokesperson on our family's doings in the middle of the twentieth century.

Why did I wait so long? As a schoolteacher with classes to prepare, papers to grade, teams to coach, and meetings to attend, and as a husband and father helping Irene raise our four children, I could probably enter a plea of "too busy." Nevertheless, had I the intent back then, perhaps I could have done the job, but it would not have been the same job. Though I have probably forgot some anecdotes of family life and I have certainly missed some interview opportunities, I hope that I have brought to the subject a perspective that has improved with age.

It has been hard to reconstruct with absolute certainty what I thought or felt sixty or more years ago. With some notable exceptions, I don't know now what I knew or thought I knew then. Therefore, I have tried to present a narrative point of view that is appropriate to my age and maturity at the time under discussion while maintaining a fairly consistent and, in the literary sense, omniscient prose style.

The military history presented in this book is a synthesis of what I have learned in my research. I have provided this history as a convenience for the reader who is not a student of World War II in the Mediterranean Theater. It also provides a context in which to see my father in action and to read his letters. I have not attempted to correct or update history, only to find and tell one man's story in the midst of it. For the most part, I have tried to follow the mainstream of revealed historical events. However, I realize that there may be differing interpretations of some of the events mentioned herein. I acknowledge that in places I have selectively emphasized certain details to underscore something in the narrative. Nowhere, though, have I intentionally distorted or misrepresented events so as to mislead the reader.

I know that Dad, Mom, Anne, and I were but one family of the thousands set in motion by the mobilization of 1940. However, I do not think that we were terribly conscious of being part of a sociological phenomenon, and I do not presume to speak for any except our family. In fact, I was probably more aware of the people who were not on the move than I was of those who were. In the spring of 1942, when I got to the last of the five schools I was in that year, I think I found it odd that my classmates had been at the same desks in the same school for the entire year. The traveling that we did was the norm because it was what we were doing.

While living in Columbus during the war, I recall only one new family moving into our neighborhood. None of my friends in Columbus had a father in the service. The fathers of kids I knew, contemporaries of my father, were a little too old for conscription and had not chosen to enlist. The military tradition in which Dad grew up and that had led to his National Guard service made him and us different. Again, though, I did not dwell on why Dad was overseas while the fathers of my friends were at home. That was just the way things were.

I know, too, that we were luckier than many families on the move. We did have supportive family in Ohio and New York to whom Mom and Dad knew they could turn if the going got too rough. Without doubt, these strong family bonds, affording comfort and stability, meant a great deal in our lives. But for Anne and me there was a more immediate and more pervasive stability in the way Mom and Dad took care of us. We would not know if the going got too rough. What we did know was that they loved us and that they would take care of us, and we believed them when they told us that everything would be all right.

Because my father did not return from the war, then, I am telling his story. I suppose, too, that if one cannot entirely separate the teller from the tale, this is in some small way my story, as well. From records and recollections I have gathered the details that make up as much of the story as I can tell. As I tell it, I realize that among the interviews I missed is the most important one: the one with my father.

ACKNOWLEDGMENTS

First, it cannot go without saying that I am deeply indebted to my late wife, Irene, for her love and support in our nearly forty-eight years of marriage. Among the countless acts of kindness and of love was her reading this book in its early drafts and offering insightful suggestions. I hope she would approve of the result.

In the course of my research and writing, many people and organizations have been of significant help. First among them is my sister, Anne Cushman, who was a participant in or witness to the events that make up this narrative. Through family moves and mutations over the years, Anne kept the footlocker from which come most of the letters to, from, and about Dad cited in the text. I am grateful to Anne also for reading and critiquing the manuscript.

Three other readers merit special thanks. On my first visit to the National Archives, I met Rick Atkinson, who was finishing research for *An Army at Dawn* and would go on to write of my father in *The Day of Battle*. Rick read my work in early manuscript form and provided encouragement and excellent advice along the way. He also graciously passed along useful documents dug up in his own research. One such document brought up the name of Dr. Kurt Piehler, Director of the Center for the Study of War and Society at the University of Tennessee. Dr. Piehler read my manuscript and recommended it to Fordham University Press, where Robert Oppedisano, Eric Newman, and the staff provided support and expertise in the making of this book. And Sally Nicholson Brooke brought her copy-editing experience and ear for and love of the language to critiques of the manuscript in its late stages.

Tim Nenninger introduced me to the relevant holdings at the National Archives and Records Administration facility in College Park, Maryland, and answered numerous questions. David Keough and the staff at the U.S. Army Military History Institute, Carlisle Barracks, Pennsylvania, helped me find my way through the Institute's holdings. At the U.S. Military

Academy Library at West Point, Susan Lintelmann did much to facilitate my research. Jane Yates at The Citadel Archives and Museum in Charleston, South Carolina, was most gracious and helpful in making available the diaries of General Clark as well as the relevant volumes of the Fifth Army History.

The George C. Marshall Foundation and Library let me examine the Truscott papers there. The Ernie Pyle State Historical Site in Dana, Indiana, supplied copies of Pyle's articles on the Sicilian campaign, and Patty Cottingham of the Scripps Howard Foundation gave me permission to quote from them. The New Jersey State Archives and the state's adjutant general's office provided records of Dad's and Jack Senior's National Guard service. The McCormick Research Center in Wheaton, Illinois, and the Smithsonian Institution's Museum of American History were helpful, too.

The U.S. Army Human Resources Command offered up Dad's "Individual Deceased Personnel File." The Combined Arms Research Library, Army Command and General Staff College, Fort Leavenworth, Kansas, found material pertaining to courses attended by both Dad and Jack Senior. The Donovan Research Library at the Infantry School at Fort Benning, Georgia, provided several monographs on specific unit actions in Italy. The Center of Military History at Fort McNair, in Washington, D.C., published several of the books to which I refer in the text and helped me obtain biographical data on several general officers mentioned in the narrative.

Edouard L. Desrochers, archivist at the Phillips Exeter Academy, filled in some gaps in Dad's record there and provided background information about Robert Bates. Kate Dombrowski, director of public relations at Cheshire Academy, provided clues to my father's doings at the Roxbury School. Staff members at Porter Sargent Publishers in Boston supplied information about other schools mentioned in the text. The alumni offices at Wells College and Cornell University supplied yearbook records of Mom and Dad at college. The staff at Historic Fort Wayne supplied information about the army post where Dad was born.

To the staff at the Mason Library in Great Barrington, Massachusetts, I am deeply grateful for their prompt responses to my requests for interlibrary loans. Ramune Kubilius at the Galter Health Sciences Library, Northwestern University, provided information about the Twelfth General Hospital. The Huntsville, Ontario, Library generously sent me information about the Bigwin Inn, and the *Muskoka Sun* kindly permitted me to quote from Douglas McTaggart's series of articles about the inn. Other public libraries deserving of my thanks include those of Cheyenne, Wyoming; Hamilton, Ohio; Hoboken, New Jersey; and New York City.

I am grateful, too, to the Ninth Infantry Division Association and to the Society of the Third Infantry Division for helping me locate the veterans of those distinguished divisions who kindly shared with me their wartime recollections of my father. These men are acknowledged individually in the veterans' section of the sources.

Years ago, William V. Toffey, Dad's first cousin, gave me copies of my great-grandfather's Civil War letters. Henry G. (Red) Phillips generously gave of his trove of information about the Battle of Maknassy. Dean Fisher provided recollections of his father, Fred, our benefactor in Pine Bluffs.

George Biddle's two books, *Artist at War* and *War Sketches*, document the bond of friendship that developed between the artist and my father. I am grateful to Michael Biddle, George Biddle's son, for permission to quote from the two books and to reproduce sketches of my father.

With warmth and grace, on a lovely afternoon in early June 2004, Silvano Casaldi showed my family and me the soft Italian countryside that once was the beachhead and beyond and led us to a spot that might be where Dad fell.

To James Gilbert for the graphic embellishments to the maps of North Africa, Sicily, and southern Italy, and to Marion Gaenzle for her translations of German documents, I am indeed grateful.

Cheryl Raifstanger and the staff at Kwik Print in Great Barrington produced countless photocopies of the manuscript itself and of numerous documents related to the manuscript and its preparation.

Grateful as I am to all of these people, as well as to some whom I may have inadvertently failed to mention, the interpretation of the material they supplied and its use in this narrative are of my own doing. Any errors in interpretation and application are of my own making.

U.S. Army War College.

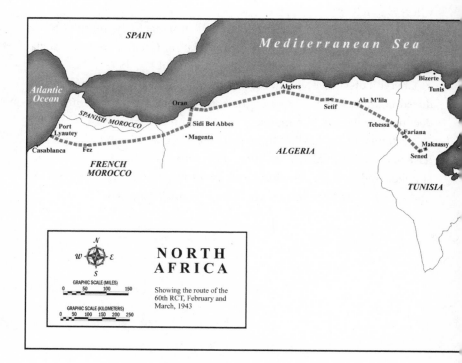

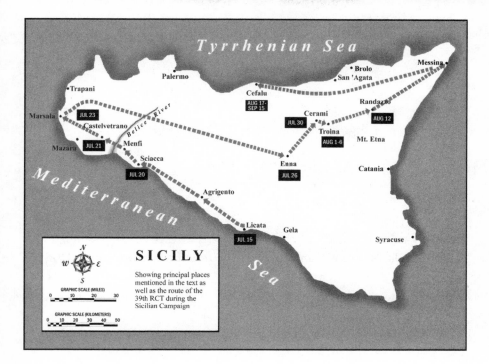

Tyrrhenian Sea

Palermo

Trapani

Messina

Brolo
San 'Agata

Cefalu

AUG 17–SEP 15

Randazzo
AUG 12

Cerami
JUL 30

Troina
AUG 1–6

Mt. Etna

Marsala

Castelvetrano

JUL 23

Belice River

Mazara

Menfi

JUL 21

Sciacca

JUL 20

Enna
JUL 26

Catania

Agrigento

Licata

JUL 15

Gela

Syracuse

Mediterranean Sea

SICILY

Showing principal places
mentioned in the text as
well as the route of the
39th RCT during the
Sicilian Campaign

GRAPHIC SCALE (MILES)
0   10   20   30

GRAPHIC SCALE (KILOMETERS)
0   10   20   30   40   50

N   W   E   S

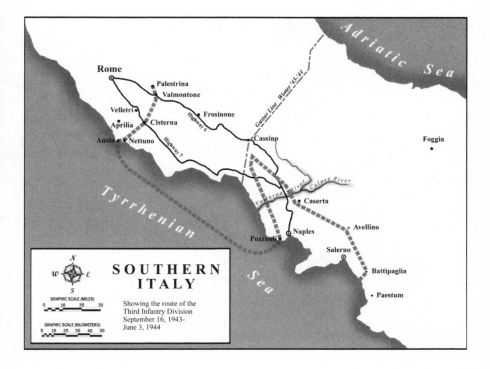

Adriatic Sea

Rome

Palestrina

Valmontone

Velletri

Frosinone

Aprilia

Cisterna

Highway 6

Gustav Line Winter '43–'44

Anzio

Nettuno

Highway 7

Cassino

Foggia

Volturno River

Calore River

Caserta

Avellino

Pozzuoli

Naples

Salerno

Battipaglia

Paestum

Tyrrhenian Sea

**SOUTHERN
ITALY**

Showing the route of the
Third Infantry Division
September 16, 1943–
June 3, 1944

GRAPHIC SCALE (MILES)
0   10   20   30

GRAPHIC SCALE (KILOMETERS)
0   10   20   30   40   50

N   W   E   S

"War is a game for the young."

—Lt. Martin W. Lanham, in a letter from France, October 11, 1918 *chapter one*

THE FIRST LETTER

Dear Dad,
Bill Hershberger is *dead*. He was found in his room on Saturday.
John

That is probably the first letter I ever wrote to my father. There may have been an earlier one, but I doubt it, because until I wrote that letter, our family—my father, mother, sister, and I—stayed close enough together to stick to voice communication. Furthermore, I was then less than three months past my ninth birthday, and in all likelihood my previous epistolary efforts were parentally induced thank-you notes to grandparents and a few great aunts and uncles. Because each of our parents was an only child, my sister and I were without genuine aunts and uncles, though various friends of our parents were given honorary titles. But our grandparents on both sides of the family had plenty of siblings, many of whom were apparently delighted to bestow on Anne and me at Christmases and on our birthdays traditional avuncular blessings. So age and occasion had limited my letter writing in those days.

The letter is postmarked Columbus, Ohio, and dated August 6, 1940, my mother's birthday. That event passes unobserved in my letter to my father. I'm sure he knew it was her birthday and had written a letter, or had sent a card, or would call that evening. He didn't need to be told it was his wife's birthday, but I was pretty sure he needed to know about the sudden death of a local ballplayer.

I don't remember much about writing the letter, but it looks as if I wrote it or at least started it on the eighth floor of the Beggs Building, overlooking the State House in Columbus, Ohio. That's where my grandfather worked as an agent for the Travelers Insurance Company. When we visited my maternal grandparents in Columbus, one of my favorite pastimes was to accompany my grandfather, Homer, to his office. It would be two more years before I would experience the greatest of all possible

Columbus adventures—an Ohio State football game. For now, going to the office was fine. There I would amuse myself by looking at the assembled Travelers agents and Ohio State football captains who looked back at me from the framed photographs on Homer's office walls. Usually I could find Homer, a small man despite his prowess as an Ohio State quarterback in the 1890s, kneeling or sitting in the front row, but in some of the large gatherings of insurance agents he was harder to find. He took great delight in showing me the picture of some convention on the Boardwalk at Atlantic City in which he appeared twice—once at each end of the back row. When I tired of looking at the pictures, I would sit at Homer's big black typewriter, hunting and pecking away.

Obviously, my typing was not yet adequate for a letter telling my father of Bill Hershberger's death. On the front of the envelope, I had crossed out Homer's business return address, and on the back flap I had typed the address of Homer's house, where we were staying while Dad was away, the same red-brick house where Mother had grown up, and where she and Dad had been married ten years earlier. The letter is written on what appears to be a piece of business stationery. On one side I had started to type the day and date before giving in to impatience and turning to longhand on the other side and drawing several lines an inch or more apart to guide the unfolding of the terse message.

This was one of those rare times when Dad was away for more than a day or two. For three years when we lived on the second floor of a large white frame house on a pleasant street in Wyoming, Ohio, Dad had traveled Ohio for the Aridor Company, selling bottle caps. Most of his travels were day trips, and occasionally he took me with him. Once we called at a pickle-processing plant where the employees were still in a state of excitement because one of the workers had just drowned in an enormous vat of brine. Maybe we called on the Crampton Cannery, the subject of one of the first bits of poetry I committed, apparently indelibly, to memory. After persuading that producer to join the growing list of happy Aridor customers, Dad telegraphed the home office in Chicago: "Roses are red, violets are blue / Crampton Cannery's signed up too." It must have been on a visit to Greenville, in west-central Ohio, maybe to celebrate the Crampton coup, that we stopped at the Darke County Fair, a montage of trotting races, carnival rides, and booths displaying some of the fruits and vegetables not destined for Crampton's cans and jars with Aridor's caps. In his business travels Dad would have had to spend some nights away from us, but never long enough for a letter to reach him.

This time Dad was away for extended period. He was training with the New Jersey National Guard at a place called Pine Camp, in the fastness of New York State up near the St. Lawrence River and Canada. To get the letter to my father, I carefully copied the address just as someone had written it out for me: Captain John J. Toffey, Hdqrs, 44th Division / APO #44 / Canton, NY. I doubt that I knew what the various components of the address meant, only that I had to have them there to reach Dad over in New York.

Though I don't remember writing the letter, I do remember first learning of the death that prompted it. We were driving from Cincinnati to Columbus, as we often did in those days, along Route 3, the old 3 C's Highway (connecting Cincinnati, Columbus, and Cleveland). Exactly who was in the car is unclear. Perhaps it was the three of us—Mom, Anne, and me—going up to Columbus to stay with Mom's parents while Dad was away at Pine Camp. Perhaps Homer and Granny (formerly and mellifluously Aurelia Belle) had come down from Columbus to get Mom, Anne, and me. If Homer and Granny had come to get us, Homer was definitely driving, because Granny, who wore pince-nez glasses, had never learned how to drive a car, which she continued to refer to as a "machine." Whoever was in the car on that August Sunday in 1940, we were family and comfortable.

As we drove along, we were listening to a broadcast of a game between our Cincinnati Reds and the Boston Bees. The action was in Boston, but the broadcast was from Cincinnati. The telegraph key would click for a while, and then an announcer would tell us what had just happened, fleshing out his narration with images to make his word picture more real. "Frey steps out, picks up some dirt, looks for a sign from Gowdy at third, and steps back in. Tobin sets himself on the rubber, peers in for his sign, shakes off one, then nods, winds, and delivers."

I don't recall the particulars of the game, but I do remember one of the announcers saying that Willard Hershberger had committed suicide. I don't know if I understood all the implications of the word "suicide," though I did know that to commit suicide was different from executing a suicide squeeze. We thought this was a metaphor for something that had happened earlier in the game. What had he done? Tried to stretch a single against a strong throwing arm? Tried to score from third on a comebacker in the infield? It was several innings before we realized that Willard Hershberger had killed himself in his Boston hotel room.

Hershberger was the backup catcher for the National League Champion Cincinnati Reds. A good catcher and hitter, Hershberger's role was in support of the great Ernie Lombardi, MVP in 1938, when he led the league with a .342 batting average while slugging .524, and who finished his career with a lifetime batting average of .306. Hershberger was naturally relegated to pinch-hitting and to catching the second games of double headers.

Hershberger had spent seven years on minor-league teams from El Paso to Newark, where, as a member of the great Newark Bears team of 1937, he had been voted the International League's outstanding catcher. Since the parent Yankees had a catcher named Bill Dickey, Hershberger came to the Reds in 1938 as part of a rebuilding effort that would take them from last in the league to fourth that year, then to league champs in 1939, and, two months after Hershberger's death, to champions of the world.

All of us were rabid Reds fans. Dad had always been a baseball fan. With roots in Washington, D.C., and New York, he had grown up surrounded by Senators, Yankees, Giants, and Dodgers. Mom and Dad began domestic life in New York, where I was born (Brooklyn, actually), and where legend has it that Dad had been at one or another of the city's three ballparks when Mom went into labor.

After we moved from Chicago to Cincinnati in 1937, I saw Dad's enthusiasm up close. He once sent a telegram congratulating Lou Riggs on the occasion of the light-hitting infielder's crucial base hit. He would also take me to Crosley Field when the Cubs were in town so that I could see Dizzy Dean pitch. During the Cubs' pregame batting practice, Dad lifted me over the railing along the left-field foul line and told me to go out into left field to get Ole Diz's autograph. Mercifully, Dizzy sent me back to the stands, promising to come over to where we sat when he was through horsing around with other players while they shagged flies. Dizzy signed our scorecard that day, but I never got to see him pitch. But if I missed Dean in his twilight, Dad and I did see at least one memorable pitching performance. In 1938 we saw rookie Johnny Vander Meer toss the first of his two consecutive no-hitters. As the record books will tell you, it was against the Boston Bees on a Saturday afternoon in June—June 11, to be precise—and a knothole day. As a member of the knothole gang, I showed my card and got in for some nominal charge and then joined Dad where we usually sat, behind third base.

I don't recall a special attachment to Willard Hershberger; my heroes were Bucky Walters and Frank McCormick. I don't recall asking Hershberger for his autograph at the ballpark or seeing him dining in Milders Inn, a favorite eatery of the Reds in Hamilton.[1] But he was one of ours. And ballplayers didn't die, literally, while a game was going on. Only former ballplayers died, whatever that meant to a nine-year-old, and when they did, Dad would deliver to the rest of us an anecdotal eulogy.

But this was mid-season. The Cincinnati papers provided eulogies of sorts. According to one, Hershberger "was the favorite of thousands of fans and idol of almost every woman who ever went out to the ballpark." "Before every ladies' day game," the paper went on, "Hershy was the center of a ring of women, all demanding autographs and some even offering to take him into marriage for the first time." Popular with his teammates, "he could take kidding better than anyone else on the club and one could always get a hearty laugh out of [him] with a joke. He rarely drank or smoked. As the paper summed him up, "Morally he was perfect. He seldom went out, except for an occasional movie, and spent most of his evenings reading magazines and books on hunting and fishing."[2]

On that Saturday afternoon in Boston, Hershberger had not accompanied the team to the ballpark, saying that he would be along later, to catch the second game. When he did not show up, the club's traveling secretary Gabe Paul called him. Hershberger told him he was sick and couldn't play, but would come right out to the park anyway. When he had not appeared by the end of the first game, manager Bill McKechnie asked Dan Cohen, a Cincinnati shoe-store owner traveling with the team, to go to the hotel to check on Hershberger. Cohen found the catcher lying over the bathtub. Around 2:30, apparently, alone in his hotel room during the first game of the double-header, Willard Hershberger took his own life by cutting his throat with a straight razor.

In the third inning of the second game, someone whispered the grim report to McKechnie. He left the team in charge of one of the coaches and returned to the hotel. The next morning, he told the press that Hershberger had been depressed since the Reds had lost to the Giants the previous Wednesday, when the Giants scored four runs with two out in the last of the ninth. The big blow was Harry (The Horse) Danning's home run off of Bucky Walters. "It was my fault. I called for the wrong pitch," Hershberger had told McKechnie later. "I alone was to blame for the defeat." McKechnie admitted that Hershberger had seemed depressed after the loss and recalled that Hershberger had told him, "My father took his own life, and so will I."

What did Hershy's death mean to the Reds? Grown men wept openly. The club announced that it would pay Hershberger's full salary to his mother in California, and the players agreed to give her her son's full World Series share if they won the pennant. To handle the catching, Bill Baker, Hershy's roommate and the third-string catcher, would back up Lombardi, and Dick West would be called up from Indianapolis. After a late season injury to Lombardi, the club activated forty-year-old coach Jimmy Wilson, who, as it turned out, would catch six of the seven Series games, bat .353, and steal the only base of the series.

What did Hershberger's death mean to me? At the time, it was something that I had to tell Dad. It seemed more important than did the death of the worker in the vat of brine. It was even closer than my paternal grandfather's death. Was its impact upon me so great that I could write about nothing else?

In that summer of 1940 America was, of course, still in a Great Depression. Although at that time 17 percent of Americans were unemployed, Dad had a job. We were not among the two and a half million Americans whose only income was from government programs. Half the men and even more of the women earned less than $1,000 a year, and less than 1 percent of the taxpaying population earned more than $2,500 a year. Though nearly one-third of the homes in America had no running water or indoor plumbing, ours did. Though more than half of all homes in America were without central heating, ours had it. Both Mom and Dad were among the minority of Americans who had gone beyond the eighth grade and the 25 percent who had graduated from high school. Mom was among the 5 percent who had finished college. Dad wasn't.[3]

On August 3, 1940, the Cincinnati paper that headlined Hershberger's suicide also announced that as the presidential campaign opened, the first Gallup poll showed Wendell Willkie leading in all northern states except Washington and Montana and in the electoral vote, while FDR led in all the southern states and in the popular vote. In Hamilton County, Ohio, a river's width from being southern, the cry was "No third term!" The Republican Cincinnati paper recalled that four years earlier Alf Landon had led FDR in the early going.

Europe had been at war for almost a year. Hitler had overwhelmed France and the Low Countries by the spring of 1940, and in late May and early June, 300,000 Allied troops were evacuated from Dunkirk in less than a week.

On August 3, those who read beyond Hershberger's death learned that Winston Churchill was warning the British people to be ready for a "mass Nazi attack at any time." And while British troops worked to prepare their island's defenses, German bombers were often seen in the skies over England, Scotland, and Wales. But on August 6—Mom's birthday and the day I wrote Dad about Willard Hershberger—Hermann Goering was meeting with his senior Luftwaffe commanders to fine-tune the plans to eliminate the RAF.[4] Before the Germans turned their full attention to the savaging of London, however, British bombers managed to attack some German ports and manufacturing centers. After one such raid, German propagandists quickly arranged a tour of Hamburg to show the world that Britain's claims of massive destruction were without foundation. Instead of rubble, the world press saw canoeists paddling on shady canals.

Across Europe on that same day, "Fears of Communist disturbances in Hungary and of disorders in Rumanian-held Transylvania complicated the Balkan situation . . . as Bulgaria, Hungary and Rumania prepared for an attempt to settle their boundary differences in a manner acceptable to the Axis Powers."[5]

On this side of the Atlantic, in Washington, the Japanese ambassador protested to Undersecretary of State Sumner Welles President Roosevelt's recent embargo on aviation fuel. Having bought from the United States 106,000 barrels of gas for their planes as they attacked China, the Japanese found the embargo to be "an unfriendly act."

In the U.S. Senate, a drive was underway to rally the votes needed to pass the Burke-Wadsworth compulsory military service bill. Strong opposition foretold a close vote, and some were already preparing compromise legislation.

In Columbus that Sunday morning, Granny and Homer took us with them to Central Presbyterian Church, a venerable pile of red sandstone on south Third Street, just around the corner from Homer's office. Here Dr. Frank Throop presided, and once—perhaps that very Sunday—proclaimed from the pulpit that Solomon in all his glory had more gold in his treasure house than the United States had in the depository at Fort Knox. I wondered how he knew.

That morning the choir might well have sung "Heavenly Father, We Beseech Thee," or one of the other anthems Homer had written.

After church we returned home for Sunday dinner. Homer began, as always, by saying grace. When he had finished, Granny looked up and said, "Homer, I didn't hear a word you said." "I wasn't talking to you," Homer replied, gently. Granny and Homer kept the Sabbath quiet. Homer did, however, like to tell about the little boy who had accompanied his father to church on a Sunday morning and to a ballgame in the afternoon. As he was going to bed that night, the boy said to his father, "I don't understand. In church this morning we sang, 'Stand Up, Stand Up for Jesus,' and at the ballgame a man yelled, 'For Christ's sake sit down.'"

After supper we gathered around the radio. On this Sunday night, regular network programming gave way to an address to the nation by General John J. Pershing. Though he had retired as Army's chief of staff in 1924, General Pershing remained America's most distinguished soldier. Pershing told us,

> A grave danger for us lurks in the present world situation. . . . More than half the world is ruled by men who despise the American idea and have sworn to destroy it. They know that while one great people remains independent and free because it is strong and is brave, they can never crush finally the people they have conquered. . . . It is not hysterical to insist that democracy and liberty are threatened. . . . Only the British are left to defend [them]. By sending help to the British we can still hope with confidence to keep the war on the other side of the Atlantic Ocean, where the enemies of liberty, if possible, should be defeated.[6]

While Pershing urged support of President Roosevelt's proposed lend-lease agreement with Britain and while the politicians maneuvered in Washington, the largest army the nation had ever assembled in peacetime was starting three weeks of training. That is what my father was doing in upstate New York on that Tuesday in August 1940: training with his National Guard outfit, New Jersey's Forty-fourth Infantry Division.

On Wednesday, August 8, General Hugh Drum, commanding the First Army, spoke to 12,000 officers and senior noncommissioned officers, telling them that the United States must stop basking in "the sunshine of peace and the security of two oceans" and must avoid "the doctrines of the supremacy of the military defensive which have led to the ruin of France and forced England to face so many disasters." General Drum went on to call for national industrial mobilization organized for the rapid production of large quantities of materiel and for the rapid creation of a manpower pool.[7]

Six years earlier, another general, my grandfather, then commanding the New Jersey Guard, issued a similar warning. His audience—the Jersey City Rotary Club, assembled for its annual Armistice Day program—was much smaller. The general called for military preparedness while local clergymen called for "mental and spiritual preparedness." In its lead editorial, *The Jersey Journal* agreed: "Our nation does need both kinds of preparedness, and at the same time. Both are woefully lacking." The *Journal* went on to say, "In one brilliant part of his address, Gen. Toffey remarked that at the end of the [First World] war we were all determined that this must never be again." To quote the general,

> What must never be again? Is it war? . . . Shall the nation never rise again in its might to defend itself, its commerce, its citizens, from aggression, from the oppression of the willful rulers of willful nations? God forbid that the time ever come when our flag will float over a helpless nation, indifferent and impotent in the face of invasion—whether that invasion be of our country or of our vested rights as a nation.
>
> What, then, should never be again? One thing certainly, my friends. The needless exposure of the nation to defeat because of the lack of reasonable provisions for defense.[8]

For three weeks in August 1940, the troops of the First Army played war games in upstate New York. The equipment they played with was outmoded or lacking altogether. Some trucks played the parts of tanks; some .30 caliber rifles represented .50 caliber machine guns. Pieces of drainpipe represented antitank guns, and pieces of stovepipe were mortars. Springfield 1903 rifles far outnumbered the M-1. Troop movements and logistical support were badly handled. Inexperience and ineptitude took their toll. Though eleven months had passed since Roosevelt had declared a state of "limited emergency . . . for the purpose of strengthening our national defense within the limits of peacetime authorizations," our army was not ready for war.

Then, on August 27, Congress authorized the War Department to call into federal service 300,000 guardsmen and reservists for a period of twelve months. Three weeks later Congress authorized the first peacetime draft in the nation's history. The National Guard and Army Reserve officers who had listened to General Drum's call for military and industrial mobilization suddenly had a lot to think about. Where would they be sent? Would those who had jobs still have them at the end of their year of service? Would they be able to keep up mortgage and car payments on their army pay? Would they be able to bring their families with them? Should they? For my father and all those others who had heard General Drum speak, there was much to ponder beyond the death of an obscure ballplayer. Perhaps as he thought about the year ahead, Dad reviewed the events by which he, husband, father, and bottle-cap salesman from southwestern Ohio, as his father and grandfather before him had, would go to war.

chapter two

YOUNG JACK

My father was born into the Army. It happened on Saturday, August 31, 1907, at Fort Wayne, near Detroit, Michigan, where his father, a captain, was serving as adjutant of the Seventh Infantry Regiment. The most complete record of my father's first year is in a little book entitled *Our Baby's History*, which not only documents the first months of my father's life but also gives a sense of what constituted special moments in the life of an infant in the first decade of the twentieth century. We learn what he weighed at birth, when he was given his first carriage ride, when and where he was baptized, when he first wore "short clothes," when he cut his first tooth, when he first crawled and walked, and what he got for his first birthday.

There is no comparable chronicle of my father's boyhood. To reconstruct it we must look to the fragments that we have of his father's military career.[1] "Jack Senior," as he was known in the family after my father was born, was actually a "junior." He was born in New Jersey in 1874, to the first in a line of John J. Toffeys and to Mary Elizabeth Sip. In 1895 he was commissioned a second lieutenant in the New Jersey National Guard and had made first lieutenant when, three years later, he passed an examination resulting in a commission as second lieutenant in the Regular Army. Remembering the *Maine*, blown up in Havana harbor on February 15, 1898, we may assume that Jack Senior's move to the Regular Army was related to an American military buildup. Whatever the reason, it was not universally popular among officers of the Regular Army. At Fort Sheridan, Illinois, his first post after graduating from West Point, Second Lieutenant George S. Patton Jr. found his fellow junior officers to be, historian Martin Blumenson records, "much like the [West Point] cadets except for a fewer number of gentlemen among them. Some were awful, 'not even decent,' particularly former militia members who had entered the Regular Army after the war with Spain. Patton and others referred to them as 'the sin of 1898.'"[2]

Promoted to first lieutenant and commanding a company of the Fourth Infantry Regiment, Jack Senior went to the Philippines, where he saw action against Emilio Aguinaldo's insurrectionists. After the defeat of Aguinaldo, Moro tribesmen kept rebellion alive for several years. The army's ongoing attempts to subdue the Moros became a proving ground for young officers on career tracks.

Back in the States in 1905, Jack Senior married Helen Bonner of New York and Stamford, Connecticut. The young couple set up housekeeping at Fort Wayne, and two years later their son was born.

"In the army there's sobriety; promotion's very slow," says an old West Point song. Jack Senior remained a captain for thirteen years—from 1904 until 1917. In 1908 he returned to the Philippines, this time taking his family with him. Back in the States in 1914, while the youth of Europe girded for what some of them thought would be the glories of war, Jack Senior served with General Frederick Funston at Veracruz and later with General Pershing in pursuit of Pancho Villa along the Mexican border. Here, again, Jack Senior soldiered with and in some cases commanded officers who would be the generals of World War II.

From Indianapolis, where in 1916 Jack Senior was directing an officer training camp, we have the first record of my father's formal education. A medal in a family footlocker testifies that in 1916 J. J. Toffey III won the Kingham Prize for Improvement in Writing at the Brooks School. How proud young Jack's parents must have been of their eight-year-old son as Principal Brooks pinned the golden medal over his heart.

In 1917, Jack Senior's outfit, the 329th Infantry, was ordered overseas, but Jack Senior was promoted to colonel and sent to Camp Pike, Arkansas. Under his command in the 329th was a young West Virginian named Martin W. Lanham. Lt. Lanham sailed for France with the rest of the regiment, and on October 11, 1918, he wrote to my father, then eleven years old. In a hand schooled in penmanship he filled nine pages of stationery supplied by the Knights of Columbus Overseas Service.

The lieutenant reports that upon reaching France, he transferred to the First Infantry Division—"The Big Red One." He then regales young Jack with war stories: that he captured some German officers and an officer's horse; that he picked up a couple of pairs of field glasses, one of which he promises to give to Jack Senior; that he had been living on raw cabbage and crabapples before his outfit captured a Boche supply train. "It was just like going shopping with everything free," he says.

The fun abated when the regiment went into the line on October 1. For six days the Germans hammered his outfit's positions with explosive shells and gas. One night Lanham was burned by the gas and inhaled enough to make him vomit violently. Weakened and sick, he remained with his unit for four more days, until a shell knocked him down an embankment. There he lay until the odors of the torn bodies returned him to consciousness.

The young lieutenant goes on to tell the younger boy of winding up in a hospital bed with real linen—the first he has felt since July. He has his clothes and shoes off for the first time in twelve days. He gets a bath and real food. He speaks of friends killed or wounded in the recent fight but still draws satisfaction from the knowledge that his outfit whipped the crack First and Fifth Prussian Guards. He tells his young correspondent how in the gas ward where he was being treated, he "watched a Hun slowly die in terrible agony from the effects of our gas." The scene makes him think "how [the Boche] had wanted to make the war inhuman and how it was being sent home to them now."

Lanham says he is glad to hear of Jack Senior's promotion, but he hopes the war will end before Jack Senior is sent over to France. As he sees it, "Somehow there is a lot of satisfaction in thinking of one's friends safe in good old America. With me it is different. I am young and strong and can stand the hardships. In fact I would not want to miss them—but it is a game for the young."

Lieutenant Lanham urges his young reader to be good and true and to make his parents proud of him. He hopes that after the war young Jack will visit him in West Virginia and meet his parents and his sister. There the lieutenant and the boy could "ride, fish, and play ball" for days at a time.

After the war, Jack Senior did a brief tour as recruiting officer for the state of Kentucky, duty that proved to be both difficult and dangerous, inasmuch as the "illiterate mountaineers often forcibly resisted with arms any attempts on the part of recruiting officers to interest them in military affairs." Nevertheless, during his tour, enlistments from Kentucky increased.[3]

While Jack Senior commanded the Thirty-fifth Infantry Regiment at Schofield Barracks, in the Territory of Hawaii, young Jack attended Honolulu Military Academy, where he was again decorated for action in the classroom. During a football game there, Dad remembered, he had the wind knocked out of him. As he lay there on the field slowly collecting his lost breath, his mother appeared over him. Though the physical pain was quickly gone, the embarrassment lasted for years.

In 1924, Jack Senior was assigned to the staff of the Chief of Infantry in Washington, D.C. Here lessons learned from mistakes made in the fields of France in 1917 and 1918 were written into the field manuals used by instructors and students in the various courses that made up the curriculum of the Infantry School at Fort Benning, Georgia.

About the time that Colonel Toffey and his family came to Washington, a young reporter named Ernie Pyle arrived from Indiana to take a job as a cub reporter with the *Washington Post*. Some years later he recalled the words of welcome with which his new editor greeted him: "You'll probably like Washington. But let me warn you: don't stay here too long. It's a nice easygoing city and people get in a rut, and if you stay till you get to liking it too well, you'll never leave. You'll just settle down to a pleasant routine and never amount to anything."[4]

For the sojourn in easygoing Washington, Col. Toffey and his family made their home at 2712 35th Place NW. Staff duty in Washington brought with it a busy social life that included an invitation to dine at the White House with President Calvin Coolidge and the First Lady. To keep the house and cook and serve the food, Jack Senior and his wife hired a young man named Arcenio Pajarillo, recently arrived from the Philippines. Like many of his countrymen, Arcenio knew that working for the Americans offered a better life than what might be available in his own country.

Young Jack would get to keep only one foot in Washington, however. His parents decided that their son should finish his secondary-school education at the Phillips Exeter Academy in New Hampshire. Why Jack's parents chose Exeter is not a matter of record. It is perhaps no more than coincidence that General John J. Pershing, just retired as Army Chief of Staff in Washington in 1924, and whom Jack Senior knew from service in the Philippines and on the Mexican border, had enrolled his son in Exeter the previous year.

Exeter was rich in a tradition of excellence that extended back to 1781, when John Phillips founded it "for the purpose of instructing youth, not only in the English and Latin grammar, writing, arithmetic, and those sciences wherein they are commonly taught, but more especially to learn [sic] them the great end and real business of living." Or, as the Latin inscription over the door of the main building put it, *Huc venite pueri ut viri sitis*: "Come hither boys that you may be men."[5]

Through this door in the fall of 1924 walked young Jack as a new lower middler (sophomore). Was he happy at Exeter? Did he thrive in the busy world of classes, sports, collegial classmates, and austere faculty authority figures? Some twenty years after he left Exeter, Jack's mother wrote to Dr. Louis Perry, the principal at the time, to tell him that "Jack *loved* Exeter as few young men can—and always said, 'If I ever have a son I would like to send him to Exeter.'"

In the summer of 1925, young Jack attended a month-long course at a Citizens Military Training Camp at Fort Monroe, Virginia. These camps, established around 1920 and lasting until 1940, provided military training for young men between the ages of seventeen and twenty-five. After four summers of CMTC, a young man could qualify for a commission as a second lieutenant. In 1925 there were some thirty-four thousand young men attending forty camps around the country. To promote the program the government engaged the services of no less a figure than Babe Ruth. The Babe would say, "If I had a son, I'd want him to attend a Citizens Military Training Camp." Then he would autograph a bat and ball for presentation to each outstanding soldier-athlete.[6]

Jack returned to Exeter in the fall of 1925, his father reminds him in a four-page letter, for "a good education, physical up-building, and a value received for the money spent." March 1926 was not a good time for Jack. His first-term grades were poor, and a case of measles put him in the school infirmary. He was tired, listless, and depressed.

His parents wrote sympathetically, his father acknowledging "you have had hard luck with your studies and the term since Christmas has not been a very prosperous one considering the work and study you have put in and the amount of money spent." They cite the struggles against serious illness of two old army friends—Beverly Browne and "Uncle" Johnny Turner—as examples of the human spirit meeting real adversity. They look forward to the upcoming holiday as a time when their son can return to Washington for a "sensible" vacation, and have "to put aside the idea of dances, late parties, lack of proper rest, and all that sort of thing." His father includes a check for $35 to cover travel expenses and provide a little pocket money. His mother just writes a little note to cheer up her son, and perhaps to cheer herself with the prospects of spring in Washington and of seeing her son in a week's time.

Jack did not return to Exeter after the spring vacation. When summer came and his erstwhile schoolmates were beginning the long vacations dreams of which had sustained them through the bleak midwinter, Jack was off to boarding school again. The school this time was the Roxbury School, in Cheshire, Connecticut.

Under various names the school traced its origins back to the eighteenth century and claimed as alumni Gideon Welles, Rockwell Kent, and J. P. Morgan. Its purpose, it said, was to prepare its students for "all colleges, and especially for Yale."[7] The 1927 edition of the school's yearbook, *The Rolling Stone*, reports that to his colleagues Jack was known as "Spider" and "Baby Face," that he was an end on the varsity football squad, and that his college of choice was Princeton.

But Jack did not go to Princeton. Instead, he went to Cornell, where the record is again sketchy. He remained at Cornell for no more than two years. He was a member of Chi Phi, rowed, and was in the Reserve Officers' Training Corps (ROTC). Though he may have declared himself an engineering student, the only relic of his studies at Cornell is an anecdote about an English class. One day he dropped by the class during a discussion of Chaucer. Puzzled by the Middle English in which Chaucer wrote, Jack is said to have left, muttering that he had been under the impression that the class was to be conducted in English. Whatever Jack did or did not do at Cornell, the memories of experiences among the gorges above Lake Cayuga stayed with him years after he left, and he continued to sing the songs of Cornell and to pass them along to his children, always ending the medley with "Far Above Cayuga's Waters."

The best thing to happen to Jack at Cornell occurred on October 12, 1928, the day he met Helen Howard, a student at Wells College, some twenty-five miles up the lake. The meeting took place at Cornell's Kappa Alpha house, where Jack and his Chi Phi fraternity brothers were living after a fire of unknown origin had made their house uninhabitable. Helen was beginning her junior year at Wells, majoring in English and performing in college dramatics. Though two years older, Jack had not completed that much college. On that October evening, so family legend has it, Helen was wearing a dress cut low in the back. Jack told a friend that he wanted to meet the girl who could hold that dress up. At the time, Jack was seeing a lot of a girl from Chevy Chase, and it was rumored they might soon become engaged. They were not.

Though Jack and Helen had a wonderful year above Cayuga's waters, it was Jack's last at Cornell. The next year he was in New York, having taken a job in the brokerage firm of Harris Upham and earned a civil-service appointment as a subinspector in the United States Engineer's Office in New York at $110 per month. As it turned out, 1929 was not an ideal year in which to begin a career as a stockbroker, but Jack stayed with it while courting Helen. He could board the Lehigh Valley Railroad's Friday night train up to Ithaca, take Helen to the football game and the Chi Phi house party, carouse with his fraternity brothers, and catch the Sunday night train back to New York.

Or Helen would come to New York for the weekend. Either way, they saw a lot of each other, and between weekends they wrote or talked on the phone. Helen's passion for mail and telephone calls during her senior year is noted by her classmates, as is her signature expression, "Did I tell you about the time Jack . . . ?" Perhaps on a trip to the theater in New York she and Jack had heard what became Helen's special song of 1930, "A Little Hut in Hoboken."[8] Did it suggest life after college?

Jack's life, then, was an extension of college, except that between weekends with Helen in Aurora, Ithaca, or New York, work had replaced classes. Jack easily fit with the young college crowd in Manhattan, young men whose demeanor was inconsistent with something called "the Great Depression." Charlie Saltzman, like Jack the son of a career officer, had graduated with distinction from West Point and after a Rhodes Scholarship and tour of duty as White House aide resigned his Regular Army commission to pursue a career in business while retaining a commission in the New York National Guard. Hugh Troy brought his elaborate pranks and often outrageous practical jokes down from Cornell in 1927 to amuse or exasperate the city. Ted Geisel, out of Dartmouth and Oxford, came to New York to pursue a career as a cartoonist, making "Quick, Henry, the Flit," a household slogan and signing his work "Dr. Seuss."

At some point during his time in New York, Jack posed for the illustrator Elbert McGran Jackson. The resulting painting became the cover of the June 29, 1929, issue of *Collier's*. It shows a handsome, well-built young man saluting. He is wearing a polo helmet, bathing-suit top, and riding britches. Over his shoulder is a bag of golf clubs. From his belt hangs a baseball glove. In his left hand he holds a canoe paddle, tennis racquet, and fishing rod. The picture in entitled "The Loafer."[9]

On December 29, 1929, Helen's parents announced the engagement of their daughter to Mr. John James Toffey Jr., "son of Col. and Mrs. James [sic] Toffey of Governors Island, N.Y." The following August 16, Helen and Jack were married in a small, informal ceremony in her parents' home in

Columbus. The *Columbus Dispatch* reported that after a wedding trip the couple would reside in New York.[10]

Though few were invited to the wedding, many received announcements and responded with gifts. One hundred twenty-three are logged into "The Bride's Gift Book." Among all the silver and pewter are recorded several gifts of money, perhaps the perfect gift for a couple starting out in the Great Depression. Helen has carefully logged all the gifts into the book in her neat, round hand, noting the date on which each gift was acknowledged.

Two gifts got special attention. Jack records the $500 from his Aunt Marie and Uncle Billy Beach with flourishes. In the column labeled "Acknowledged" he writes "My God Yes" and in the "Remarks" column paraphrases the old crapshooter's cry with "Baby gets new shoes." From friends of Jack's Aunt Edith, came another check, this one accompanied by "A Rondeau for Jack and Helen, Charmingly entitled A Wedding Gift":

> A wedding gift, no doubt, should be
> A thing of worth and artistry,
> Expressing by sheer charm, no less,
> Its tribute to your happiness.
> (I hope my dears you *do* agree.)
>
> But here beside the summer sea,
> 'Tis hard to find, I must confess,
> A thing that *anyone* might guess
>   A wedding gift.
>
> So, happy ones, herewith from me
> A bit of paper—commonly
> Known as a check. In time of stress
> Use it for coal, or drink, or dress.
> 'Tis sent with love—That's certainly
>   A wedding gift.

To this the newlyweds replied in kind:

> To answer the poetic muse
> In words of ordinary use
> Would cause Olympic gods to blush
> For one whose phrases will not rush
>   Along.

Come, Keats and Shelley, give a lift
To thank the Faulkses for their gift
And find me words of amplitude
To show these friends our gratitude
In song.

A Wedding Gift, you say, should be
A thing of worth and artistry.
But in the face of present dearth
These two young things prefer the *worth*
You see.

We bless you for your happy thought,
By simple pen and paper wrought,
Imbued with magic, none the less,
To give us both much happiness,
Indeed.

(Refrain:)
Our finances are all a wreck
And so we thank you for the check.

The young couple in such financial shape lived wherever they could in New York. For a couple of months they lived in Aunt Edith's apartment in Manhattan; then for a while they lived with Jack's parents on Governors Island. Early in 1931 they were able to rent an apartment of their own at 2 Grace Court in Brooklyn Heights. Here their first child—I, that is—was born.

A year later, in June 1932, Jack Senior was given the most prestigious assignment of his career, command of the Twenty-ninth Infantry at Fort Benning, Georgia. This was the Army's showcase field regiment, providing the demonstration troops for the Infantry School. Furthermore, it was the only full-strength regiment in the Army. A tour as commander of the Twenty-ninth was a prelude to a star. There was one slight drawback. Jack Senior's wife didn't want to leave New York for the red clay of western Georgia.

At the same time, the Forty-fourth Division, the New Jersey National Guard, needed a commanding general. By late summer, after several people had recommended Jack Senior, he emerged as Governor Harry Moore's choice, and on December 29 Governor Moore appointed him major general in command of the National Guard, effective January 1, 1933.[11]

The general and his wife took up residence in Summit, New Jersey, and shortly thereafter my father enlisted as a private in his father's outfit. The day after enlisting, he was discharged in order to accept a commission as a second lieutenant to fill a vacancy as aide to the commanding general created when the previous aide was promoted to major. On his enlistment papers Dad notes as military experience four years at Honolulu Military Academy, a summer at the Fort Monroe CMTC, and two years of ROTC at Cornell.

In 1934 and 1935 Dad completed Army extension courses in the 20 and 30 series. Among these were "Weapons and Musketry," "Scouting and Patrolling," "Military Law—Courts Martial," "Supply and Mess Management," "Care of Animals and Stable Management," "Defense Against Chemical Warfare," "Solution to Map Problems," "Defensive Combat and Organization of the Ground," "Combat Orders—Infantry," "Offensive Combat of Small Infantry Units," "Tank Operations," "Training Management," "Signal Communication," and "Mobilization."[12]

In addition, Dad took part in the Guard's summer training held at Camp Moore, Sea Girt, New Jersey, while we lived in the commanding general's quarters with Jack Senior and my grandmother Helen, to whom I gave the name "Deo," apparently my youthful replication of the "dear" that I heard others call her. From those days I remember going with Dad to see the burned hulk of the *Morro Castle*, an unfortunate luxury liner than had run aground at Asbury Park in September 1934.

In 1935 Dad joined the Aridor Company, a bottle-cap manufacturer with headquarters in Chicago. We moved to the Chicago suburb of Hinsdale, settling into a house at 348 Ravine Road. Thus separated by about a thousand miles from the Forty-fourth Division, Dad was transferred to the inactive reserve. In January 1936 my sister Anne was born. Writing to Sy Austin, his fraternity brother and best man, Dad calls her a "swell new daughter," saying she is "an awfully cute little girl . . . and is a real good one too." To his old friend Dad sums up life in Chicago thus:

> It's like years to me since I saw any of you and yours. I'm a hermit out here. I work plenty hard here but still like it. I think there is a future for me too. No one has to be passed. I'm production boss and factory superintendent, and it's a nice job. I get to Wheeling, W. VA. once in a

while on business, but N. Y. and the East look way off until summer brings vacation to me.

He asks Sy about his law business, his love life, and "the boys & gals I once knew." He says that *Mutiny on the Bounty* has just arrived at the local movie house. "Wow! Are we hicks." Still, "Helen is grand and very happy out here. It's a pretty good town and the job is good. We don't exactly roll in money but we have hopes. It's been an expensive winter."

In 1937, the Aridor Company sent Dad to Cincinnati, Ohio, to direct regional sales. We moved into the second floor of a duplex at 124 Stearns Avenue in suburban Wyoming. Though Dad spent a lot of time on the road, he and I had our father-and-son doings in Cincinnati: ballgames at Crosley Field and backyard catches at the end of which I had to throw him ten straight strikes before going in for supper.

Though Dad had been out of sight of the New Jersey National Guard, he was not out of its mind. In early September 1938, the Deputy Adjutant General wrote Dad that he would lose his commission for failing to meet minimum standards of training. After protests and appeals, it was worked out that he could train with the 147th Infantry of the Ohio National Guard and enroll in 40-level extension courses. On the basis of reports of his training with the 147th and the opinion of Major General Winfield S. Price, now commanding the New Jersey Guard, that Dad was "an asset to the military service," he was allowed to retain his status in the Guard.

A year later, the war in Europe having begun, the New Jersey Guard discovered that Dad had not yet taken the special physical examination requested of National Guard officers by the secretary of war. Again, arrangements were made between New Jersey and Ohio for Dad to be examined in November 1939. Six months later Dad received a letter telling him that at six feet and one inch in height and at 208 pounds, he was seven pounds overweight. On June 8, 1940, at 197 pounds, he was fit for duty. Two months later he would be on maneuvers with the Forty-fourth Division, and in another month he would be called to active federal service.

chapter three

FORT DIX AND THE
FORTY-FOURTH DIVISION

When Dad finished maneuvers at Pine Camp that August and returned to Cincinnati, the choices available to my parents were probably three: Mom, Anne, and I could stay in Cincinnati at least until Dad's military assignment became clearer; we could go to Columbus, move in with Granny and Homer and await further developments; or we could pack up and follow Dad wherever he was sent. At this point, mobilization did not seem to mean that war was inevitable. As President Roosevelt had said and would say again to the American people, "Your boys are not going to be sent into any foreign wars. They are going into training to form a force so strong that, by its very existence, it will keep the threat of war away from our shores."[1]

Anne and I were not privy to the discussions, nor did we contribute to making the decision. Mom and Dad decided we would stay together. Would the decision be hard on their marriage? It *was* their marriage. Surely for our parents it would create hardships and moments of discomfort and extreme anxiety (which they almost always succeeded in keeping from us), but it enabled them to stay together, and that was how they chose to live their marriage. Because by traveling Dad had earned our living, he knew well the importance of a dependable automobile; as a soldier he knew that we were likely to be in for a lot of travel in the coming months. Hence the new blue Plymouth "Tudor" Deluxe sedan in our driveway.

Early one September morning Dad took the car around to Ned Blackwood's Standard Oil station, where a couple of attendants filled it with gas, checked the oil and tires, and washed the windshield while Dad and Ned chatted about Reds baseball and the implications of American mobilization. Back home a few minutes later, Dad began carrying suitcases and boxes downstairs and loading them into the car. Then a moving van pulled up in front of the house, and three men put everything else into the van and drove off. I think Mom was saddest to see the Acrosonic spinet go that Dad had given her for her birthday or their anniversary a year or so before. My Lionel train set from a Christmas past was too big for inclusion in the car. Mom told us that everything in the van was going to be put into storage and kept for us until we found a proper place for it.

Katie and Henry Bond, Hugh and Mary Sydney McDiarmid, Bill and Louise Ibold, and Shirley and "Ramp" Wrampelmeier, friends of Mom and Dad, came to see us off, as did Bonnie and Barry McKay, kids whose backyard abutted ours. Hugs and handshakes and valedictions exchanged, the four of us piled into the Plymouth, Dad driving, Mom beside him, Anne and I among the bags and boxes in the back seat. So as the World Series came to Cincinnati, we left for Fort Dix, New Jersey, the first stop in what would turn out to be two years of nomadic travel and adventure, two years until we would see again the piano and the Lionel train.

The trip to Fort Dix took us first up to Columbus for more good-byes. The route between Columbus and the East we would travel many times, and its memories remain: Route 40, the National Road, with its old stone mile markers, Mail Pouch tobacco and Burma Shave signs; Zanesville, with its "Y" bridge; the Ohio River at Wheeling; McCulloch's Leap; mountains and slagheaps; Carlisle, with its military barracks and Molly Pitcher Hotel; the rich farmland of the Pennsylvania Dutch; the Delaware River into New Jersey; and, finally, Fort Dix.

Camp Dix had lain dormant since the end of World War I, except for some use in the 1930s by the Civilian Conservation Corps and Citizens Military Training Camps. Now, as Fort Dix, it would house and train the men of the Forty-fourth Division and serve as a reception center for enlistees and draftees. It was woefully unprepared for the influx. Existing barracks could house only about fifteen hundred men. By mid-September some two and a half thousand civilian carpenters and mechanics were working to build the barracks, mess halls, supply rooms, headquarters, motor pools, hospitals, chapels, and rec halls to accommodate the twenty thousand people soon to inhabit the place. But it would be several months before the whole division was in barracks. Tents would be used in the meantime. Five-foot wooden walls and a Sibley stove would add a degree or two of comfort as fall deepened into winter.[2]

By September 21, about twenty-five hundred officers and men of the Forty-fourth Division had arrived at Fort Dix, enough for the commanding general, Major General Clifford R. Powell, to move his headquarters from

Trenton. General Powell's arrival would occur without the two ruffles and flourishes and thirteen-gun salute to which his rank entitled him. "We are here for serious business," the general said, "and we want no pomp or panoply."[3]

All through September 1940 the world as we knew it wondered when Germany would launch its cross-channel invasion of Britain and marveled at the heroics of the RAF against Hermann Goering's Luftwaffe. Those who read and understood the news from abroad contemplated the implications of the pact that Germany, Italy, and Japan entered into on September 27, in which, among other things, the three governments agreed "to assist one another with all political, economic and military means if one of the three Contracting Powers is attacked by a Power at present not involved in the European War or in the Chinese-Japanese conflict."[4]

Troops arriving at Fort Dix were short of uniforms and equipment. No unit could fall out in matching uniforms; some would be in khakis, some in blue fatigues. At first weapons, too, were obsolete and in short supply. Some companies drilled with sticks for rifles.[5]

A week after training had begun, Fort Dix received a visit from the chief of staff of the Army's General Headquarters, Major General Lesley J. McNair. General McNair was the man immediately in charge of mobilization and training for the entire U.S. Army. Maintaining that he was not on an official inspection but merely trying to get a sense of how things were going, General McNair said he was generally pleased with what he found at Fort Dix. He brought with him nine members of his Washington staff. Among these were Lieutenant Colonel Frederick J. de Rohan and Lieutenant Colonel Mark W. Clark.[6]

The rash of building at Fort Dix did not include housing for families. Mom and Dad rented a white frame two-story house on a dairy farm in Jobstown. In the kitchen stood an icebox, the cooling element of which was a twenty-five- or fifty-pound block of ice. Sometimes the iceman would bring a new block; sometimes Dad would, with big tongs and a piece of canvas over his shoulder to protect his uniform. The icepick was one of the most valuable utensils in the kitchen.

I enrolled in the fourth grade. Early that October much more important to me than the Tripartite Pact or General McNair's visit was rooting our Reds through their seven-game World Series with Detroit. Detroit won the first game in Cincinnati behind twenty-one-game winner Bobo Newsom, while the Tigers pounded the Reds' twenty-game winner, Paul Derringer.

That same day, for the second time in two months, death visited baseball. Bobo Newsom's father died in his Cincinnati hotel room. The next day the Reds' Bucky Walters held the Tigers to three hits to even the Series. The teams split the first two games in Detroit, Tommy Bridges beating "Milkman" Jim Turner in Game 3 and Derringer returning in Game 4 to beat Dizzy Trout. Newsom returned to pitch Game 5, which he dedicated to his father, and shut out the Reds on three hits. Back in Cincinnati the next day, Bucky Walters pitched a five-hit shutout and hit a home run to beat Schoolboy Rowe and even up the Series. Derringer for the Reds and Tommy Bridges for the Tigers were the obvious choices to pitch Game 7; instead the Tigers came back with Bobo Newsom on one day's rest. The finale was all that a seventh game should be. The Tigers got a run in the third inning and Bobo shut out the Reds until the bottom of the seventh, when they got the two runs they needed. Both pitchers went the distance. It was Newsom's third complete game in seven days. Bobo Newsom may have been a tragic hero, but our Reds were champions of the world.

At the time the Forty-fourth Division was mobilized, Dad was a captain assigned to division headquarters, where he served as an aide to General Powell. In that role he probably first met de Rohan and Clark, the two lieutenant colonels, during General McNair's October visit. In that role, too, he once arranged for me to ride to New York with the general in his big olive drab staff car with the red license plate displaying two white stars above the front bumper. Once, to my utter delight, Sergeant Poinsett, the driver, switched on the siren for a moment to clear a minor traffic obstacle and move us importantly through.

December 7, 1940, was a milestone of sorts in our house. It was the first radio broadcast of the Metropolitan Opera of that season, and it was the first broadcast sponsored by Texaco. Though her piano was sitting in a Cincinnati warehouse, Mom retained her love of music, and the weekly radio broadcasts of the opera were a staple of her cultural existence. She knew her opera and loved it. She delighted in having Anne and me listen to passages that we would recognize from somewhere else, like the "Bridal Chorus" in *Lohengrin* or the Lone Ranger's theme song in the overture to *William Tell*. Sometimes, too, she would tell us operatic anecdotes. There was the time in 1938 when an off-duty opera star, listening at home to a broadcast of *Aida*, heard the tenor falter in his first-act aria, jumped in a cab, and was at the opera house in time to finish the performance. Then there was the performance of *Lohengrin* in which the swan failed to arrive on cue at the end of the opera. According to Mom, Lauritz Melchior turned to the singer next to him and coolly asked what time the next swan boat was due.

Shortly after Christmas we were on the road again. Dad was promoted to major in January 1941 and sent to the Battalion Commander and Staff Officer course at the Infantry School at Fort Benning, Georgia. Because Dad and Mom knew that this assignment would last only until mid-April, we did not accompany him. Instead, we retraced our steps west to Columbus and settled in with Granny and Homer as Dad headed south to Georgia. The Infantry School at Fort Benning must have brought to Dad memories of Jack Senior's short-lived command of the Twenty-ninth Infantry eight years earlier. Mom went south once to visit Dad for two weeks while Anne and I remained in Columbus. A reporter for *The Columbus Citizen* wrote that on her visit to Fort Benning Mom found that "the old army life is considerably changed. There is a much more serious air about the entire regime of life and duties in camp." Of the peripatetic army life, Mom said that it would be good for everyone at least once in a lifetime "to move to another city where our families, schools and backgrounds weren't known and where we would be accepted or rejected purely on our own personal merits."

In his course at the Infantry School, near the confluence of the Chattahoochie River and Upatoi Creek, Dad acquired not only the professional tools of his trade that made up the curriculum, but also a grimly satiric takeoff on a school hymn coincidentally sung to the tune of Cornell's "Far Above Cayuga's Waters," which Dad had learned at Ithaca. It went something like this:

> Far above the Chattahoochee,
> By the Upatoi,
> Stands our dear old Alma Mater
> Benning School for Boys.
> Forward ever, backward never;
> Follow me and die
> To the ports of embarkation,
> Next-of-kin, good-bye.

Back at Fort Dix, as a result of his promotion and the course just completed, Dad was moved out of division headquarters and made executive officer of the second battalion of the 114th Infantry Regiment. One day he took me to meet his regimental commander. "Colonel," said Dad, "may I present my son, John? John, this is Colonel H. Norman Schwarzkopf." I was meeting the host of *Gangbusters*, one of my favorite radio shows. The colonel had achieved national recognition as head of the New Jersey State Police at the time of the Lindbergh baby's kidnapping, about which I had heard a little from my parents, but it was *Gangbusters* that put him on my map, and now he was my father's commanding officer.

By the spring of 1941 most of the division's logistical problems had been solved, though a shortage of firing ranges at Fort Dix required that elements of the division go periodically to Indiantown Gap or A. P. Hill Military Reservations, in Pennsylvania and Virginia respectively. The serious business of training men for combat that did go on at Fort Dix that spring and summer afforded lots of things to entertain Anne and me. There were parades on Saturdays, and sometimes we would even watch Dad as he lectured troops on some piece of new equipment or an infantry tactic. One afternoon we watched as he introduced a new quarter-ton vehicle called a "Jeep." Sometimes he would take us over to play on the obstacle course. A couple of afternoons a week Mom, Anne, and I would drive over to the post for a retreat formation and supper with Dad at the Officers' Club. The club had a marvelous jukebox that featured movies of the bands and vocalists performing the songs that we selected.

One afternoon while we waited at the club for Dad, a young lieutenant came up to us and spoke to Mom, asking if she was the wife of Major Toffey. In the course of the conversation it came out that we had been living in Cincinnati before entering federal service. "Oh," said the lieutenant, "my cousin works in Cincinnati." "What does he do?" replied Mom. "He plays baseball there," was the answer. "What's his name?" we all asked. "Bucky Walters," the young lieutenant said. When Dad arrived, Mom smiled, introduced the lieutenant to Dad and said, "Jack, you really should get to know your junior officers better." Dad said to Bucky's cousin, "Son, if there's ever anything in this man's army that you don't like or is uncomfortable or inconvenient, you be sure to let me know."

In July 1940, just before Dad went off to Pine Camp, the regular army had about 14,000 officers and an actual enlisted strength of 243,095. By July 1941, through the first peacetime draft in the country's history and through voluntary enlistments, the total strength of Army field forces stood at 1,326,555. In the summer of 1941 the Army had on duty with National Guard units 17,753 officers. Fewer than half of these had been through a service school such as the one Dad had completed at Fort Benning. Twenty-two percent of the National Guard first lieutenants were over forty years old, more than nine hundred captains were over forty-five, and a hundred lieutenant colonels were over fifty-five. Much the same could be said of the regular army officer corps. Weeding out the overaged, overweight, physically unfit, or incompetent officers was not going well. General McNair wrote to Chief of Staff General George C. Marshall in June 1941, "The principal obstacle [to effective weeding out] now is that commanders lack either the guts or the discernment to act."[7]

I knew none of this at the time. We didn't wonder what we were doing at Fort Dix; it was simply where the family happened to be. Anne and I didn't think much about being part of a much larger whole engaged in preparing an army for a war that now seemed to be fast approaching. Though Mom did not express to Anne and me her anxieties about what might lie ahead, she had written them to her cousin Nathaniel Howard, Editor of the *Cleveland News*. He replied,

> Dear Helen—It takes me this long to answer letters. Thanks for yours and I am so glad to learn Jack is on his way to being a general. He has always been a general to me. Sounds like a popular song title. I have no means of settling your qualms about the future. It is quite possible that we are entering a phase of history in which the so-called world revolution has hardly started yet, and in which Hitler, Roosevelt, and the Reds are preliminary incidents. If that is the case, nothing now makes much difference. It is only pretense of the most unenlightened character to think we can possibly be isolated from the remainder of the world. Perhaps we can settle the first phase by quick and direct action. That I hope we do.

After conveying some family news, Nathaniel asks Mom to "tell the general the Indians never were much good and no one is disappointed, but to keep his eye on the Pirates."

One Saturday afternoon in late June, Dad took me over the river to Philadelphia to see a ballgame. The Yankees had come down from New York to play Connie Mack's Athletics. The Yankees won and Joe DiMaggio doubled and singled to extend his hitting streak. And one day Dad took me deep-sea fishing. I became seasick. Dad said I would feel better if I ate something and handed me a mustard-slathered piece of baloney between two thick, soggy slices of white bread. After I dropped it overboard, I did feel better. When Dad and his friend had boated a couple of fish, we went home.

In mid-July Granny and Homer drove east from Columbus to take Mom and me on a tour of New England, while Anne, who didn't travel particularly well, stayed with Deo and Dad's aunts and uncles on Long Island. Memorable were the New Hampshire seacoast, a visit with Mom's college English professor in Maine, the Old Man of the Mountain and Flume Gorge in New Hampshire, and Granny's constant consulting of Duncan Hines's *Adventures in Good Eating* and *Lodging for a Night* to determine where we would eat and sleep.

Meanwhile the Forty-fourth Division left Fort Dix for two weeks of maneuvers at A. P. Hill Military Reservation. The division moved out in two convoys totaling twenty-two hundred vehicles. The longer stretched for eighty miles along the highway and took nearly four hours to pass a fixed point. The other was about half that size. General Powell announced that a "lack of training funds to pay bridge tolls" dictated the routes taken by the convoys. Just across the river into Philadelphia a convoy caused havoc when it tangled with a parade of Elks. Generals Drum and McNair came down to Virginia to view the exercises.[8]

As Dad went about his duties at Camp A. P. Hill, on the south bank of the Rappahannock River, he must have thought of his grandfather, the first of three generations of John J. Toffeys gone for soldiers in New Jersey regiments. In December 1862, Dad's grandfather, then eighteen years old, had fought in a real battle in the cold and mud at Fredericksburg, a few miles upstream from where Dad's regiment was playing war games.

In a letter to his parents written shortly after he enlisted, the first John might have been putting into nineteenth-century prose what many of the young men at Camp A. P. Hill eighty years later were thinking or saying to explain why they joined up. Wrote John, "I suppose you think it queer that I enlisted. I could not see young men of my own age going off without going with them and if I should be spared to return I know I will never regret having helped to crush the rebellion." Of the battle at Fredericksburg he wrote,

> Seven of our regt. were wounded, our col. had his sword struck with a piece of shell and our brigadier general was seriously wounded while encouraging the skirmishers, and we all think if he had not been wounded we would have very likely been brought in close action, as he

is a very brave man. Within 100 yards of us one of the Penn. regts. advanced and the enemy fired on them and they commenced firing back. We could plainly see the officer riding up and down with hat in hand encouraging his men and then see him fall and his horse run riderless about the field. We could see the Colours fall and then rise again. But we being in an open field and they having a woods and strong breastworks to fight from, it was impossible to drive them from their position.[9]

From his first combat experience the young private concluded, "It is very nice to read of a battle, but to be as near to one is not so nice and I never want to be as near one again." He would be, though, most notably eleven months later as a first lieutenant at the battle of Chattanooga. While leading his company of the Thirty-third New Jersey in a charge, he was severely wounded through the hip. For gallantry in this action he was awarded the Congressional Medal of Honor.

Young John saw no more battles in the Civil War. Because of his wound, he was transferred to the Veterans Reserve Corps and assigned to duty at Lincoln General Hospital in Washington. While there he would witness a dramatic event in his country's history. As he told his parents:

On Friday evening I understood that President Lincoln and Gen. Grant was going to attend Ford Theatre and I concluded that I would go, not to see the play particular, but to see those *great men*. While sitting looking at the performance about $1/2$ 10 o/c a shot was fired. I took no notice of it, neither did any of the audience, as we thought it to be part of the performance, till we saw a man leap from the President's box and light on the stage. He lingered for a second and then shot off like an arrow. Everyone was struck with astonishment until he had disappeared behind the scenes and it was announced that the President was shot.

He goes on to tell of having caught a sweating, riderless horse thought to be the one that John Wilkes Booth had ridden, and he concludes by saying,

The night the president was murdered I done something that I have not done in a good while and that was to cry. The tears showed themselves before I knew it. We officers are to wear the badge of mourning for 6 months. I am going down tomorrow to see the President's remains as I understand it is to lay in state.[10]

Later, John would testify at the trial of the conspirators and attend their executions.

> It was an awful sight. When I entered the yard the first thing I saw was the scaffold with four (4) dangling ropes so soon to hold their victims. Just on the left of the scaffold were four yawning graves waiting for their tenants with the coffins or boxes near them. Soon the prisoners came out and after the sentence was read and a few remarks and prayers from the chaplains, they were swung off. I do not care to see any more executions—except Jeff Davis'. I think I could help hang him myself.[11]

Early in August 1941 Dad interviewed the sergeants in the regiment. His findings show some of the problems facing a National Guard division as it prepared to fight a war. Fifty percent of the sergeants were married. Of these three-quarters found it "a financial strain to be in service." Many had come in to do their year, were intelligent and capable, but found it difficult to "devote their best efforts to the service while mentally concerned and upset" about their families and their civilian jobs. Noting that no outfit can be better than its noncoms, Dad found that "Most of our non-commissioned officers are excellent men, but their imagination, instructive ability and training for combat is seriously hampered, in fact 'snowed under' by a welter of administrative duties." The sergeants thought that some sort of housekeeping units could be formed to relieve combat troops of seemingly petty and distracting chores. Dad concludes: "if all our officers throughout the Forty-fourth Division were as good as most of our enlisted men, we could have a remarkable outfit."[12]

On Saturday, August 16, 1941, Mom and Dad celebrated their eleventh wedding anniversary. Perhaps they had an early dinner at the Officers' Club or went to a movie. In any event, they were back home in time to listen to *Chicago Theater of the Air*. These weekly entertainments were the idea of and a vehicle for Colonel Robert McCormick, editor and publisher of *The Chicago Tribune*. The broadcasts originated in the studios of Colonel McCormick's radio station WGN ("World's Greatest Newspaper") and sent out over the Mutual Broadcasting System. The programs consisted of musical selections from light operatic favorites, which Mom loved. During intermission, Colonel McCormick would deliver a speech.

The colonel was known for his conservative, isolationist, and anti-British sentiments. He got his colonelcy with the First Infantry Division—

"The Big Red One"—in France in 1918. He cherished his association with the division, naming his Wheaton, Illinois, estate "Cantigny" after the division's headquarters in France. McCormick regarded himself as an authority on, among almost everything else, military matters.

The colonel's address on August 16 had to do with the superiority of German military tactics and training to America's. He acknowledged the valor of our soldiers in every war and on every field. "But," he added, "valor without military education only means suicide." Before returning his audience to the music of the evening he asked: "Do you realize that the German private soldiers have had vastly more instruction than our regular soldiers, than our National Guard officers, than our reserve officers?" He concluded with what he called "the most momentous statement in my life."

> With all of the billions we are spending on armament; with all of the millions of men conscripted and to be conscripted; with all of our threats to make war on Hitlerism, we have not yet begun a system of training which would allow our boys to defend themselves for a day against these educated soldiers.
>
> If our boys should be recklessly thrown into battle with only the kind of training they have been receiving, they would be destroyed as certainly as were the Australians so cruelly sacrificed in Greece and Crete.[13]

The colonel's remarks did not sit well with my father. He had been born and brought up in the profession of arms, and he had been working hard at the profession for nearly a year. It was one thing to elicit and forward through channels the criticisms expressed by his regimental noncoms; it was quite another to hear McCormick criticize from the outside. He took personally the colonel's impugning of his training and by extension his competence as an officer. He quickly fired off a letter to the colonel, a copy of which, alas, no longer exists. We do have the colonel's reply, however. That he thanks Dad for his "polite" letter strongly suggests that it wasn't. The colonel does send along four copies of the speech.

A couple of weeks later we listened to President Roosevelt's Labor Day message.

He told us,

> We are engaged in a grim and perilous task. Forces of insane violence have been let loose by Hitler upon the earth. We must do our full part

in conquering them. For these forces may be unleashed upon this nation as we go about the business of protecting the proper interests of our country. . . . I know that I speak the conscience and determination of the American people when I say that we shall do everything in our power to crush Hitler and his Nazi forces.[14]

Just after I began the fifth grade, *Life* published an article that shook the world as I was beginning to know it. According to *Life*,[15] the curveball did not exist; it was only an optical illusion. And *Life* had Gjon Mili's high-speed, stop-action photographs of the great Carl Hubbell to prove its hypothesis. I took the matter to Dad, who reassured me, saying that you can't believe everything you read—and besides, it was obvious that nobody connected with the article had ever batted against King Carl.

In a world thus shaken by *Life's* revelations, it was only fitting that we would have to move again. This time the whole division was packing up and heading south to take part in the Carolina Maneuvers. On the eve of its departure the division held a big parade and the band played "Auld Lang Syne." We watched the troops load up and move out. Then we packed the Plymouth and followed Dad and the division south.

As we drove south we listened to the World Series. With our Reds out of it, we rooted for the Dodgers against their uptown rivals, the Yankees. The teams split the first two games; in the third Brooklyn's venerable Freddie Fitzsimmons was shutting out the Yankees for seven innings until the opposing pitcher, Marius Russo, hit a line drive off Fitzsimmons's leg. Fitzsimmons had to leave the game. Brooklyn's ace relief pitcher Hugh Casey was promptly pounded for four hits and two runs while getting one man out. The next day Casey entered the game in the fifth inning and took a 4–3 lead into the ninth. With two out, he threw a third-strike optical illusion past Tommy Henrich, fooling Dodger catcher Mickey Owen as well, and allowing Henrich to reach base and prolong the inning. The Yankees scored four runs, won the game, and led the Series three games to one.

The next day, Monday, the Yankees ended the Series and the Carolina Maneuvers began. For the next two months these war games would involve 350,000 men in exercises throughout southern North Carolina and northern South Carolina. Mom, Anne, and I found accommodations for the duration at Miss Margaret's Rooming House in Society Hill, South Carolina, a village at a road junction on the south bank of the Great Pee

Dee River. Miss Margaret had one of the town's three telephones. Here we ate family-style with the transients, and Anne and I were introduced to such items of regional cuisine as grits, black-eyed peas, collard greens, okra, and fried bananas. The bananas were good. At Miss Margaret's, too, we saw a bit of what could well have still been the antebellum and even colonial South. In back of the house was a big cauldron in which the help boiled the laundry every Monday, and beyond that was a cotton field, pretty well picked over by the time we got there, but still with a few bolls clinging to stalks for Anne and me to gather up.

The Welsh folks who had settled Society Hill in the eighteenth century had named their local school St. David's Academy after the patron saint of Wales. Here I enrolled and became a member of the sixth grade, perhaps because of the fund of book learning I had acquired up north or because I was one of the two or three kids who regularly wore shoes to school. Mom tried to get Anne to go, but she took one look at the prevailing dress code and refused to set foot—shod or not—in the place.

On a rise beside Highway 15, Society Hill's brief main street, stood the town's elegant Baptist church, red brick with white trim. Sometimes we went there for the Sunday morning service. Once we followed the other churchgoers as they filed down the slope toward the river to witness baptisms. The minister stood waist-deep in a pool cut into the riverbank, where he received several white-robed congregants, then immersed each in the waters of the Great Pee Dee River. In the Episcopal Church of our parents and the Presbyterian Church of our maternal grandparents, Anne and I had never seen the like.

On the eve of the Carolina Maneuvers, as he had at Pine Camp fourteen months earlier, General Drum assembled his officers at First Army headquarters in Monroe, North Carolina, and told them why they were there. War was inevitable and imminent, however the country would be brought into it. Debate, always appropriate in a democracy, must yield to action. "Force, and superior force only, will save us in this national crisis." A well-trained, combat-ready army was that force.[16]

Dad would often get to Society Hill on weekends and would even stop in unexpectedly during the week if the 114th was maneuvering nearby. One Saturday Dad and I got into our Plymouth and headed down the road to Hartsville, about fifteen miles away. Dad pulled off the road by a diner at the edge of town. The place was nearly empty—just a man behind the counter and another seated on a stool at the near end of the counter nursing a Coca-Cola. "John," Dad said, "I want you to meet Bobo Newsom." Bobo shook my hand and told the counterman to give us all a Co'Cola. Bobo came from Hartsville, it turned out, and owned the diner. Between baseball seasons, he sat on his stool and passed the time of day with all who dropped in. Bobo and Dad had talked for a while about American League seasons gone by, and Dad asked what Bobo thought about the *Life* article on the curveball. Though I didn't understand all the words in Bobo's answer, I don't think he cared for the article.

From Miss Margaret's all I saw of the Carolina Maneuvers was an occasional convoy of jeeps or trucks moving through town. The soldiers all wore blue or red armbands. I knew that the blue meant good guys. More precisely, the maneuvers consisted of two main parts. In the first, through October and into early November, the three corps of the First Army conducted exercises within their assigned areas. In the second and culminating part during the last two weeks of November, the First Army (blue) did mock battle with the Third Army's IV Corps and the Second Armored Corps (red). Though the blue had some 200,000 men to the red's 110,000, the red had 765 tanks. But the blue had 764 mobile antitank guns. Rules governing tank and antitank action did not always replicate combat, however. In the Carolinas, umpires could declare neutralized all infantry within a hundred yards of a tank of any size. On the other hand, a tank could be put out of action by a .50-caliber gun or a bag of flour representing a hand grenade. In addition to large-scale testing of tanks in offensive warfare and effective defenses against them, up near Fort Bragg, North Carolina, the maneuvers tested the efficacy of parachuting troops into combat.[17]

As the maneuvers began, General Powell was relieved of command of the Forty-fourth Division. Reasons cited by the press included unsatisfactory morale and discipline in the division, as well as a high desertion rate when men learned that their year of federal service would be extended,[18] a condition that led to the acronym OHIO (Over the Hill in October.) Other personnel problems surfaced during the maneuvers. The First Army would lose 20 percent of its strength between December 1941 and March 1942. The primary cause for the loss of officers was the War Department's limit on the age at which each officer rank was too old for combat. The Forty-fourth Division stood to lose fifteen officers and nearly sixty-four hundred enlisted men.

Nevertheless, the Carolina Maneuvers were declared a success. General Drum said that these exercises showed a 40–50 percent improvement over those held in Louisiana in September. General McNair was pleased but guarded in his assessment of the maneuvers. Said McNair,

> The question is repeatedly asked, "Are these troops ready for war?" It is my judgment that, given complete equipment, they certainly could fight effectively. But it is to be added with emphasis that the losses would be unduly heavy, and the results of action against an adversary such as the German might not be all that could be desired.[19]

On Saturday, December 6, as we were packing up to leave Society Hill, Mom was listening to the Metropolitan Opera's broadcast of *Die Valkyrie*. She told us that Helen Traubel was singing the role of Brunhilda for the first time. She also wanted to surprise us with the music of the Valkyries' ride in the third act. Herr Wagner's music provided a fitting prelude for the events of the next day.

On Sunday, December 7, 1941, the Forty-fourth Division left its headquarters in Wadesboro, North Carolina, to begin the journey back through Civil War country to Fort Dix. The convoy carrying the infantry units would spend nights at Ingram and Sperryville, Virginia, and at Gettysburg, Pennsylvania. The other convoy would bivouac at South Boston and Culpeper, Virginia, and at Gettysburg. Before either convoy had reached its first day's destination, the men of the Forty-fourth learned of the Japanese attack on Pearl Harbor. What had been a war game was now war.

I heard the news of the attack on Pearl Harbor in Miss Margaret's Boarding House. I think we were listening to a concert by the New York Philharmonic when the program was interrupted. My knowledge of world geography was slight at best, but because Dad had lived in and around the places being talked about on the radio—Pearl Harbor, Hickam Field, Schofield Barracks—and had told us about them, they were closer or more real to me than to others hearing the news on that Sunday afternoon. I think my reaction was that of many Americans who had no idea of what they were talking about. What did the Japs think they were doing attacking the mighty United States? They'd be sorry. We'd whip them in six months.

Mom had a quite different reaction to the news. She was terrified. What had probably been a vague anxiety in the back of her mind ever since we left Cincinnati was now up front, very real, and horribly immediate. She knew that it meant that she and Dad were about to be parted; that she was about to lose her husband—perhaps for a long time, perhaps forever. All that he had been doing on active duty for fifteen months, culminating in the maneuvers just ended, had been preparing him for just this. He would go and go soon. Where or when hardly mattered now; his going was inevitable.

In the trucks heading north the men of the division wondered what would happen to them. Many were looking forward to ten- or fifteen-day leaves over the upcoming Christmas holiday. Others anticipated being discharged either because their year was up or because they were over the twenty-eight-year age limit then in effect. When at last they climbed stiffly down out the trucks at Fort Dix, they found out that all leaves and furloughs had been canceled and that there would be no discharges. Suddenly everyone was in "for the Duration." Troops in some units were told to pick up the full field equipment that they had been using in the Carolinas and be ready for assignment to guard duty at defense plants. By the end of the month, civilians were taking over some of the administrative and housekeeping chores, just as the sergeants of the 114th had recommended back in August.

We drove back north to await Dad's next deployment. Though rumor, anxiety, and uncertainty gripped an army and a nation newly at war, such wartime austerities as rationing were not yet in full operation. Life went on. Dad's best man and best friend from Cornell, my godfather, was getting married in Scarsdale, New York. Both Dad and Mom were in the wedding party, and Anne and I were wedding guests, in Deo's charge. Dad had to get special permission to step out of uniform long enough to wear the cutaway assigned to the groomsmen. Mom wore gold velvet.

More tangible than the memories is a letter the officiating minister was moved to write to Dad: "Dear Major, It was indeed an *inspiration* to meet you both at the wedding rehearsal and the wedding and I sincerely I hope that we will meet again. It is a *great comfort* to know that men like you are in our army looking after our sons, and all my love and prayers go out to you." He concludes with a blessing: "Now, with all my New Year's wishes & hopes & prayers for the victory—your arms—for our Nation & our war-torn world, & for you and all dear to you."[20]

And Mom had especially liked the prayer offered at the end of the ceremony:

Almighty God, we ask thy special blessing upon these two dear friends who have this hour consented to join themselves in this sacredly beautiful comradeship, and as they shall now journey together over life's hills and across its plains, may their journey be illumined not only by the love-light within their own hearts, but by the loving light of thy Eternal Presence, mile after mile, and upon them and all dear unto them this day, may Heaven's favors continue to abide, through Jesus Christ, our Lord. Amen.

In the year ahead we would journey over our nation's hills and across its plains, mile after mile, from the Atlantic to the Pacific and back again as our family tried to stay together as long as the world at war would allow.

chapter four

COAST TO COAST, 1942

In January 1942, the 114th Infantry was ordered to Camp Claiborne, Louisiana. Dad went with the regiment, while Mom, Anne, and I cleared out of the house in Jobstown, loaded the car, and drove out to Columbus, where we picked up Homer, who would drive with us the rest of the way.

Memories of the sights along the way are few and dim, except for the Irvin Cobb Hotel in Paducah, Kentucky, recommended by Duncan Hines because of its "splendid reputation for fine Southern hospitality and food."[1] Tiger, our peripatetic cat, was with us, and we had to sneak her into the hotel.

We probably motored along the old Natchez Trace, the history of which Homer explained. I liked the word "trace" and the romance the Natchez Trace implied. When I wasn't tormenting Anne or she me, I thought I could glimpse Indians gliding through the woods, or maybe boatmen returning to Cincinnati on foot following their float down the Ohio and Mississippi Rivers. Somewhere in Mississippi, I think, we visited one of the antebellum plantations with a driveway lined with live oaks leading to a hoop-skirted hostess waiting between white columns on a wide veranda. We crossed the Mississippi at the Natchez end of the trace and headed southwest toward Oakdale, the sleepy little town where we would live for the next two months.

The house was a wooden one-story affair painted white and raised off the bare sandy ground on concrete blocks. The house came with the family of a Captain Mahoney. Anne recalls Oakdale as the nadir of her nomadic childhood, chiefly because of the Mahoney's young son Skipper, who, but a year or two old, attached himself permanently to her. Perhaps it was to escape Skipper that Anne, now six, decided that school had more appeal than it had had in Society Hill four months earlier. Off she went every day, leaving a distraught Skipper with his nose indenting the screen on the front door. After school, Dad and I would throw a baseball until I had thrown ten straight strikes or darkness had fallen. I also learned to roller-skate. No booted skates these, mind you, but adjustable metal platforms on four metal wheels.

Camp Claiborne was not the amusement park that Fort Dix had been. It was huge, at one time the largest army post in the continental United States. At Claiborne the Eighty-second Division, the "All-American" Division of World War I, Sergeant York's old outfit, became the Eighty-second Airborne Division, and the 101st Division became the 101st Airborne—the "Screaming Eagles." And out of the ashes of the old cavalry came the Third Armored Division. For the 114th Infantry, though, it was just another place to pitch tents and continue training.

Exactly what the 114th Infantry was doing at Claiborne I don't think Dad ever told us. Maybe the camp was used the way Indiantown Gap and Camp A. P. Hill had been—for its ranges and ample terrain on which a regiment could maneuver. Maybe in the confusion after the attack on Pearl Harbor, as officers and units were being sent hither and yon at the drop of an order, someone decided that the war effort would be significantly aided by sending the 114th to Camp Claiborne. Meanwhile, a regiment at Camp Claiborne was ordered to move to Fort Dix.[2]

The 114th picked up a new commanding officer, Colonel Manton S. Eddy.[3] Born in 1892, Eddy was commissioned in the regular army in 1916, and in May 1918, as a captain commanding a machine-gun company in the Thirty-ninth Infantry Regiment, went to France.

Twenty-three years later, Eddy caught the attention of his superiors during the Louisiana Maneuvers, where Mark Clark, George Patton, and Dwight Eisenhower played key parts. While the 114th under Colonel Schwarzkopf maneuvered in the Carolinas, Eddy was assigned to general staff duty as G-2 (intelligence) at III Corps headquarters in Baltimore. Soon, though, he was on his way back to Louisiana with his new command.

At the end of February 1942, the regiment got orders to move again, this time to Fort Lewis, Washington. By February 1942, seventy-one thousand men had been shipped from the States to the Pacific. Most of these were bound for Australia, with others assigned to Alaska, the Central Pacific, and the islands crucial to maintaining our supply routes. Two divisions on the West Coast were preparing to repel a Japanese attack on the American homeland.[4] Would Fort Lewis be the port of embarkation for the 114th, or would it be home to the regiment augmenting the force defending the Pacific Coast? That we were allowed to accompany Dad suggested it might be the latter.

Toward the middle of February, Dad went into the camp hospital for minor surgery. From there he wrote to Granny and Homer that he was recovering nicely and was able to "sit easier and longer in one place." He said he expected to be released in the coming week, when we would begin our drive to Fort Lewis. He tells Granny and Homer that their daughter "is a real soldier's wife—she takes 'em as they come & looks on the trip to Lewis as a nice ride and excursion together for the first time in a long while." He says that a friend has put them in touch with an "apartment hotel housekeeping type of place and we should land same in either Tacoma preferably (nearer Lewis) or Seattle." He adds that he can tell them nothing about the permanence of the move but will keep them posted. He then outlines the itinerary, a southern route through Dallas, El Paso, Los Angeles, and then north to Fort Lewis. This route, he points out, would enable us to avoid snow and "the perils of big mountains." Because the army has allowed him eleven days for the journey, we can take our time.

Today Rand McNally figures this route to be 3,152 miles long and that it should take fifty-two hours and eighteen minutes of driving time, an average of 60.26 miles per hour. In 1942, even before the imposition of the wartime speed limit of thirty-five miles per hour, we figured we were lucky to average forty miles an hour, at which rate it would take us about seventy-nine hours of driving time to reach Fort Lewis. Dad's ability to "sit easier and longer in one place" would be sorely tested.

Along the way, we would play our travel games. Other times Mom and Dad would recite poetry or lead us in song. Dad liked the poems of Robert Service, especially when 'a bunch of the boys were whooping it up in the Malamute Saloon" or "There [were] strange things [being] done in the midnight sun by the men who moil for gold." There were the songs of World War I, college fight songs, the songs of Stephen Foster, folk songs like "Casey Jones" and "The Wreck of Old 97" and songs from *The Mikado* and *H.M.S. Pinafore*. There were different words to the same tune. Dad would sing of West Point's "sons of slum and gravy;" Mom would sing Friml's "Song of the Vagabonds." Dad would sing "Army Blue"; Mom would give us "Aura Lee." But above all stood the works of Rudyard Kipling. Mom had told us about how, on the occasion of Queen Victoria's diamond jubilee, Kipling had written his hymn to humility, "Recessional," with the recurring "Lest we forget." Dad was partial to "Danny Deever," and in my mind Kipling's elephants piling teak on the road to Mandalay were akin to the farmer's elephant I had once seen plowing bottomland on the road to Columbus. And of course there was "Gunga Din," the movie version of which Dad and I had seen several times when it first came out three years before.

In those days before chains of franchised food or lodging provided predictability, travelers had to pick their stops. We had the Duncan Hines book with us, but more often than not had to rely on billboards to announce a place that we would then check out as we pulled off the highway. Dad drew upon his civilian experience as a traveling salesman in advising us that if we weren't sure of the quality of the cooking in a diner or a "quick-and-dirty," we should order fried eggs and ham because you could tell if either of these was spoiled.

With gas it was different. We were now committed to Texaco because it sponsored the Saturday opera broadcasts that Mom liked. Or maybe because they offered "registered rest rooms" when we pulled in to "fire up with Fire Chief." In all our travels, though, no filling station attendant in his green uniform sporting the "red star with a green T" would sound like Milton Cross. I also wondered why every Texaco station wanted to "Marfak" our car and what would happen to the car if we let them, but no one ever told me. In a pinch, we would settle for Sinclair, the brand Homer bought in Columbus, or Mobil. I preferred Mobil's flying red horse, because some baseball announcer used to describe Harry Craft, the Reds' fleet outfielder, as getting on his flying red horse to chase down a fly ball in deep right center field.

When we didn't have a friend or relative with whom to lodge for the night, we stayed at a cabin in a motor court on the outskirts of town. Usually the cabins were plain wooden structures that once had had a fresh coat of white paint. Some boasted other attractions, like a small zoo displaying a prairie dog village, maybe a mangy coyote, and always a rattlesnake or two.

West of Roswell, New Mexico, Dad pointed out El Capitan rising about twenty miles away to over ten thousand feet. Nothing in our experience prepared Anne and me for such dimensions. Approaching Columbus from any direction we would see the AIU tower sticking up out of the Ohio farmland, and for years it was the entire Columbus skyline. But in the clear desert air El Capitan stretched the imagination.

Southwest of Alamogordo, New Mexico, we went through White Sands National Monument when the principal attraction was sand, not missiles. Our next stop was Las Cruces, New Mexico, where we stayed with a childhood friend of Mom's. Her husband had been an usher at Mom and Dad's wedding, but we had seen them from time to time in Columbus. They had separated, and "Aunt Mamie" moved to New Mexico with her two children. Her daughter Molly was my age and better looking than Elizabeth Taylor in *National Velvet*.

In southwestern New Mexico we were in the country in which Jack Senior and other veterans of the Philippines roamed during the dispute with Mexico that preceded the entry of the United States into World War I and where the army had pursued the Apaches in the 1870s and 1880s. Visions of Mangas Coloradas, Cochise, and Geronimo danced in my head as we continued westward.

Our entrance into California was extraordinary. Thus far, crossing a state line just marked so much progress in the trip. But the California border was different. Signs counted down the miles to the state line, where we had to pull off the road. A man in a uniform approached and told us we would have to unload the car so that he could search for contraband agricultural products.

"I'll be goddamned if I'm going to unpack this car," Dad said. "I spent an hour packing it this morning and I sure as hell didn't put any goddamned plants in there. You want to look in the trunk, you unpack it." Though the man seemed somewhat startled, he did remove the suitcases and boxes one by one until the trunk was empty. Then he straightened up and said, "Thank you, sir. You may now proceed."

"I'll be goddamned if I'm going to repack this car. Once a day is enough. You took the stuff out; you put it back. And hurry it up. We're wasting time standing around this goddamned circus." The man hesitated only a moment before he began to reload the car until Dad took over. As we pulled away from the checkpoint, Dad called out the window, "I hope you all get admitted to the Union some day."

We crossed southern California without further incident. Mom, who had come out here when she was a girl, handled most of our orientation. We spent one night in Riverside, where we splurged and checked into the Mission Inn, built "amid surroundings that are duplicated nowhere else."[5] As we worked our way through Los Angeles we paused to look at one of the movie studios. Then on to the Pacific Ocean. Mom, ever the English major, thought we ought to look at each other with a wild surmise.

It was time to turn right, up the coast. In San Francisco Dad drove us around the Presidio, the favorite post of many a Regular Army man, and then over the Golden Gate Bridge, singing "Open up your Golden Gate, California here I come." Several motor courts, Mt. Hood, and the Columbia River later, we arrived at Fort Lewis with a day or two to spare, time enough to get us settled before Dad had to report to the 114th.

The friend who was supposed to have gained entry for us into the Tacoma housing market had failed. No apartment was waiting for us. Nothing was, and it began to look as if nothing would be. We looked for a long-term rental of a cabin in a motor court as a last resort. Even a good soldier's wife can take 'em as they come for just so long. For the first time that Anne and I were aware of, Mom was in tears. Here we were, thousands of miles from home without a place to live.

Then Dad learned of a cottage on the grounds of the Tacoma Country Club, and suddenly we had a place to live. A pleasant one-story building not far from American Lake, it was better than the home we had recently left in Louisiana and we didn't have to share it with anyone. Cottage 20 was surrounded by all that one expects of the Northwest—vast expanses of green, even in early March, a beautiful lake and our own personal view of Mount Rainier. Anne and I found sandbags in the halls of our new school and learned to get under our desks during air raid drills.

At Fort Lewis the 114th Infantry was replacing the Seventh Infantry. The regiment into which Dad had been born at Fort Wayne had gone to California to join the rest of the Third Infantry Division in amphibious training.

With Colonel Eddy's background in counterintelligence, the 114th was guarding defense plants in and around Seattle. Chief among these, of course, was Boeing's sprawling aircraft plant. Once when we were traveling around with Dad, he pointed out a shabby-looking brick building that overlooked the port of Seattle, saying that his outfit was keeping an especially close eye on the people who passed in and out of that building. For the most part, though, Dad performed his duties with the regiment, and Mom took care of domestic life in Cottage 20 and waited for the orders that would someday come.

The war news was not good. Though Americans were not yet fighting the Germans in large numbers, we were getting clobbered in the Pacific.

And for Dad, who had accompanied his father on one tour of duty in the Philippines, Arcenio's homeland, words like Manila and Corregidor and Bataan were concrete images.

In March the orders began to come. Colonel Eddy was ordered back east to an assignment that would shortly earn him two stars and command of a division. Soon afterward—sometime in April—Dad, too, got orders. He was not going to fight on some small island in the Pacific. Instead, he was to report to Fort Leavenworth, Kansas, to attend a month-long course for officers who would be the cadre for the new divisions that were being added as fast as the army could enlist or draft the men to fill them. He was assigned to the Eightieth Infantry Division, a reserve division that would exist only on paper until its officers and noncommissioned officers were ready.

Once again we were packing up and hitting the road. This time we would return to Columbus, as we had when we went to Fort Benning the year before. He would drive us to Columbus and then return to Leavenworth by train. While Dad spent his last duty day with the regiment, we put everything back into the suitcases for the crack-of-dawn start the next morning. At suppertime I noticed that Tiger was missing. When she had not appeared by nightfall, we began to worry and to search. Someone pointed a flashlight up into a tall pine tree and lit Tiger's eyes. She was on the first branch, about thirty feet up, apparently having forgotten her climbing skills or suffered an attack of acrophobia.

"Oh, well," said Dad, "she'll come down when she's ready. Let's get some sleep. We've got a long drive ahead of us tomorrow." Later that night, Dad said to Mom, "Damn it, I can't sleep with that cat up the tree. I've got to get her down." He went out and called some more, with the same lack of response. Finally, he pulled his uniform on over his pajamas and drove to the signal company headquarters at Fort Lewis. He procured a set of telephone lineman's climbing irons, returned home, and, taking off his uniform, strapped on the irons over his pajama pants and started up the tree. He plucked Tiger from her perch. Tiger, in a wave of relief, sank all her claws deep into Dad's shoulder. Dad bellowed in pain and dropped her thirty feet to the ground, where Mom grabbed her before she could take off again. Dad scrambled back down, took the irons back to the post, and returned in time to catch a couple of hours' sleep before taking his family back across the country.

Coast to Coast, 1942 : 45

This time there was no avoiding the mountains. Our route would take us through the Cascades at Snoqualmie Pass and along the Yakima River, then south across the Columbia and into Oregon, where we picked up U.S. 30. At Pendleton Dad talked about the big rodeo that they had there every year, and as we crossed the Powder River, he startled us all by suddenly yelling, "Powder River let her buck!"—the battle cry of the Ninety-first ("Wild West") Division of World War I.

In Wyoming, we felt almost as if we were home, because we thought of Wyoming, Ohio, where we had started our wanderings a year and a half before. East of Rock Springs we crossed the Continental Divide. From there on the trip would be all downhill, at least until we got to the Mississippi River. Somewhere between Laramie and Cheyenne, we ran into a snowstorm. Dad hoped that we would drive out of it, but before we could, we found ourselves stuck. Dad climbed out of the car, rummaged in the trunk until he found the bag of chains, and began putting them on the rear tires, singing "When It's Springtime in the Rockies" as loudly as he had saluted the Powder River and as ironically as he had taken leave of the California border guard on the journey westward.

On our fourth day on the road, a couple of miles from the Nebraska line, the Plymouth quit. We were in the tiny town of Pine Bluffs, Wyoming. Dad nursed the car into the first garage he saw, a Ford dealership owned and operated by Fred Fisher.

An Ohioan by birth, Mr. Fisher had gone to work for the Ford Motor Company in Dearborn, Michigan, in 1917. He worked his way west before settling in Pine Bluffs in 1923. Because in his youth a horse had kicked him, shattering his knee, he would not be taking up arms for his country. Instead, he would collect, cut up, and ship tons of scrap metal. He also was the founding force behind the town's honor roll, on which were recorded the names of all the young men from the town and surrounding country who had gone off to war.[6] Perhaps his helping us was another small contribution to the war effort, though Mom and Dad suspected that this generous man would have helped us under any circumstances.

Mr. Fisher looked under the Plymouth's hood for a while, scratched his head, wiped his hands on an oily rag stuffed in the back pocket of his overalls, and suggested that we leave the car with him overnight and get a room in the Jamison Hotel, just up the street. He could tell us more about the car in the morning.

Fixing the car wouldn't be difficult—maybe a day's work, but to find the necessary parts, order them, and wait for them to be delivered could take a couple of weeks. There was, he reminded us, a war on. We didn't have a couple of weeks. Dad had less than a week to get us to Columbus and then report to Fort Leavenworth. Mom and Dad began to plan our next move: we would leave the car at the garage and take the eastbound Union Pacific train next morning. The train would take us to Omaha, where Dad would leave us and make his way to Fort Leavenworth, while Mom, Anne, Tiger, and I continued on through Chicago to Columbus.

The only trouble was that the train didn't stop in Pine Bluffs. After a couple of phone calls, Dad had to read to someone at Union Pacific headquarters his orders to report to Fort Leavenworth. In a few minutes the same man authorized the station agent to stop the train for us. The agent then bent over his telegraph key to contact the station agent at Burns, eighteen miles west of Pine Bluffs. The agent in Burns would attach the stop order to a pole with a hoop on one end. When the train came roaring through Burns at about seventy miles an hour, one of the train crew would lean out, slip his arm through the hoop, and bring the message on board. A few minutes later the train would begin to slow for the unscheduled stop at Pine Bluffs.

Back at the garage we unloaded the car and began to sort our possessions into five piles, designated "with Dad to Leavenworth," "shipped to Dad at Leavenworth," "with us to Columbus," "shipped to Columbus," and "left in the trunk of the car." Tiger was checked through to Columbus in the baggage car.

The next morning, after a real western breakfast in the Jamison Tavern, we picked up what we would take with us and walked to the station. As we stood on the platform, we noticed people beginning to come toward the station. Word was that the eastbound train was going to stop that morning, an event rare enough to cause a small crowd—the only size Pine Bluffs could manage—to assemble. The train came in, all steam and bells, as conductors and porters alit to see what had caused the unscheduled stop in this little town. Up we climbed and off we went across Nebraska's prairies along the Platte River.

Dad left us in Omaha to make his way down the Missouri River to Fort Leavenworth, and we rode on to Chicago, where "Uncle" Bobby Peck, an old cavalryman himself and longtime family friend, met us and saw us safely from one station to another and onto the Pennsylvania Railroad's train to Columbus. Homer met us, along with Fred, the ever-present gate-man at Columbus's Union Station. Granny stayed at home to make sure that everything was in perfect order, as it always was.

We settled in at 1622 Clifton Avenue—Mom and Anne in guest rooms on the second floor, and I with the entire third floor to myself. It was a large bedroom with windows overlooking the street and a small back room with windows overlooking the backyard, the alley, and the backs of the houses on the next street over. I was higher than the two cherry trees in the backyard.

It was still early May, and Anne and I were reminded that school was still in session. Anne was driven out East Main Street to suburban Bexley and a preschool run by "Aunt" Neetie, who had been in Mom and Dad's wedding. I walked a few blocks to Eastgate, a public school between the house and Alum Creek. Actually I had briefly attended Eastgate the year before, while Dad was at Fort Benning, so it was a return of sorts. Of course I had been in a lot of other schools since my first hitch at Eastgate, four in the current school year alone. At Eastgate I was assigned to the fifth grade, in which I had begun the year in New Jersey all those miles and states ago.

From Kansas, Dad wrote that school was going nicely. The big news, however, was that General Joseph Patch, the division's commanding offi-cer, and Dad, his aide, would travel from Leavenworth to Camp Forrest, Tennessee, to make "certain arrangements for the arrival & reception of the outfit." A couple of weeks later Dad wrote that he heard from Fred Fisher. The car was ready, and the bill was $77.40. In another week, Dad would finish the course, take the train back to Pine Bluffs, get the car, and drive to Camp Forrest. There he and his classmates would begin to train the soldiers who would make up the Eightieth Division.

Leaving Anne and me with Granny and Homer, Mom took the train to Tennessee to visit Dad and find a place to live. A couple of miles outside of Tullahoma was Camp Avoca, a former summer camp for orphans run by the Knights of Pythias. The camp offered housing for the Toffeys and families of other officers of the Eightieth Division. Mom came back to Columbus, packed us up, and off we drove to Tullahoma.

Camp Avoca seemed like a great summer place. It began at a small lake, but I've seen larger ponds. A road stretched from the lake up to a large wooden main building. On either side of the road were white cabins; ours was the second from the lake on the right. A little bigger than a cabin in a motor court, it had a sitting room and two small bedrooms with a bathroom in between and was sparsely furnished. Anne and I slept in double-decked cots the olive drab paint of which suggested they had been requisitioned from a quartermaster warehouse. To offset the lack of a kitchen, Dad and two other officers got the families at Camp Avoca to pool their resources, hire civilians, and create our own mess using the camp's kitchen and dining room.

The living was easy. During the hot Tennessee summer, we'd spend a lot of time in the lake or on the beach. In the evenings after dinner, when Dad came home, we would get into one of the boats, paddle across the lake and try to catch fish. The lake provided plenty of fish, mostly bass that would swallow hook, line, and sinker. Dad fished about as often as anyone and almost never caught anything. That is, until one day we got a message from the Railway Express agent at the Tullahoma depot that there was a package for Dad and that he should come and get it.

As soon as Dad got home, he and I drove into town and pulled up next to the depot, centrally located right in the middle of the town's main street, billed locally as the widest main street in the country or maybe the world. In fact the train tracks ran right down the middle of the street, like the trolley tracks on High Street in Columbus. The Railway Express agent had us sign for the package and pointed to a big green wagon with spoked wheels and a handle long enough to hitch a team to. On it was a wooden crate, maybe four or five feet long by a foot and a half wide and almost a foot high. Dad smiled as he wrestled the crate as far as it would go into the trunk of the car. Then we drove back to camp and parked the car around behind our cabin. I hurried up the hill so as not to miss supper, but Dad just kept smiling and walked casually down to the lake, where his buddy Jim Bellah was waiting. More accustomed to deep-sea fishing, Bellah fished Lake Avoca almost as vigorously as Dad. Bellah, a captain at the time, I believe, worked in the division's G-2 (intelligence) office. He and Dad had been classmates at Fort Leavenworth in May and had become good friends. Dad described Bellah as "a grand guy, a fascinating globe-trotter, author & soldier of fortune who comes to us as our new G-2 from the 1st Division." He said that Bellah had flown for the RAF in World War I. Later on I would notice James Warner Bellah's stories in the *Saturday Evening Post*, some of which became screenplays for *Fort Apache* and other John Ford–John Wayne cavalry films.

After supper people usually strolled down by the lake in the cool quiet of the coming evening to chat and watch the fishermen. Frogs and birds made what little noise there was. But this evening's tranquility was pierced by a coarse cry from across the lake. "My god, he's huge!" In a furiously rocking boat two men stood precariously. One held a fishing rod that bent dangerously close to breaking; the other had a metal pole with a hook on the end. "There he is. Quick, gaff him!" cried the man with the rod. The other lunged forward, thrust the gaff into the water, and pulled sharply upward. "Got him!" he gasped. "Holy mackerel! Look at the size of him! Let's get him in the boat." There was more struggling as the two heaved something up over the side and into the bottom of the boat. As they sat down and began to pole back across the lake, I realized that the men were Dad and Jim Bellah.

Drawn by the battle across the water, strollers gathered as the boat squished to a stop in the sandy shore. From the bottom of the boat Dad lifted the largest fish I had ever seen. It was a beautiful silver, and just behind the head, near the gill, blood oozed from the wound made by the gaff. "God, Jack! What is it?" "How much does it weigh?" Dad just smiled and the fish twitched as Dad flexed his forearm muscles. Self-styled experts on Appalachian game fish offered opinions about what kind of fish Dad held. Dad said nothing; he just carried the huge fish up the hill and gave it to the people in the kitchen to clean and prepare for supper the next day.

The following morning a reporter from a Chattanooga newspaper called Camp Avoca, but couldn't get much of a story. That evening, as officers and their families came into the dining room, a few stopped to read a small, elegant card pinned to the bulletin board announcing the gift to Major and Mrs. John J. Toffey of a thirty-six-pound Grand Cascapedia salmon. Every June, Dad's uncle, Billy Beach, went fishing in Canada, and every year he sent us a salmon. In the past Uncle Billy's fish supplied our family with more meals than we could keep track of. We ate it hot, we ate it cold; we ate it in fillets and in croquettes; we had it in salad, we had it in sandwiches. We had it however and forever. Packed securely in ice, this fish had made the journey from the Gaspe Peninsula to Tullahoma in good enough shape to fool a lot of people at Camp Avoca.

As July burned into August, life at Camp Avoca grew grimmer. First there was the death of the officer. His body, floating face down in the lake, was discovered one evening. Anne and I never got close to the body or the details, but it was said that he had taken his own life. We never knew why. But the officer's death in that weedy lake did not get the attention that Willard Hershberger's had two years before.

Then the communal mess, which suffered financially all summer, had to close. Without real cooking or refrigeration in the cabins, Camp Avoca began to pale as housing. Mom and Dad looked in the surrounding towns and finally found a house to rent on the campus of the University of the South, on a mountaintop in Sewanee. It was the best house we had lived in since Cincinnati. Uncle S. K. (for Sebastian King) Johnson, Granny's brother-in-law, had attended the university at Sewanee before he went off to be gassed in World War I, and Mom and Dad found three faculty members who remembered young "Seba."

Some time that summer, Dad returned to troop duty with command of a battalion of the 317th Infantry. Though he was pleased with the progress being made by his troops, he said that he would "like to get going and get to war." As he explained it to Homer, "One's enthusiasm for drill and training on the fields on [sic] Tennessee dampens when one has done it for two years in the hope of someday taking his troops into combat." But, he adds, "No doubt I'll have the opportunity in the not too distant future and need not be impatient."

On September 3, he wrote again to Granny and Homer that his outfit had been firing on the rifle range from dawn until dark and that he had taken me out to the range. He said I enjoyed it. He also tells them of a rumored transfer to the Ninth Division, "hot and set for overseas." He recognizes that a move to a combat-ready division is hard on Mom, but he praises her for being "level-headed and smart & courageous and faces 'em as they come." He adds, "It is our present plan that when orders come we'll go as far as we can together in the car."

Late one afternoon Mom had taken Anne and me to the dentist in Tullahoma. Outside his office, a train stood on the tracks in the middle of the street. It was filled with troops shipping out. Through the open windows of the olive-drab coaches, some soldiers were smiling and talking to people on the street. I noticed tears in Mom's eyes. When I asked her why, she said that the sun was in them. Of course, I knew that her eyes watered a lot in August because she was allergic to goldenrod.

A couple of days later, Dad's transfer came through. The Ninth Infantry Division was stationed at Fort Bragg, North Carolina. The division commander was Manton S. Eddy, now a major general. Following the Carolina

Maneuvers the previous fall, Generals McNair and Marshall had apparently decided that at fifty-nine years of age, the commander of the Ninth, General Doyle, was too old to lead a division in combat. So Eddy, who had caught General Marshall's eye at the Infantry School in 1929, was selected to train the Ninth Division under General Doyle and then to take command of it in the last phases of training before going into combat.[7]

In the three weeks between his two letters to Granny and Homer, Dad likely took steps to hurry the opportunity to lead troops in combat. I imagine, though cannot prove, that he wrote to General Eddy asking to be brought over to the Ninth. And I imagine General Eddy telling his G-1 to "get Toffey over here." Sometime in mid-September, we packed up the Plymouth and headed south toward Chattanooga, where seventy-nine years earlier, Dad's grandfather had led his company of New Jersey volunteers in combat and won the Medal of Honor. Heading eastward into North Carolina, we crossed the Great Smoky Mountains and then the tail of the Blue Ridge before starting down the long Piedmont, which in turn gave way to the sand hills and cotton fields surrounding Fort Bragg. We were back to within seventy-five miles of Society Hill, our home almost exactly a year earlier.

Dad reported to Ninth Division headquarters at Fort Bragg, where General Eddy promoted him to lieutenant colonel and told him he would command the Third Battalion of the Sixtieth Infantry Regiment. At regimental headquarters he reported to Colonel Frederick J. de Rohan, who had been given command a couple of months earlier. Colonel de Rohan had served in the coast artillery in the United States during World War I. When he got his Regular Army commission, he switched to the infantry, attending the usual schools at Forts Benning and Leavenworth as he moved up in rank. Intelligent and articulate, he seemed to some to be better suited for staff than troop duty.[8] At any rate, Dad now found himself working under the man who with Mark Clark had accompanied General McNair on his visit to Fort Dix in October 1940.

About the time we got to Fort Bragg, one of the Ninth Division's regiments—the Thirty-ninth—was detached and shipped to Scotland. Ten days later, the Sixtieth moved to a staging area about six miles from the main post. Dad and Mom must have known that Dad was about to go overseas, though they did not discuss the situation with Anne and me. Soon after we got to Fort Bragg, Dad's mother and two aunts came down from New York for what was billed to us kids as a visit, but was in fact good-bye. Meanwhile the training went on. Once or twice we went with Dad and watched the men of his battalion climbing down what he called cargo nets into mock landing craft. As one soldier later said, "We did it so often that we could do it in our sleep." Though the division had been having amphibious training since early February, Dad would occasionally have to tell somebody to keep his hands on the vertical ropes so they wouldn't get stepped on.

With Dad squared away with his new outfit, Mom, Anne, and I found housing in the Colonial Auto Court outside the post in Fayetteville, North Carolina. The court's layout was familiar to us from our western trip—cottages set beneath long-leaf pines in a semicircle around the office. Though small, they seemed substantial—like real houses in miniature. It was here, our radio perched in an open window, that we listened to the 1942 World Series. Our Reds had finished the season in fourth place, losing as many as they won, twenty-nine games behind the Cardinals. In the absence of the Reds, as loyal National Leaguers, we could root for the Cards. For Dad they brought back memories of the Dean brothers and the Gashouse Gang of the early 1930s. And I liked the Cardinals' battery brothers, Mort and Walker Cooper, as well as Marty Marion at short and the outfield of Stan Musial, Terry Moore, and Enos Slaughter. Big John Mize was gone from first base, but in his stead the Cards had Johnny Hopp. I thought his name better suited a middle infielder, and I liked it when the announcer would say, "Hopp up," as Johnny came to bat. Of course the Yankees won the American League pennant again, with the power of DiMaggio, Keller, Henrich, Dickey and the pitching of Bonham, Borowy, Ruffing, and Chandler. The Yankees were clear favorites to win the World Series again. But we sat on the stoop and listened and rooted. In the first game the Yanks got to the Cards' ace Mort Cooper. Despite the Cards' four-run rally in the bottom of the ninth, Red Ruffing beat the Cardinals and it looked like déjà vu all over again. But the next day, Johnny Beazley went the distance to beat the Yankees 4-3. The Series traveled to New York for the next three games, all of which the Cardinals won. I remember Dad at some point expressing outrage that the Cards' manager, Billy Southworth, chose to pitch to Bill Dickey in a crucial moment, rather than intentionally walking him. However, the usually dangerous Dickey did no damage, and Beazley returned in the fifth game and dueled Ruffing for nine innings. Whitey Kurowski broke a 2-2 tie with a two-run homer in the top of the ninth.

On October 5, the Cards won the Series. The next day, Brigadier General Lucian K. Truscott Jr. arrived at Fort Bragg to take command of the Sixtieth Regimental Combat Team—that is, Colonel de Rohan's Sixtieth Infantry Regiment, augmented by artillery, armor, and engineer units. The Sixtieth was detached from the Ninth Division on October 8. General Eddy said that the regiments of the division would soon have the opportunity to make history. He said their success would shorten the war by at least a year; failure would prolong it indefinitely. He added that the Ninth Division would reassemble somewhere at the end of the year. The next day General Truscott addressed the officers of the Sixtieth about amphibious operations and the lessons learned at the Dieppe debacle.[9] Whatever the Allies may have learned at the expense of so many Canadian soldiers captured or killed, the raid was an inauspicious beginning to Allied amphibious operations.

The other big name in amphibious operations was Gallipoli. In the years between the two wars, American officers had studied the failed British attempt to take the Dardanelles in 1915. In the summer of 1941, General Douglas MacArthur believed that the Japanese, too, had studied Gallipoli, and "hence would never launch an attack against a coast heavily defended by modern weapons."[10] Many of the officers who had studied Gallipoli probably noticed that Winston Churchill, the principal proponent of the campaign, was now Britain's prime minister.

Another visitor to Fort Bragg was Major General George S. Patton Jr., who would command the force of which the Sixtieth would soon be a part. The men were formed up on a parade ground facing the reviewing stand, behind which stood the post hospital. Accompanied by the ruffles and flourishes to which his two stars entitled him, the pistol-packing Patton dismounted his staff car and mounted the reviewing stand. Nurses in the windows of the hospital applauded politely. The general turned to them and waved. Then he turned back to the troops and began to speak. In a voice more high-pitched than seemed to fit so distinguished a commander, he told the troops that they were well trained, that their cause was just, and that they would prevail in the battles that lay ahead.[11] Then he said,

> I can't tell you where we are going. But it will be where we can do the most good. And where we can do the most good is where we can fight these damn Germans or the yellow-bellied Eyetalians. And when we do, by God, we're going to go right in and kill the dirty bastards. We

won't just shoot the sonsabitches. We're going to cut out their living guts and use them to grease the treads of our tanks. We're going to murder those lousy Hun bastards by the bushel.[12]

Another recorder of the scene described it thus:

Lofty, high-blown phrases gave way to the gutter talk that Patton . . . assumed was the way soldiers still talked. "Grab those pusillanimous sons-a-bitches by the nose and kick 'em in the balls," was one of his milder expressions. As Patton continued in this vein, one by one the hospital windows . . . slammed shut and the white-clad figures disappeared. One first sergeant said to another, "If those tough old birdies can't take Georgie, he must be getting pretty raw."[13]

If Dad knew where he was going, he didn't tell us. Secrecy was on everyone's mind. "Loose lips sink ships!" bawled ubiquitous billboards. One evening three days before the regiment left Fort Bragg, Captain Dick Kent, the Third Battalion's operations officer, said half to himself as he turned out the light, "I wonder where we're going." "Port Lyautey," his wife answered sleepily. He sat bolt upright. "How the hell do you know that?" he asked. "I was playing bridge with Colonel de Rohan's wife this afternoon, and she told us." "My God!" thought the captain. "If my wife knows, Hitler must know."[14]

Mom always said afterward that she and Dad parted on October 12—the same date on which they had met at a college house party fourteen years earlier. I don't remember the date or the occasion of our Fayetteville farewell. We said goodbye to Dad as we had all those times before when he left the house in Hinsdale or Cincinnati to go on a business trip, or when he had gone from Fort Dix to school at Fort Benning or on maneuvers to Camp A. P. Hill or Indiantown Gap, or when he left us on the train in Omaha to go to school at Fort Leavenworth. We were used to good-byes. As usual, he told me to take care of Mom and Anne until he got back. As we piled in the car and started driving north to Columbus, where Granny and Homer awaited and where we would wait out the war, the sun was in Mom's eyes again.

chapter five

FRENCH MOROCCO

We were probably still in North Carolina when the Sixtieth Regimental Combat Team pulled out of its staging area at Fort Bragg and headed for its port of embarkation at Norfolk, Virginia. Upon arriving on October 14, Dad's Third Battalion boarded the *Susan B. Anthony*, a twelve-year-old former Grace Line passenger steamer of 504 feet and 8,101 gross tons. Taken over by the navy in 1942, she was outfitted with one five-inch and four three-inch guns. She could carry somewhat more than two thousand troops. Originally christened the *Santa Clara*, the *Anthony* quickly acquired from some of her soldier-passengers the nickname "Tombstone Annie" in recognition of the particular stones added as ballast to compensate for the new armament topside.[1]

It rained all day on October 14, and was still raining as troops began to arrive and load around midnight. General Truscott was not pleased with the loading. The navy had promised twelve checking teams, but only six were on hand, and the officers in charge of checking teams were incompetent and used no initiative. According to the general, "Only Lt. Col. Toffey, of the 3rd Battalion, showed excellent initiative and planning in detraining and embarking his battalion."[2] When one of the port's checking teams showed up on the pier beside the *Anthony*, Dad ran them off. He said that he and Lieutenant Lusk of M Company would see to their own loading because in combat he didn't want his men to reach for ammunition and find toilet paper.

On Tuesday, October 20, now aboard the *Anthony*, Dad wrote Mom the first of the letters that would be our principal means of communication while he was away.

> Dearest Helen
>
> I am safe, well and happy and working very hard.
>
> I received your wire from your first night's stop and assume you have gotten home by now after not too uncomfortable a trip.

Bet old John and Anne had a good trip—Sure hope the new home is nice and that the furniture fits it and that you experienced no difficulty in obtaining same.

I would surely like to see you all but know you are comfortably fixed and doing OK, especially if the kids have gotten school under way. John must go to a good school—I feel very definitely about that and do hope he likes the Academy & the gang.

Circumstances prevent my writing any matter pertaining to my present activities or exact whereabouts or for that matter the weather conditions.

Suffice to say that I miss my dear little family very much. I've made some grand new friends in whom I have the utmost confidence.

Mail from me will be scarce for a time, but eventually it will get normal again, I'm certain.

God bless you all—Lots of love to you the kids and your folks.

Devotedly, Jack

P.S. Tell Homer that like Stonewall Jackson I carry his present in my haversack.

A month earlier, a hundred miles up the Peninsula, Douglas Southall Freeman, too, had thought of Stonewall Jackson as he put the finishing touches on the first volume of *Lee's Lieutenants*, his monumental study of Confederate command and commanders. He concludes his foreword thus:

In times less out of joint, publication of this study would have been delayed until it could have appeared in its entirety. The disadvantages of issuing a three-volume work as if it were a serial story are manifest; but something, perhaps, may be gained by printing in the first year of this nation's greatest war, the story of the difficulties that had to be overcome in an earlier struggle before the command of the army became measurably qualified for the task assigned to it. If the recountal of the change of officers in the first fifteen months of the war in Virginia seems discouraging, the events that followed the reorganization of July, 1862, are assurance that where the supreme command is capable, fair-minded and diligent, the search for competent executive officers is not in vain. The Lee and "Stonewall" Jackson of this war will emerge. A second Manassas will follow the blundering of backward-looking commanders and of inexperienced staff officers during the Seven Days' Battle the new army must fight.[3]

At 7:00 on Friday morning, October 23, the ships set out to sea. America's first combat operations over the next seven months would confirm Freeman's assertion that military history can repeat itself. As the convoy left American waters, the troops on board began to earn a 20 percent pay increase for overseas duty.

The armada—Task Force 34—was under the command of Rear Admiral H. Kent Hewitt aboard his flagship, the cruiser *Augusta*, which had carried FDR to his meeting with Churchill earlier in the summer. The task force included 102 vessels out of Atlantic ports from Casco Bay, Maine, to Bermuda, and covered an area of approximately twenty by thirty miles in the North Atlantic.

On Saturday, October 25, 1942, the mission and destination of Task Force 34 were revealed to troop leaders. The Sixtieth Regimental Combat Team would, as the colonel's wife had told her bridge companions, attack Port Lyautey on the Atlantic coast of French Morocco, about eighty miles north of Casablanca.

Port Lyautey would be one small target of a grand operation to be called Torch by the British and American planners who had decided, while Dad had been fooling the folks at Camp Avoca with the big fish, to launch the long-awaited second front by invading the French territories of Morocco and Algeria. General Eisenhower was named supreme commander of the joint operation, with Mark Clark, who in two years had jumped from lieutenant colonel to major general, as his deputy commander. As Task Force 34 steamed toward Morocco, two other task forces were departing Britain on their way through the Straits of Gibraltar to the Algerian landing sites.

Within Task Force 34 were three attack groups. Troops in the Southern Attack Group would attack Safi and secure its airfield. The Center Attack group, the Third Infantry Division, would take Fedala, just north of Casablanca. The Northern Attack Group, code-named Sub-Task Force Goalpost[4] and consisting of the Sixtieth Regimental Combat Team, would seize Port Lyautey. When all three of these groups were safely ashore, General Patton would assume overall command from Admiral Hewitt.

The crews sailing these ships were new to active duty. On one cruiser, half of the sixty-five officers were recently called-up reservists. Only nine had been in the navy more than three years. Of the 1,050 enlisted crewmen, more than half had never before been to sea. To drive the landing craft to the beaches, the navy had recruited men with small-boat experience from fishing ports and boat yards along the New England coast. To

Lieutenant Commander Samuel Eliot Morison aboard the *USS Brooklyn*, Task Force 34, with its thousands of untested soldiers and sailors, was like "a football team forced to play a major game very early in the season, before holding adequate practice or obtaining proper equipment."[5] A "major game" seems, in retrospect, hyperbolic. It looked more like a scrimmage against the French before tackling Germany, the first major opponent on the schedule.

The young men of Task Force 34 wondered about French resistance they would encounter in Morocco. True, the free French were our allies, but the French puppet government in Vichy did not want to do anything to incur the further wrath of Germany, who might then seize the rest of France or its colonies. Though the Allies had been carrying on secret diplomatic negotiations with French officials in North Africa, no one knew for certain if the French would fight us.

On November 3, Dad wrote again:

> Dearest Helen & Kids,
>
> After your grand letter and wire telling of your safe arrival home it is hardly fair that a letter should take as long as this to reach you but c'est la guerre or something. . . .
>
> As this is being written I find it quite difficult to sit still and upright because of quite a bucking and pitching of my home away from home. The past couple of weeks have been very pleasant—Nice friends, cooperative efforts and packed full of work and interest—And lots of swell food—Never have I eaten so much so often and I'll bet I've gained about ten pounds on account of the way the blue clad brothers feed us.
>
> Understandably by the time this reaches you Time Life and the daily papers will have broken the military secrecy which we must of course maintain—So you probably know my whereabouts or can guess at it with some accuracy. . . .
>
> Not much I can write you now darling except that I do miss you all very much—and a week from today I will be a success or failure in this game—for by that time our plans will be in effect and no doubt the results of our operations will be world wide news.
>
> We find ourselves extremely calm and quite self-assured as we face the kick-off and my boys are plenty confident of their ability to do a job and I'm sure the results will make a definite change in the course of

things to come. You can feel confident that we are giving 'em a hell of a ball game in any event.

If we can carry all the wonderful stuff we have to fight with, God help the other guy. He is surely in for it. . . .

It is hard to write without names, places & plans being mentioned but enough to say we are safe, well and ugly and someone is going to catch a hell of a lot of pent up fury when we turn it loose.

God bless you all and remember I'm thinking of you and will be back to you before too very long.

My love to you all. Devotedly, Jack

The convoy enjoyed good weather and, aside from one submarine sighting, smooth sailing. Meetings took up most of the daylight hours as the ships zigzagged at fourteen knots. In addition to the assault plans themselves, the meetings covered "Habits and Customs of Inhabitants of French Morocco," "German Army Uniforms and Organization," "The Career of General Erwin Rommel," and French lessons. On deck, soldiers were introduced to the new "bazooka" shoulder-fired antitank weapon.

Meanwhile, as we had told Dad in our first letters to him, Mom, Anne, and I had reached Columbus and moved into a stucco town house that Granny and Homer had found at 1799 East Long Street, a few blocks from their house on the east side of Columbus. In a few days a moving van arrived from Cincinnati with Mom's piano, my Lionel train, and the rest of our belongings that had been in storage for two years. The spinet fit neatly against a living room wall. The train I carried to the third floor, where once again I would live in spacious solitude. We were prepared to like our house, the neighborhood, and the city. In better accommodations and with a greater sense of stability than we had had in two years we would wait for Dad to come home.

Such stability meant school. This time it was The Columbus Academy, an independent school for boys about a mile from our house. My new classmates had been in school for more than a month by the time I entered the sixth grade. A few of my classmates I had known from previous sojourns in Columbus; others were the children or grandchildren of people Mom or Granny and Homer knew.

Autumn in Columbus was Ohio State football. Homer, a star before the turn of the century, a Varsity "O" man and regular at the annual Captains Breakfast, was delighted to initiate me into the ritual of a game in Ohio

Stadium. During lunch at the Faculty Club, Homer would introduce me to the celebrities of Ohio State sports. Then we joined the crowds in the great concrete horseshoe of the stadium. To celebrate its opening twenty years earlier, Homer had written "The Stadium Song." One Saturday noon, as we started across the Oval, the chimes in the tower of Orton Hall began to play "Ohio State," a hymn that Homer had written and for which he had won a prize in 1916. We always got to the stadium early. Homer loved the band and made sure we were in our seats before it made its dramatic entrance.

Despite a wartime schedule that included games against Fort Knox and the Iowa Seahawks, 1942 was a great year to root for the Buckeyes, and in my letters I kept Dad abreast of how the season was going. Under the legendary Paul Brown Ohio State became national champion, posting a record of nine and one. As a Varsity "O" man, Homer had access to the locker room after the games. Here I would stand in silent awe as Homer introduced me to Les Horvath, Gene Fekete, Paul Sarringhaus, Lin Houston, and Bill Willis. As players peeled off uniforms and equipment, some would chat with Homer about how the game had changed since his playing days. For Homer, who had contributed to both, the university's music and its football meant a great deal.

Far to the east of Ohio Stadium, as the Western Task Force approached the Moroccan coast, Dad wrote again from the *Anthony*:

My Dearest Helen & Kids—

Just a line before we actually boil over the side and get started on our real job—It has been quite a trip—most interesting and enjoyable to me—

Our ship's Captain—an amazingly interesting man—has treated me royally and amused me with the most thrilling recountings of the raising of the S-4, S-51 and *Squalus*—in which he participated.

The men have stood the trip pretty well. Seasickness was not a major problem—and I feel confident that when you read about what we do in the next 24 to 48 hours you'll be proud of us, and some of the boys on the other side will begin to wonder if maybe they weren't wrong. . . .

We are calm, cool and collected as we wait for the gong, and you can bet we'll give somebody an awful cuffing around in the good old American way. We've had time to plan and work details and we have the equipment, men and leadership with which to do a job. I hope the newspapers and magazines get the facts for you. . . .

Tell the kids I sure miss them and have just worlds of interesting stuff to tell them when I'm allowed to write about it all. John's eyes would pop out if he knew all the facts and figures on this job we are doing.

Please don't worry at slowness of mail. We'll try to keep in touch and keep you really posted on what goes on. Right now I'm fat—well & happy. Miss my family—and I'm ready for the gong.

God bless you all and may you have a grand winter. I'll see you before too very long I feel certain.

Don't worry. We'll do our best in a big way.

Devotedly, Jack

Just before midnight on November 7, exactly on time, the navy got the troops to their unloading areas off the Moroccan coast. In the Northern Attack Group, the last nine miles lacked the precision of the first forty-five hundred. Last-minute course changes by the lead battleship *Texas* caused some of the transports to become lost. Unloading was delayed. Then a French ship passing through the convoy signaled a warning to the shore. Meanwhile, the Algerian landings were under way, and the radio had broadcast messages from President Roosevelt and General Eisenhower to the people of Morocco. Day was breaking. The element of surprise was long gone.

Dad's Third Battalion was supposed to land about one-third of its strength on Red Beach, about four and a half miles north of the mouth of the Sebou River, and the rest on Red Beach 2, just north of the mouth of the river.[6] When the landing craft were finally loaded, the minesweeper *Osprey* led them north parallel to the beach. At 0600—6:00 in the morning, to civilians—they turned toward the shore. In a last-minute switch, Dad ordered all the boats to follow him so that the entire battalion could land together on one beach. As they were heading in, two French planes strafed and bombed the boats, destroying two, but without casualties. The navy put the battalion ashore about five miles north of their designated Red Beach. As they came ashore, they met no enemy gunfire and knocked down the two planes that were strafing the beach.

Behind the beach a steep escarpment covered with scrub pine prevented the easy movement of vehicles inland. The first bulldozer ashore started pulling vehicles out of the surf. Then it began making a road up and over the escarpment. From the beach the Third Battalion moved inland for two and a half miles before turning south. By noon it had reached Hill 58 and dug in overlooking the airport across the river.

Accompanying the battalion was a naval fire control party directing the fourteen-inch guns of the battleship *Texas* to targets of opportunity. Early in the afternoon of November 8, General Truscott established his headquarters at Mehdia Plage, just south of the mouth of the Sebou River, and tried to establish communications with his battalion commanders. In his memoir the general speaks of being unable to reach the Third Battalion by radio. "No word from Toffey's battalion until late in the morning when returning landing craft reported that he had landed on Red Beach 2." (Actually, he had been put ashore well north of either Red Beach or Red Beach 2.) A little later he says that Colonel de Rohan had had no word from Toffey's battalion. And again, "There was a vague report that Toffey's battalion was on the river opposite the airfield." A page later he writes, "Toffey we knew to be on the river opposite the airfield."[7]

On the second day, the Third Battalion launched a two-pronged attack. K and M Companies moved southeast toward the western side of the Port Lyautey bridge, and I Company crossed the Sebou River to create a diversion at the airfield. Neither operation was completely successful. On the airfield side of the river, I Company got lost and had to dig in and await daylight. K and M companies managed to drive the French off the bridge, but in turn were driven back by French machine-gun fire. Leaving a platoon to cover the west end of the bridge, the two companies returned to Hill 58.

As the sun rose the next morning, Dad deployed one company to attack the airfield. From Hill 58 he watched as the *Dallas*, an old destroyer converted to a transport, carried a raiding party up the Sebou River through French gunfire. Just past Hill 58 the *Dallas* ran aground, its raiders scrambling over the side to launch their attack on the airfield. Meanwhile I Company attacked from where it had dug in the night before.

Dad, an artillery observer, and a squad from I Company went to check on the Port Lyautey bridge. There they found French artillery massed along the Rabat-Tangier road beyond the bridge, to which they directed the big guns of the *Texas* as well as fire from two destroyers and an air strike by navy dive-bombers. The airport having yielded to the Third Battalion, General Truscott told Dad to organize a perimeter defense for airport security, and P-40s were on the airfield by 10:00. A couple of hours later, infantrymen and tanks secured Port Lyautey.

Meanwhile, to the south, the First and Second Battalions were finishing their missions. Colonel de Rohan took charge of the Second Battalion's assault on the Kasba, an ancient fort above the south bank of the river, where French Foreign Legionnaires fired from the battlements as the Americans stormed the fort. Unable to break through the main gates, Colonel de Rohan called an air strike, and 250 Frenchmen surrendered.

On November 11, the twenty-fourth anniversary of the end of World War I, hostilities in French Morocco ended with a formal ceremony at the Kasba. In three days of fighting, Sub-Taskforce Goalpost had captured Port Lyautey, winning "a vital airdrome, a seaplane base from which to engage in the critical battle of the Atlantic against Axis submarines, and a focal point of transportation routes through northeastern Morocco to Algeria and Tunisia." In taking the airfield, seventy-nine Americans were killed. None of the P-40s at the airfield flew a mission in Morocco. Allied casualties for the whole of the Moroccan campaign of November 8 to 11 were 530 killed, 887 wounded, and 32 missing.[8]

On November 12 Dad found a moment to dash off a quick note:

Dearest Helen & Kids,

Safe, well and happy in French Morocco—Nice fight—They can't take it. I sure miss you all. Am hot, tired, dirty, happy and aside from that there is nothing to say. Our navy can sure shoot. So can our artillery & so can theirs. At present there is an armistice.

I must cut this short. More soon. Send lighter and fluid. No more clothing needed—Could use pair of Jodhpur shoes—a la artillery officers—size 9 1/2 D.

All my love. More soon. Love to all. Jack

In his report of the Third Battalion's operations Dad says that "the navigational ability of the naval wave commanders and coxswains leaves much to be desired." He repeats his great regard for the naval fire support and finds communications between shore fire control parties and their ships to have been excellent. On the other hand, communication between battalions and regiment and battalions and Goalpost was "extremely unsatisfactory." In response to General Truscott's assertion that he did not hear from the Third Battalion, Dad offered this:

The 3rd Battalion Landing Team got receipts acknowledging every message sent to the 60th Combat Team or to Goal Post, but received no answer to specific questions asked. We were in constant receipt of messages requesting information, receipt of which had already been acknowledged. The 3rd Battalion Communications Section was outstanding in its performance of its mission, and its work was highly satisfactory to the undersigned.

He recommended Distinguished Service Crosses for five men from K Company, Silver Stars for eight men of M Company and fifteen men of L Company, a battlefield commission for one M Company sergeant, and a promotion for another.

In a separate message to General Truscott written three weeks later, Dad recommended for the Silver Star René Malvergne, who had piloted the *Dallas* up the Sebou River. Dad notes that Malvergne had volunteered his services and "was invaluable in rendering G-2 information on the subject of French Morocco." On November 8, wearing an American uniform, he boarded the *Dallas*. For three days, said Dad, Malvergne was "constantly on the bridge, utterly disregarding his personal safety." He made possible the landing of the raiding party that attacked the airport. Dad also points out that had Malvergne been captured in an American uniform, he may well have been shot as a spy. General Truscott awarded the Silver Star to the man Dad called "a gallant French gentleman."[9]

The after-action assessment of Goalpost was not all kudos. To be sure, the invaders had seized their objectives without heavy casualties. Still, the inexperience of the American troops was clear almost everywhere. In addition to being frustrated by poor communication between his headquarters and the attacking battalions, General Truscott was annoyed with reports of small American units surrendering before they were in real danger of being surrounded or annihilated.[10] This time the foe had been the French; next time the enemy would be the Germans, who would almost certainly present a more formidable front. We would have to be better.

Far to the east in the Libyan desert, German General Erwin Rommel, his army defeated at El Alamein despite Hitler's order that he "show [his troops] no other road than to victory or death," learned of the American and British task forces approaching Africa. Even then, six months and thousands of casualties before the end of the fighting in Tunisia, Rommel realized that the invasions to his west "spelt the end of his army in Africa."[11] On November 20, while walking with Hans Von Luck, one of his Panzer commanders, Rommel said,

What I was afraid of weeks ago will occur: our proud Africa Army, and the new divisions that we have landed in northern Tunisia will be lost. First the loss of Stalingrad, with 200,000 battle-tried men; now we are losing Africa too, with elite divisions. . . . Luck, the war is lost. We've got to seek an armistice with the Western Allies. We still have something to offer. This assumes, of course, that Hitler must be forced to abdicate; that we must give up the persecution of the Jews at once and make concessions to the Church. That may sound Utopian, but it is the only way of avoiding further bloodshed and still more destruction of our cities.[12]

For at least one distinguished German general, the tide of battle had already turned.

As peace and quiet settled over Port Lyautey, the Sixtieth Infantry needed a place to live. The cork oak trees of the Mamora Forest, six miles south of Port Lyautey, provided excellent cover, and here the battalions of the Sixtieth moved in with headquarters, field kitchens, and latrines. The men dug, cut logs, and scrounged packing boxes and ammunition crates to fashion the walls of their huts. Then they fastened together their GI shelter halves to make the roofs. The cork bark fueled many a fire.

Settled into postcombat life in French Morocco, the men of the Third Battalion were eager to explore what they considered, however imperfectly, to be the exotic pleasures awaiting them in Port Lyautey. Perhaps some men, remembering the 1938 film *Algiers*, assumed that every Kasba in North Africa came complete with Hedy Lamarr. Otherwise Hollywood offered little by way of orientation. *The Road to Morocco* was released on November 11, the day the fighting stopped. *Casablanca*, shot in the summer of 1942 and scheduled for release in 1943, was rushed into theaters on November 26, Thanksgiving Day, so that the American capture of that exotic city could figure in the picture's promotion.[13] In his letter of December 6, Dad sums up what the young Americans could expect outside the cork forest:

> War is as Sherman says and has no similarity with cinema or story-book versions. Positively no beautiful svelte spies with fancy boudoirs, brandy and such. All the femininity here has a strong garlic and unwashed odor as well as a four plus case of syphilis. The country possesses nothing that one can buy. We have plenty of money; so have the natives & French but there is *Rien! Rien! Rien! Pas de savon, pas de rhum, pas de cognac, pas de chocolat. Rien! Rien! Rien!* [Nothing, nothing, nothing—no soap, no rum, no cognac, no chocolate. Nothing, nothing, nothing!]

He does, however, find "a little champagne, local and quite good, for 30 francs (or 40 cents) the bottle." He admits that his "French is anything but perfect; however it is beginning to come back as the demands to use it arise." And contrary to conventional army wisdom, he writes, "The American food packers deserve a decoration for the splendid job they've done for our boys. Our emergency battle rations were better than the average French Christmas dinner and now that we are fairly well established we eat like barons." Moroccan restaurants, Dad says, were off-limits because there is only enough food for the citizenry and because "the sanitation is lousy."

Dad also wrote Anne and me on December 6:

> This country is very much like Florida or parts of California—plenty of oranges and grapefruit grow here. The people are mostly French and Arabs with many more Arabs than whites. The Arabs are Mohammedans and wear flowing robes looking like dirty burlap bags. These Arabs are mostly from Syrian or Arabian descent and are brown or black in color and speak a guttural sing-song language that is hard to learn or understand.

From Columbus, Anne wrote Dad on December 7. Her letter reads in its entirety: "Dear Dad, how are you. The dog and the cat seem to disagree. The dog tries to make friends and Jo spits. Mom is fine. I am sorry that I can't say more. Love, Anne."

Meanwhile, the men of the Dad's battalion began to mingle with the locals. One soldier, on his first trip to town, carried with him for barter a carton of Twenty Grand cigarettes. He quickly learned that the local girls accepted only "Lucky Streeek."[14] In as long as it took the troops to look upon Port Lyautey as Fayetteville with olive trees, it became obvious that some reminders were in order. At a battalion formation, Dad reminded the men that they were not a conquering army; that success in the future would depend on good relations with the French and the Arabs. On the other hand, Arab merchants inflated the prices on what food and wine they could find to sell. The troops complained but paid. Price ceilings might have to be established. Meanwhile, men going into town would have to improve their appearance; excessive drunkenness and indiscriminate knocking on the doors of private homes or hotel rooms would mean company punishment; accosting Arabs and beating up cab drivers would mean a court martial; conviction for rape could bring a death sentence.

Furthermore, officers who failed to control their men or correct inappropriate behavior would forfeit half their pay.[15]

For those who did not want to partake of the meager indigenous pleasures at inflated prices, there was the American Red Cross in the person of Olivia Kammerer. In Port Lyautey, she quickly commandeered a sleazy saloon and turned it into a club, invited the town's French colonial mothers to tea, and persuaded them to allow their daughters to attend the club's dances by promising chaperonage and transportation to and from the club in American trucks.[16]

The Sixtieth Infantry in bivouac was beset with rumors. Though the regiment was far from German airbases and the Luftwaffe had more urgent targets in Tunisia, one rumor had it that gliders had landed saboteurs in the area. Another said that American soldiers were being murdered, their bellies slit open, their bodies stripped clean. Yet another had it that the troops of Operation Goalpost would be going home.

But they would fight a lot more before they went home. Their next field of battle lay more than a thousand miles to the east. To move the men and equipment of Operation Goalpost would require considerable planning; to get them ready to fight the veterans of Rommel's Afrika Korps would require more combat training. And train they did every day except Thanksgiving Day, when the mess sergeants prepared a respectable replica of a traditional Thanksgiving dinner—turkey with all the trimmings.

After the welfare of the men in his battalion, Dad's principal worries were financial. He wrote to ask if the allotment he had set up for Mom had started coming through. Likewise, he wondered whether the war bonds were being taken out of his pay. To be on the safe side, he sent Mom a couple of money orders for $180. He also endorsed to Mom a check for $50 that the Army had paid him to cover our travel from Camp Forrest to Fort Bragg back in September. He asked Mom to send $3.00 to the *Infantry Journal* to pay for his subscription.

But a bigger financial matter had come up. The Eightieth Division sought reimbursement for the loss of $1,167.84 incurred by the Officers' Mess at Camp Avoca, and a board of inquiry decided that "a fair and equitable settlement" would be for Dad and two other officers to pay 50 percent of the loss and that all the other participants should pay the other 50 percent. The division figured Dad's share to be $215.86. He told Mom to pay it if she could, while he directed a protest to the division commander, asking for a review by a higher authority.

Meanwhile, Dad named his jeep "Helen" and had Mom's name painted on the side. Through December the regiment lived in the cork forest, played in Port Lyautey, pulled lots of guard duty, and trained on the surrounding terrain.

The Public Relations Section of the Western Task Force issued periodic news bulletins. In the issue of December 23, 1942, readers learned that British bombers had hit Munich and that American planes over Tunisia were hitting German and Italian supply lines. On the home front, UCLA would represent the West Coast in the Rose Bowl against the University of Georgia Bulldogs. And the Associated Press voted the Yankees the biggest sports flop of 1942 for losing the World Series to the Cardinals. The paper also reported that the Merchant Marine would soon receive a new ship named the *Lou Gehrig*, after the great Yankee first baseman.

In December, General Eddy arrived in Morocco, and Dad was glad to have him back. Earlier Dad had written, "We are anxiously awaiting the arrival of M. S. Eddy & the regathering of our parent unit—for reasons of settling down and removal of certain elements of harassment and picayunishness which, contrary to my hopes, do not cease in war." Dad notes that "The mimeographs and typewriters landed soon after we did and have been delivering effective fire ever since the last French volley died away." A couple of weeks later, he wrote, "M. S. Eddy looked pretty good to me today, and I was sure glad to see him. Hope he takes over pretty soon as we always worked well together and frankly I have missed same & him." A week later he added, "M. S. Eddy's arrival has given the Claiborne touch to training and early rising these days and I must say it does snap the outfit up a lot and give it a familiar feeling which I like—and enjoy."

For the Third Battalion, Christmas 1942 was a special event. The chaplains, of course, held services for the faithful and the seekers of faith. For the secular celebration Dad reduced the traditional twelve days of Christmas to three, writing, "We've got a tree in the battalion area and will trim it with tangerines and such other items as we can locate to add color etc." For the Christmas feast, Dad, using all the resourcefulness at his command, found thirteen hundred steaks, which were washed down with plenty of good liquor. The troops, many spending their first Christmas thousands of miles from home and family, had a great time. In their diaries and memorials written years afterward, they speak glowingly of that Christmas in Morocco.

In Columbus that Christmas, I was put into a Sunday-school pageant. I was to be the third wise man. Though somewhat reluctant, I was not new to this sort of thing. In our last year in Cincinnati I had been the second shepherd. At home there was some discussion about whether going from second something to third something constituted a demotion. I held that going from shepherd to wise man more than compensated for the numerical downgrade. The third wise man's gift was, of course, myrrh: "its bitter perfume / breathes a life of gathering gloom / Sorrowing, sighing, bleeding, dying / sealed in a stone cold tomb." My associates brought gold and frankincense, which I thought were more suitable to the occasion. My role as prophetic magus being lost on me, I thought that myrrh was a lousy Christmas present and was embarrassed to be bearing it.

Life in Morocco had settled into a "sort of groove . . . with lots of guard duty and training alternated and nothing very constructive or interesting afoot." "I'm somewhat disappointed," Dad wrote on January 4, 1943, "in the lack of vigorous and intelligent training as well as the lack of effort to get any going."

But in a letter to me dated the previous day, Dad sounded positive and reasonably happy:

> Dear John—I enjoyed your letter when you told me about the football game and meeting the Ohio State players. Yesterday we heard a rebroadcast of the Rose Bowl game—and enjoyed it very much indeed. Things here are going along just as normally as if we were on maneuvers at home, and except for missing you and Mouse and Mom I like it O.K. Of course I'm anxious to see your new home and live in it with you. Mom has written me that you are doing very well in school and I'm certainly proud of you and glad to learn of your success.
>
> Someday I'll have plenty to tell you of interest but right now I'm only permitted to say that we are somewhere in Africa and we see many strange and different peoples and things. We keep busy and seem to be doing as well as can be expected. We ate turkey on New Years Day—and all our wants are simple ones except as I said above about missing my family.
>
> Well son I hope we can all be back together again before another holiday season rolls around. Lots of luck to you in Basketball and Baseball. My best to all your pals.
>
> Devotedly,
> Dad.

On December 23 the Sixtieth Combat Team gave a big party for the French and the Task Force Headquarters. Though Dad says it will break the monotony and add a chance to dress up for an occasion, it was to be a "stag affair and I should imagine stiff and not too much fun." Another break in the monotony came on December 27, when Dad and an officer identified only as "Walters"[17] traveled thirty miles north toward the Spanish frontier to have lunch with Donald Carleton, his "charming and beautiful French wife and two extremely cute kids." Carleton, an American, had been farming in Morocco for more than twenty years. In putting away "turkey, cauliflower, wines, pudding, aperitifs, hors d'oeuvres, etc." Dad says he ate about six meals in one and "proudly displayed my family snapshots." On another occasion Dad visited with the pilot of the *Dallas*, René Malvergne, and his wife, and on January 17 he lunched with Colonel Petit, commander of the French forces in Port Lyautey, and his wife.

The big event of January, though, was the visit of President Roosevelt. On the day that FDR arrived, Dad wrote that for days leading up to the president's arrival, "Our lives have been a constant succession of anticipations of the arrival of IMPORTANT visitors. I've thought often of that portion of Tolstoy's *W & P* on that subject."

President Roosevelt and Prime Minister Winston Churchill had met at Casablanca to outline the strategy for the war in the Mediterranean, selecting Sicily as the next step on the way to Hitler's Europe. Roosevelt and Churchill agreed that only with Germany's unconditional surrender would the war end. Historians have speculated that the decision may have prolonged the war in Europe by withholding from Rommel and other high-ranking and potentially influential German dissidents the possibility of a negotiated peace.

On January 21 Roosevelt, accompanied by his advisor Harry Hopkins and Generals Clark and Patton, visited the Port Lyautey area, lunched in the field, and watched the First and Second Battalions of the Sixtieth Regimental Combat Team pass in review. The president was delighted with what he saw—men who were "tough and brown and grinning and ready, they really look as if they're rarin' to go."[18] Dad's Third Battalion did not pass before the president, having been deployed as security for the occasion. Of Roosevelt's visit Dad wrote, "It was dramatic and important—and a courageous thing to do. The G.I.'s ate it up, of course."

Until early January, Dad's letters were written on ordinary paper, usually very thin sheets, and they came in an envelope. Troops overseas knew that V-mail was coming but hadn't seen it yet. The first letter from Dad written on V-mail paper was dated January 5, 1943, but not until April did we receive V-mail letter that had been photographically reduced, a means of allowing review by military censors and making the transmission of mail more secure.

He misses us, he said, looks forward to that day not too far off when we will be together again. "The thought occurs to me often," he wrote, "whether or not I should have you meet me at some place of debarkation . . . or just appear home some time. In any case it won't be difficult to decide when and if the time rolls around." And, on January 29: "War news sounds good and of course every day is that much nearer the end. There is, however, a lot to be done. A change of scenery for me and mine is not beyond the realm of possibility." In fact, it was not beyond the next day.

chapter six

TUNISIA

The Sixtieth Regimental Combat Team was ordered eastward. Vehicles would travel in convoys, while most of the troops would travel by train. In a letter dated January 30, General Eddy put Dad in command of one of the trains. The responsibility would be great, the general said: "Each mile will bring you closer within range of hostile aircraft, saboteurs and parachutists." With the reputation of the division at stake, the general asked Dad "to do all within [his] power to make that reputation one of which we can both be proud," concluding by reminding Dad that the comfort of his men should be his "constant concern."

But the comfort of travel by train across the North African desert would be different from that afforded back home. This trip would be made by boxcar. To give historical perspective to the wretched traveling conditions, the general told Dad to "explain . . . that this trip is to be made in the same manner as their fathers and uncles traveled through France. Their sleepers will be freight cars with straw on the bottom of the '*Quarant hommes ou huit chevaux*' type"—the 40-and-8s that the old-timers spoke of on Armistice Day.

The trains headed east for some 575 miles to Tlemcen, where regimental headquarters and the First Battalion got off. The Second and Third Battalions, however, continued to Oran, where they would pull guard duty for the next two weeks. In a letter to Mom dated February 9, Dad wrote, "At present my outfit is doing the same work that I did a year ago [at Fort Lewis]—only here it is much more interesting and lively." He closed by saying: "Well, I'm still alright [*sic*]. I still miss you terribly—a condition which will not improve. Write often, darling, and don't be surprised if you hear from me directly some day. My love to all, and more to you. Devotedly, Jack."

To me on the same day Dad wrote, using a nickname for me whose origin and meaning I have never been sure of,

Hi, Snod! What's new? I heard that the big league clubs will not go south to train this spring but will remain in the north. Also I got the O.S.U. *Monthly* from Homer—which told all about the football season and which was very interesting. You surely must have seen some fine games last fall—especially that Sea Hawks game. There are a bunch of fine airplanes around where I am now and I believe that Hitler's men will really feel the effects of America's air power before too long. Plenty of very interesting stories to tell you when we get home, but of course we can't describe all the strange things we see just now as that would tell just where we are. You can be sure of one thing, John—That is, that the American people are the luckiest in the world and have the highest standard of living. People over here get very few of the needed things in life and not many baths or comforts. More soon, son. Write when you can. I'm proud of you.

Love, Dad

Two days later, on February 9, Dad wrote to Mom,

Darling—

Herewith money orders in the amount of $160, which I hope will help pay off the Avoca deal—or set up a nest egg for that farm or ranch after the war.

Things are very pleasant at the moment, what with living in a house and a recent change of scenery.

Have seen several old 44th characters and also Miss Martha Raye has twice entertained in my area and we have become big buddies. She is a scream. She will phone Deo on return to home. And if you can locate her and drop her a line ask her for first hand info of her African Adventures with Toffey. She'll keep you laughing till the war ends. . . .

Some of these days you might get a phone call from someone who has seen me in the not too distant past. Likewise I wrote Deo of an interesting and possible means of closer communication which you might check upon. . . .

Some of our local Napoleons of minor importance are predicting the end of the war in time for the World Series. Me, I don't subscribe to that train of, shall we say, thought.

Well, in any case, buy yourself a steak or a mink coat with this $160 and let me know if you ever get it or the other $180 I sent.

God bless you all. Write soon and often, and pray for the speedy reunion. Lt. Fisher and I are writing a play for afterwards. Love, Jack

At home we would get an occasional phone call or letter from someone who had come back to the States, but none that I recall from Martha Raye. Nor did the "closer communication" alluded to above pan out.

"I am told that you sang very well at Church at Xmas and that you are doing fine work in school," Dad wrote to Anne the same day. He asked for pictures of us all, the cat and dog, and the house. He told her that he has "visited some big towns in other parts of Africa lately and I now live in a house which is a very nice change." One of the companies in the battalion has a monkey for a mascot, he wrote, and he had a "pretty good police dog" for a while but hasn't seen her for several days.

On February 17, the men of M Company of the Third Battalion, guarding the airfield at Relizaine, got what would be their last shower and their last change of clothes until April 13—at least for those who made it that far.[1] The next day Dad was moved to write two letters. Anxiety and frustration about money matters prompted the first.

Darling—Your grand letter of 16 Jan reached me last nite. It was swell and the 12th rec'd from you. #11 was posted 12/18. Apparently you do not get all of mine—on or about 8 Dec. I wrote you to pay the Inf. Journal $3, Finance Officer at [Camp] Forrest $33.75 o/c an overpayment—and Avoca mess $217.86. Perhaps it finally got there or will someday. Are you getting the money orders? Have sent 180 & 160 so far. Moving out of this house tomorrow and going some place else—in the correct direction, too. Your newsy chatty letters are so like you I can't tell you how I enjoy them and only wish Uncle Sam would get more of them to me. This place has been interesting and I've enjoyed our sojourn here. Sure wish I'd get some pictures. Haven't had any mail since Deo's package end of last month—until last nite. News lately has not been too favorable for our side. Haven't seen M. S. E. [General Eddy] or his nephew [Jack Eddy, serving as his uncle's aide] for two or three weeks, but will deliver messages when I do see them. . . . Your allotment should be $398.42 and should have become effective with month of Oct. Please write two letters—giving my name, grade and 0335348. Send one to the "Office of Dependency Benefits" 213 Washington St., Newark, N.J. and one to Chief of Finance, Allotment

Div., Wash. D.C. I have confirmations indicating the increase has been recorded, so please question it. The Finance Officer check to Forrest should be made out to "Treasurer of the U.S." This letter is mostly business, so I will write another tonite telling you how much I love you and miss you. I wrote several letters about a week or ten days ago indicating that I had moved. By now you should have them. My love to you all and May I see you soon. Devotedly, Jack.

That night he wrote again, "to say that after that gruesome letter of facts and figures I really wanted to write and say I loved you very much." He adds, "I only hope that you will just remain your same self always on account I don't care about any minor matters any more. . . . Please write as often as you can and tell my kids that regardless of what their Dad does that their granddad was O.K. Love, Jack."

The next day, the Sixtieth Infantry was ordered east again, this time by foot and by truck. The men would march about fifteen miles and then be picked up by trucks and carried another thirty miles. In six days, through heavy rain and deep mud, they reached Ain M'Lila, where they were visited by their erstwhile commander, General Truscott, who recalled,

On February 24 Carleton [Col. Don E., Truscott's Chief of Staff] and I rode out to Ain Mlila to meet the first regiment of the 9th Infantry Division arriving in the forward area to join II Corps. This regiment, the 60th Infantry, had been in my command for the initial landings in North Africa at Port Lyautey. It had been only a few weeks since I left them . . . but so much had happened since then that it seemed longer. Now they were to join the fighting here, and I was to go back to the place where we had started the war together—to another command.[2]

On February 28, the regiment began to move again, southeast through Tebessa and crossing into Tunisia at Bou Chebka. The rain continued and the mud deepened. It mired vehicles and it stuck to the bottoms of the men's overcoats, weighing them down. On March 4, Dad wrote,

Lately we have been on the move and no time to write. Still pretty cold here and have had plenty of rain. We've seen lots of territory in our time over here and some amazing country—terrific as to size and space. Not unlike Wyoming and Idaho as to appearance and general ruggedness. . . . Well, the damn war can't last forever and each day is one nearer to seeing you all again. Dick Kent is now with Division, I regret to say. Hated to lose him. I'm O.K. and getting fat on canned chow so God bless our food packers. Magazines and packages are not getting thru to us. Last I got was Dec. 1942 [Reader's] Digest rec'd last week. More soon and often my dearest and all sorts of love to all of you and especially to you. Devotedly, Jack.

Four days later, after having received a stack of mail including letters, magazines, and packages, Dad wrote to say that the outfit kept moving. "It still rains and we are awfully anxious to finish Erwin Rommel and end the No. African campaign." Switching to another topic, he wrote, "John's marks are marvelous and I'm surely proud of him. Also his public speaking is a grand thing. Sure hope he will be a doctor or lawyer and stay the hell out of the army & if he does go in the army let him stay out of the infantry." From his prewar friend Bob Redpath, Dad heard that "the Giants are training at Schmaltz's Boarding House in Lakewood, N.J. this year. . . . Must close. Bed calls and I can dream, can't I. Lots of love to you all. Jack."

Anne and I shared a letter from Dad written March 5. "It is still cold here," he began, "and your dad is getting awfully fed up on living in a pup tent and sleeping on the ground." However, he wrote, before very long "this old war will end and we'll all be together again in good old Ohio or any place in the USA." He had heard that Eddie Miller would play short-stop for the Reds in the coming season, which "should strengthen the club if they ever get a left fielder."

On March 9, the Sixtieth Regimental Combat Team moved forward to Thelepte and Fariana. On March 11, Dad wrote that "we dwell among the ruins of an ancient civilization—where Hannibal started from." He reported that he was commanding the regiment while the "Col. and Exec are away temporarily" and that he hadn't "spent any money in three weeks (no chance to) nor have I drawn any pay for January or February." He added, "We should very soon now commence to put the finishing touches on E[rwin] R[ommel]. Lord knows the boys are anxious to get the job done and end it the right way." He again referred to Bob Redpath's letter, saying he had heard that Jim Bellah had married and asking what was new with the ever-nagging Avoca matter.

Bob Redpath and Dad had known each other since college days—Bob's at Yale and Dad's, briefly, at Cornell. On March 8 Dad answered Bob Redpath's letter, and in a letter to Mom, Redpath described Dad's letter as being "typical of the old-time Toffey—full of good humor and references to the Cincinnati Reds." Redpath had told Dad to keep an eye out for Dr. Dwight Fishwick, a Yale classmate of Redpath's and now a major in the Medical Corps. Dad replied to Redpath:

> Dwight Fishwick Y'28 is an old house-party acquaintance of mine— one time laughingly referred to as Bull Dog Dwight of Yale. He also caught a last-ditch pass against somebody one time, I recall. I shall watch for him and I hope I don't meet him while in the performance of his duty.[3]

The histories of World War II do not give much attention to the movements of the Ninth Division. In Tunisia, as in Morocco and Algeria before and in Sicily later, units of the Ninth were attached to other American divisions. The Allies had failed to capture Tunis and Bizerte and cut off Rommel's army in Egypt. Instead, as the winter rains set in, the opposing armies probed and sparred. Frequent changes in the Allied command structure and Axis supply shortages seem to have kept either side from gaining and holding an advantage.

Two changes in the Allied command structure were the creation of 18th Army Group—two British armies and the American II Corps—under the command of British General Sir Harold R. L. G. Alexander, and the assigning of General Patton to command II Corps. General Eisenhower told Patton that he was to relieve immediately any commander who was not getting the job done.

On the other side, there was an important command change. On March 9, General Erwin Rommel, the Desert Fox, took long-overdue sick leave and left North Africa permanently. So secret was Rommel's departure that neither the Allies nor the German home front learned of his absence, and the Allied press continued to refer to him and his Afrika Korps.[4]

The Allies now prepared to take the offensive in Tunisia. The British Eighth Army would drive west and then north along the coastal plain. In northern Tunisia, the British First Army would apply pressure on Axis troops defending Tunis and Bizerte. Meanwhile, the American II Corps would launch a series of "carefully timed, well prepared, and suitably controlled attacks to seize dominating positions along the enemy's line of communications." These operations would tie up enemy troops, secure forward airfields, and establish a forward supply center. In addition, they would "advance the training of II Corps, increase its self-confidence, and improve its morale." The enemy did not know, of course, that General Alexander had no intention of letting the Americans drive out of the mountains onto the coastal plain. He wanted only to create the impression that they might. Reaching back in history, General Patton rationalized II Corps's supporting role by likening it to that of Stonewall Jackson's flanking action in support of General Longstreet at Second Manassas.[5]

Dad wrote me again on March 13 from somewhere near Fariana.

Dear Snod—Sure enjoyed your swell letter of 11 Feb. Also I am very proud to learn of the excellent marks you have been making in school—and extremely pleased to learn about the father and son speech you made. Great work, boy. Mom writes also that you've been playing some basketball. I hope that you'll be able to start baseball soon and that you have decided on a position that you'd like to play. First base or pitcher is a good bet for a tall guy like you. Well, there is not a lot that I am permitted to write you, but I can tell you there is a lot of air activity here. We see hundreds of airplanes from Messerschmidt 109Fs all the way thru P38, P39, P40, Spitfires, B24's, 25's, 26's 17's, A20's—almost every kind in the world, and they stay busy. The country is much like that thru which you drove last April—wild and rugged. I'm feeling well and actually seem to gain weight if I don't exercise a lot. In any case I'll surely be glad to bathe regularly and often & sleep in a bed. The ground gets hard and a pup tent gets plenty small on a cold wet nite. The country we are in now has a very old history but as far as I can see that is all it does have. Once in a while we get a shot at big rabbits like Texas jacks or an occasional bird like a pheasant. They are hard to hit with a rifle. Congratulations on your good work. Love and a pat on the back. Dad

He wrote the next day as well.

My Dear Snod—Your swell letter of 25 Jan came today so I had to write you again and tell you how very much I enjoyed and appreciated the letter. We had an exciting nite last nite after I finished writing you and I got very little sleep so I can't stay up much later tonite. Glad to learn Joe [our new cat] and Colonel [our new dog] are doing O.K. Proud to learn of all your achievements and the way you look after Mom and Miss Mouse. This letter brings you a lot of love, son—and every wish for your continued success in everything you do. I know you are

developing into a fine thinking young man and I want [you] to understand how very much this means to me. Tell Mrs. Hays Hello for me
and perhaps I'll meet her husband on the Burma Road if we chase this
Rommel far enough and fast enough. God bless you all—and love and
best to you & your pals. Dad

Whatever kept Dad up most of the night of the March 13—perhaps a
harassing air raid, an artillery barrage, or a probe by an enemy patrol—was
apparently too insignificant for inclusion in the histories of the war. Still,
to the all the men in it, it brought hardship, and to some wounds and to
others death.

On the same day, March 14, Dad wrote to Mom, telling her, "We've
moved many a cold, wet mile since you last had me located and also we
put in a stop in that place I visited. Long way from there now and we'll
keep rolling." He added that he was still carrying on a ripe correspondence
with that "philosopher of the plains, Fred Fisher, of Pine Bluffs,
Wyoming."

A couple of days later, the Sixtieth moved into combat. On March 17
the First Infantry Division—Colonel McCormick's "Big Red One" of the
last war—took unoccupied but heavily mined and booby-trapped Gafsa.
Meanwhile, in continuing rain and through deep mud and high water,
Combat Command C of the First Armored Division and the Sixtieth Infantry Regiment worked their way southeast from Fariana, bypassing Gafsa
and heading for Station de Sened on the main road and rail line to Maknassy. On March 19, the Americans, halted in bad weather, reviewed their
plans.

> The plan of attack involved a march extremely taxing for de Rohan's
> [Sixtieth] combat team. It was to climb the western slopes of Djebel
> Goussa to reach the dominating terraces along its southern face, which
> rises abruptly some 600 feet above the floor of the valley, in order to
> take the enemy's hill positions from the rear. From the heights, the
> attacking force could command the entrenched positions which the
> enemy had constructed on the flats below them near Station de Sened.
> At the same time, Combat Command C would be crossing a difficult
> series of ridges and shoulders at the southwestern extremity of Djebel
> Madjoura across a valley from Djebel Goussa, protecting the northeast-
> ern flank and giving fire support. Its objective was the exit (three miles

north of Station de Sened) from this valley to the broad Maknassy Valley. Working together, the 60th Combat Team and [Col. Robert I.] Stack's [Combat Command C] would be able either to cut off the enemy force from defending Station de Sened or to compel it to hasten its retreat in order to avoid encirclement.[6]

All day on March 20 the Sixtieth toiled up the heights of Djebel Goussa while Combat Command C worked its way along the other side of the valley. However, under artillery fire, the enemy garrison either fled or surrendered to the advancing Americans. On March 21, then, Station de Sened was taken "by maneuver rather than by storm, and without the losses normally to be expected in a frontal attack. But the exertion left the infantry, particularly the Sixtieth Combat Team, too tired to begin another attack effectively."

According to the original plans issued by 18 Army Group, all that II Corps had to do now was demonstrate toward Maknassy, some twenty miles to the east. However, General Alexander revised his orders to have II Corps take Maknassy and the high ground to its east and from there send a light armored raiding party to neutralize the enemy airfields at Mezzouna. He held to his original idea that II Corps should not send any large force farther east onto the coastal plain.

By March 22, the enemy had abandoned Maknassy and taken up positions in the hills to the east. General Orlando Ward, commanding the First Armored Division, could either strike quickly into these hills before the enemy was fully organized or be a bit more cautious, let his troops catch their breath, and then undertake a more studied attack. Perhaps because he knew that II Corps was merely demonstrating and could not push through to the sea, he chose the more deliberate course of action.

About this time a newspaper reporter named Ivan H. (Cy) Peterman caught up with the Third Battalion of the Sixtieth. On March 26 he wired to the *Philadelphia Inquirer* his delayed report under the title "Debbil Djebel Wears Out U. S. Patience and Shoes."

Dat old debbil djebel, the Tunisian mountain, is helping Herr Rommel's Indian style warfare by wearing out both Allied patience and American soldiers' shoes.

It was apparent, by today's slowdown, that the Yanks are getting tired climbing steep djebel's sides studded with Axis 88 millimeter cannon and machine guns. But when headquarters announced that even armored troops are asking for new brogans to replace those worn out by mechanized forces now walking to work, the rough nature of the present battle is made clear.

Fighting their way along barren shelves, because every path is thick with booby traps and mines, Americans literally have worn out GI shoes, says Lieutenant Colonel John J. Toffey, infantry commander, who with a half dozen of his men came back from Maknassy's forward lines.

Toffey, veteran officer who was stationed at Fort Dix a long time, described newly built German pillboxes equipped with camouflaged manhole tops. These were barely visible to planes or spotters, he said, and were covered with heavy concrete or stone hoods capable of resisting shells and bombs nearly as well as the St. Nazaire submarine pens. He said every route of approach was sown with mines which killed or injured many of his command.

"The Germans during our barrage will make no reply," he continued.

"You can stand in the open and read a paper without drawing a shot," he said, "but the minute our guns are quiet and we take a step their way, all hell breaks loose again."

Colonel Toffey said he thought the Axis used automatic paving drills to dig into solid rock and expressed keen admiration for the stone masonry protecting German guns. This type of defense line was also discovered in the portions of the old Mareth line recently and suggests the nature of Hitler's European defense if the Allies don't soon reach the European mainland.

On March 22 as well, as Dad and Lieutenant Lusk were returning from a reconnaissance, two Messerschmidts caught them on the open road.[7] They dove for cover as the planes' machine guns sent bullets ripping into the dirt and cactus. The next day the battalion moved forward in trucks under frequent attacks by German Stukas, emitting their eerie screams as they stooped to harass and kill. The men by now knew that they had to begin digging whenever they hit the ground, scratching and scraping with entrenching tools, helmets, bayonets, or fingers to create even the shallowest indentation in the unyielding ground.

The enemy troops in the hills east of Maknassy consisted of some Italians and the Second Company of General Rommel's *Kampfstaffel*, or personal escort troops, under the command of Oberleutnant Harro Brenner. Their mission was to keep the Americans from breaking out onto the coastal plain and trapping the bulk of the German army as it withdrew west and north toward Tunis and Bizerte. To bolster their forces, the Germans ordered Colonel Rudolph Lang, commanding the Sixty-ninth Panzer Grenadier Regiment of the Tenth Panzer Division, to take charge of the defenses around Maknassy. The veterans of Rommel's guard recall vividly their stalwart defense, in which, in General Rommel's words, *"Die Kampfstaffel hat eine Armee gerettet"*: the guard had rescued an Army.[8] However, Colonel Lang pays little or no attention to the *Kampfstaffel* in his recollection of the action and holds his Italian allies in low regard. Indeed, as he came forward, he wrote, "Many Italian soldiers as well as vehicles of all kinds were moving to the east, with all indications of flight, individually or in groups." Lang ordered "a few energetic young officers . . . to use *all* means, if necessary even their weapons, in order to prevent even only one single man or vehicle from moving on to the east."[9]

Meanwhile, American artillery pounded the Germans. One German veteran recalls, employing uniquely Teutonic verb tenses and moods,

At Maknassy Pass I have experienced the worst and most terrible artillery fire during the entire war, the Russian campaign included. The Americans shot so abundantly like youngsters with toy-torpedoes, or if their ammunition factory would be just nearby. One day, escaping this thunderstorm, I climbed down in a well pit, just down onto the water surface. There I was relatively safe, but when the well-enclosure had been hit by a shell, I had found my eternal grave in the depth, and nobody had know, what happened to me.[10]

Lang was able to organize a strong defense against "the overwhelming superiority of the enemy forces . . . [and] by means of a flexible conduct of the fighting, every attack was smashed or intercepted, even after tens of thousands of grenades had beaten down on the men defending the spot with courage and valor."

On the night of March 22–23, the Third Battalion of the Sixtieth Infantry, attached to Combat Command C of the First Armored Division, was ordered to attack Djebel Naemia. Under a pale moon as the battalion moved up to its line of departure, Dad called his officers together and told them to go all out. After all, he pointed out, "These bastards are the cause of us being in Africa in the first place."[11] Furthermore, that very night those same bastards had destroyed "Helen," Dad's jeep, seriously wounding Dad's driver.

The Third Battalion's attack had not gone very far before encountering enemy minefields. Captain Robert Rucker, leading K Company, stepped on a mine and had his foot blown off. Colonel Lang's defenders poured artillery fire onto the Americans, driving them back and pinning them down. Cut off from his company for nearly twenty-four hours, Captain Rucker lay where he had fallen. His driver, Abe Strom, remained with him, applying tourniquets and bandages while they waited for help. Aware of what Germans were likely to do to Jews, Rucker urged Strom to leave him and crawl back to the battalion's lines, but Strom didn't. Finally a rescue party was able to reach Rucker and carry him back to the battalion aid station.[12]

Meanwhile, Dad revised his plan of attack, but again the attack faltered in the face of heavy artillery and machine-gun fire from Germans dug in on the hill. Three more times that day that battalion attacked without taking its objective. Late that same day, March 23, Dad was hit in the knee— one report says by a sniper's bullet, another by a machine gun. In any event, he was put out of action. Wallace Hawkins, a medic, recalled that he gave Dad morphine and helped him back to the battalion aid station. Albert Lubrano said that he and his 81-mm mortar team from M Company carried Dad back. Once at the aid station, Dad was further treated and then loaded into an ambulance for evacuation to a hospital. However, he refused to be moved until Captain Rucker had been brought in. Eventually he was, and he and Dad were carried off in the same ambulance.

Though Ernie Pyle did not spend much time with the Sixtieth Infantry in North Africa, his summary of the fighting there seems to describe what went on at Maknassy.

Our American troops had a brutal fight in the mountain phase of the campaign. It was war of such intensity as Americans on this side of the ocean had never known. It was a battle without let up. It was a war of drenching artillery and hidden mines and walls of machine gun fire and even of the barbaric bayonet. It was an exhausting, cruel, last-ditch kind of war, and those who went through it seriously doubt that war could be any worse.[13]

At some point in the fighting for the heights east of Maknassy, General Patton, angry and frustrated with the First Armored Division's lack of success, dressed down General Ward. "I don't want any goddamned excuses, I want you to go out there and get that hill. You lead the attack personally. Don't come back until you've got it." Ward did come back, wounded in the eye. Patton had Bradley relieve him.[14] However Patton and Bradley conducted American operations against the Germans and Italians in Tunisia, though, they would have to finish up without Jack Toffey.

chapter seven

ALGERIAN INTERLUDE

At home, we did not learn of Dad's having been wounded for two weeks. Then came the telegram, addressed to Mom at Homer's house (the only permanent address we knew when Dad went overseas). Homer and Granny grimly drove the few blocks to our house with the cold, stark news.

DEEPLY REGRET TO INFORM YOU YOUR HUSBAND LIEUTENANT COLONEL JOHN J TOFFEY JR INFANTRY WAS SERIOUSLY WOUNDED IN ACTION IN NORTH AFRICA AREA MARCH 24 REPORTS WILL BE FORWARDED WHEN RECEIVED.

ULIO THE ADJUTANT GENERAL

On March 27 and again on March 28 Dad wrote to Mom, hoping that either letter or both would beat "the War Dept.'s letter to you." "In any case," he says,

> Some guy had one with my name on it—same having struck me in the right knee and done comparatively little damage. Missed all bones but left plenty fluid on the joint. I'm not in any particular pain and should be off the shelf inside of two or three weeks. So don't worry about a thing.

He added in both letters that he was in a field hospital with doctors and nurses from New York's Roosevelt Hospital. Among them, we would learn in a letter of March 10, 1943, from Bob Redpath, was Dad's old pass-catching, house-party buddy, Bull Dog Dwight Fishwick.

From the field hospital, Dad went to the Twelfth General Hospital at Ain-el-Turck, a resort town about five miles west of Oran, "the place I moved to end of Jan." He wrote that the hospital was "run by Northwestern University doctors—extremely competent and capable." Though he found the place to be quite spread out, Dad wrote that he was able to get around on crutches, but "should be able to walk in another week and possibly return to duty before the month is out." On other matters,

The African campaign should be nearly over. The British 8th Army is wonderful and since we chased these characters off the last high ground w. of the Gulf of Tunis the British 8th has been rolling them up in a ball. Of course the future is problematical and what will happen in Europe & when is all guess work. I can't see any invasion just yet, but of course it will come in time. . . .

I hope the War Dept. has not got you upset by telling you I'm seriously wounded or something on account of I ain't and they do very tactless things. So, do no worrying.

Currently my hopes for afterwards involve a return to civilian life and a considerable amount of leisurely travel to lots of places we've wanted to stop and play in. As to work—I don't know what it'll be but I'll think of something good.

There isn't room in the airplane to tell you all I want to say—which is mainly how much I love you and how much my home and family mean to me and how anxious I am to share our lives again—but each day is nearer to the homecoming.

The first letter I had from Dad after he was wounded was written on April 5. It begins not with a reference to his wound, but to the beginning of the 1943 baseball season.

Dear Snod—What's new? By the time this reaches you the ball season should be under way and I mean I'd like to be looking at the Crosley Field Opener. At the moment I'm not too agile account of a little lead poisoning I got a week or so ago. No harm done and I'm okay. Have not been getting any mail lately because of moving around the country pretty fast. So I've no special recent news from home.

Our gang has really been in the ball game over here and it seems she is about washed up now as far as Mr. Rommel is concerned. Please keep things rolling smoothly at home until I can get there—And then boy the four of us will go places and see and do things. Mom should have a letter from me by this time. Meanwhile, good luck and lots of love to all. Devotedly, Your Dad.

And to Anne on the same day: "I suppose you are now getting ready for Easter and have some nice new dresses and pretty things for the occasion." He went on to tell her that he was in the hospital at the moment, but nothing to worry about—and I really feel pretty good and rested up. The warm weather has come here now and things are very pretty indeed. It is a beautiful spot where I am with lots of palm tress, sunshine and beautiful blue water. There are very good oranges here and I try to eat as many as I can get.

The next day Dad sent to Colonel de Rohan his recommendation that Captain Gail H. Brown of M Company be cited for "conspicuous gallantry and outstanding leadership" in the action around Maknassy on March 23, the day Dad was wounded. "Throughout the entire day Captain Brown was of incalculable value to the undersigned in exhorting a tired command to extend itself to the utmost in its efforts to capture its objective."

The word on April 10 was that with the addition of a cast to Dad's leg, recovery might take a little longer than originally anticipated. Still, he remained in good spirits, wanting for nothing except mail, including "those pictures I have been yelling for since Christmas." He still thought that he would be out of the hospital before Mom could write him there. He wrote that he missed us "worse than ever since I have time on my hands." He said that he would get "messages and proxy phone calls to [us] by any and all returning characters from here—some of which should reach you even ere this."

A couple of days later he sent a money order for $240, saying he hoped Mom "can find good practical use for same, and when I get home we'll grab off a good automobile and go places and do stuff together. But one certainty—no picnics, no hash, no Spam." He closed with "every possible wish for our speedy reunion. Hope you have some trips planned and things you want to do."

His next letter to me, written on April 13, was the first to come through the V-mail photographic process. It measured just over four by five inches, but Dad's bold, distinctive handwriting was still easy for young eyes to read. He wondered what the big-league baseball season would be like "with so many of the top stars away and others unable to play for one reason or another." He asked about my baseball team and my school year, which he guessed "is the best [I] have had in a long time—certainly since we left Wyoming."

As usual, Anne got one written the same day. Dad said that he hadn't had any mail from any of us in about a month. Trying to imagine the home front, he wrote, "I suppose Mom has got you doing some knitting or some work on bandages or such stuff as it is all very important and quite badly needed."

Anne wrote Dad on April 16, telling him that she and I had received his letters of April 5. She told him that she was going to a costume party, adding, "I was glad to hear that you had not been badly hurt. The mail man is very much interested in you. And he too was very glad that you had not been badly hurt. With lots of love, your daughter, Anne."

On April 18, he wrote that he was disappointed that the knee was taking longer to heal than he had expected. He now thought that he would be in the hospital for at least three more weeks. The Avoca matter continued to plague him. Again his thoughts turned to baseball: "I suppose by this time you have seen the [Columbus] Red Birds opener and possibly you are contemplating a journey to Cincinnati to catch the Reds in action. Sure would like to be taking you to a double-header at Crosley Field myself." He found the mail still very slow to catch up with him, and he repeated his wish for snapshots of us. He concluded, "One thing you can be sure of—the kids around here are in sad looking shape for food and clothing, Perhaps some of the stuff they are rationing at home will start finding its way to where it is needed." To Mom he sent a money order for $190.

Dad did see some baseball that spring. The hospital fielded a team that won the Oran area championship. Other forms of amusement and entertainment included weekly movies, among which during Dad's time were Hope, Crosby, and Lamour in *Road to Morocco* and Abbott and Costello in *Pardon My Sarong*. There were dances, too. So excited was the writer of the "Unit Record" of March 26 and 27 by "the best and most enjoyable dance we've had to date thanks to decorations by Nancy Gatch and music by a replacement-depot orchestra made up of musicians formerly of name bands back home, that he or she "forgot to mention that another large group of patients arrived from the front last evening."[1]

On April 22, Dad was bored.

Time hangs heavy since we've read everything and the usual rehashing has been overdone even for us. The bridge is poor and the mail seemingly one way. There is a club but 4 to 5 pm limit and wine only— and a damn long walk on crutches. Nevertheless we are very lucky and really very happy and we know it, but we must exercise the soldier's inevitable pastime of grousing.

He apologized and provided three reasons for the "4th grade penmanship of the letter: 1) It takes longer; 2) it may work better in photofilming, if any; 3) since I'm laying on my stomach it is easier than moving."

On Easter Sunday, April 25, he reported having been to a "very nice church service," eaten chicken at noon and steak at supper, and attended a ballgame. A radio provided news, Jack Benny, and ball scores. That night he wrote to Mom again:

> Darling—I just didn't feel I'd written quite enough in my other one so here is another to tell you that as Easter Sunday ends I've had a nice day—as nice as any day away from you could be, but so often I've thought of you all and followed you thru your most probable activities. Somehow I feel that we shall be together again before so very long and we can pray this will be true.

Anne got an Easter letter, too. In it Dad imagines Anne, Mom, and me having gone to church, and he wishes he could have been with us, "but maybe it won't be so long now until we're all back together." He then describes a Sunday in Oran:

> All the French people around here go walking and one sees many cute children, but they do need milk and eggs and meat and chocolate and the fine food and clothes we have at home so they can grow strong and healthy like American kids. The little Arab children are also cute but very dirty and need washing as well as all the other things I mentioned. Certainly there is nothing I need or want except mail and pictures from you all. Be good and don't grow up before I get home to see you.

Dad's spirits rose considerably a couple of days later when he got the first mail in over a month. He was still in a cast, though, and would be, he said, for at least a week, then two weeks of therapy and then limited activity. That Sunday he attended a church service again and went to a movie— *Pride of the Yankees*, "a peach but a tear-jerker."

A week later he heard that two of the Reds' pitching aces, Johnny Vander Meer and Ray Starr, stopped the Cardinals. He also heard that the present ball was not so lively. Neither, to his increasing frustration, was he. The knee was slow to heal, and he again saw at least three more weeks in the hospital. On May 3 he wrote:

Hi, John—How goes the ball season? I see the Reds have been up and down—nothing spectacular. Hope you are doing plenty of playing and wish I could have a catch with you right now. Hot weather will be here soon and perhaps I can do a bit of good swimming before too long. The war in Africa should be wound up before too very long but of course there is still much to be done before we forget the entire business and return to our homes and families and to fishing and baseball and our families and all that we love so well. Our food has been grand lately and I have to take lots of exercise on my crutches to keep from getting too fat, for I am not used to this quiet life we lead now after 8 months of strenuous activity. Perhaps some news of you all will come thru in the form of mail very soon. Meanwhile I miss you very much, send much love, and wish you good luck on the end of school. Love, Dad.

To Mom's cousin, Dad wrote that "on 23 March I got in front of some Jerry who was low and on the inside corner with one." As a result, "While Toffey basks in the lap of luxury and waxes fat and sloppy, the boys are winning without me."

Shortly after Dad was wounded and transferred to the Twelfth General Hospital, Lieutenant General Lesley J. McNair, now chief of Army Ground Forces, came to North Africa to inspect in combat the men whom he had mobilized and trained. While with troops well forward of where lieutenant generals usually go, the general caught some shell fragments in the arm. He was immediately taken to the Twelfth General Hospital for treatment and recuperation, and Ward 314, the house where Dad was, suddenly became VIP quarters.

In the years before the war, back in the old army, Dad's parents and the McNairs had been good friends. The two officers had soldiered together at Veracruz, on the Mexican border, and in Washington. General McNair was delighted to find among his wardmates young Jack Toffey. On May 8, having returned to his headquarters at the Army War College in Washington, the general wrote to Mom.

Dear Mrs. Toffey,

During my ups and downs overseas recently I found myself in the same General Hospital with your Jack. You can imagine my surprise, but I am delighted to relate that he is in fine shape. His leg is still in the cast, but he said that he is to lose it any day now—probably he has by this time. He expects to get full use of his knee again and explained to me in detail the reasons why he expects this happy result. He is taking some sort of sun baths and he is as brown as a nut—in the pink of condition except for the knee.

You probably know all this, but I write it in the possibility that you have discounted his good reports. I can tell you these things from having actually seen them.

With kindest regards and every good wish for Jack's happy reunion to you both when this affair is over. Jack is a great kid and I know how proud of him you must be.

Sincerely,

L. J. McNair (signed)

Lt. Gen. USA Commanding

Looking over what he had dictated, the general must have noticed the alarmingly ambiguous reference of the pronoun "it" in fourth line, for he inserted by hand "the cast!"

A couple of weeks after Dad had been wounded, Ed Lusk was hit by German artillery fire and knocked out of the war. On his way home he stopped off at the Twelfth General, where early one morning he went to see Dad. Dad greeted Lusk and waved him to a chair near Dad's bed. Lusk, however, thought that the other bed might be more comfortable. As he sat down, Dad yelled "No." Too late; from under Lusk came a muffled groan. The first lieutenant had sat down on a sleeping lieutenant general. As Lusk struggled to maintain composure, Dad introduced him to General McNair, as Lusk told me years later, and the chief of the Army Ground Forces arose undamaged to shake the lieutenant's hand.

General McNair's was one of several bits of "proxy" communication that Dad had said would reach us as men returned the States. From New York, Lieutenant J. F. Stack telegraphed collect on May 1, 1943: "Saw your husband in Africa. He's okay. Sends his love." From a hospital in Missouri two weeks later, Captain Rucker wrote that he had Dad's permission to say that Dad was well and safe. He added that he wished he could be back with Dad but could not because he had lost his right foot. From a hospital at Fort Devens, Massachusetts, a lieutenant who was evacuated with Dad wrote to explain "a few things the censor might not allow." After assuring us that Dad's wound was not serious and "will have no disabling effect on him whatsoever," he described the action in which he and Dad were wounded and their travels through medical channels to Oran.

The most touching of these letters, though, was the one from Robert White, handwritten in pencil at Halloran General Hospital on Staten Island.

Hello Mrs. Toffey;

Probably you won't be able to read this but I hope so. If the gov. saw this scratching they would arrest me for a spy writing in code.

I'm Robt White, your husband's driver. I drove for him ever since he came to Bragg & I can rightfully say I'm proud of it, Mrs. Toffey.

He was slightly wounded the 24th of March just above Maknassy & is probably going like a new man now for he was one man they couldn't keep down. The wound didn't even call for a cast at first for the tibia was only chipped slightly. Later they put a cast on just to stop his knee from working.

The Col. came to see me many times at the hospital for he was able to get around with crutches. I guess the doctors couldn't keep up with him for he was always visiting the men of his battalion. They all think the world of him too!

He always treated me more like a father than the Bn C.O. He's the finest man I know. Never complained and was always ready to help. I'm sorry I let him down in the most important moment.

Col Toffey asked me many times to take or accept a rating in the company but Mrs. Toffey a G.I. rating wouldn't pry me from him for he had the most nerve and the most reliable [sic] of any one I know. I'm not afraid to fight but it is a great comfort to know you aren't alone.

I guess you know all those things Mrs Toffey so I'll stop. How are those two little ones coming? Are they all right? I remember one day the Col. received a letter from the little boy; he read it over & over & if someone had said the war was over he wouldn't have been more excited.

Don't tell the Col. I said all these things or he'd think I'd gone soft but if he'd ask for Hitler I'd try & with him I'd get little Adolf.

Well it will take you two days to decipher this so I'll close. I only have a bad leg & right arm. Write if you hear from the Col.

Robt. White

Meanwhile, back in Ain-el-Turck on May 10, Dad included in his letter to me something a bit out of the ordinary. After a couple of responses to things that I had written in the letter he had just received, Dad gave me an assignment.

I wish you would get Mom to straighten out a financial matter for me. She should have gotten $398.52 every month from the govt. but I believe she has only been getting 350. Now all the difference must be collected and paid her because it has been taken out of my pay ever since the allotment started.

I, of course, was unprepared for the assignment and probably unable to do more than to show Dad's letter to Mom. The same day that he wrote me, though, Dad had written Mom expressing the same concerns about allotment matters as well as the Avoca affair, which he said "has reopened and is worrying me some. Wish you'd look into same please and let me know." The knee felt "swell" and had good motion, though it couldn't take any weight. He reported that "life here is very beautiful at the moment, and yesterday I was offered a job on graduation . . . instructor at a battle school some place near here." Then he says, "I'd like to catch a boat and see you all. Who knows—We can hope."

A couple of days later he told me about the job:

The general I am going to be working for came here to see me today and explained the job he wants me to do.[2] Which will be interesting and teaching. I'm very fortunate to get a job of this sort as it will keep me active and busy on some valuable work until such time as I'm really ready for field duty again.

Dad was sunbathing on the hospital roof on May 11 when he was surprised to spot among a group touring the hospital an old friend, Frank Vanderlip, now "somebody's aide" and living in a villa in Oran. Also in the area were Bill Ibold, a friend from Cincinnati whom Dad had previously seen in Morocco, and Charlie Saltzman, who is "most solicitous and anxious to be of any assistance—same being nice because he is truly in a big shot position around here."[3]

On May 17, Dad reported that his knee was tapped to drain off the fluid, which turned out to be not water but old blood—apparently not a good sign. More would have to be drained and Dad was back in a "posterior and half cast to immobilize the knee." He was discouraged and did not know what effect this setback would have on his future assignment.

When Dad wrote me on May 20, enough time had elapsed since he was hit to allow the veil of censorship to be raised. He is now permitted to tell me what White, Rucker, and others had already been able to tell us: that he had been wounded at Maknassy "and it was some fight. The Jerrys are good, but not good enough and my guys were better and tougher. There is a lot else to tell that is interesting and some day we'll talk about it a lot. . . . Be a good guy and take care of everything. Love, Dad."

Two days later he wrote Mom, "I understand my friend Teddy Conway has the regiment, so I lost out by being absent as I rank him about 6 months." The next day Nancy Gatch, a Red Cross worker "who paints pictures and talks about more things than fig bars and the Harry James band," took Dad and a fellow patient on a picnic that featured lettuce and tomatoes and deviled eggs, and sand "to prove we were picnicking." Dad enjoyed the outing, "although after 7 months in the field I never thought I'd fall for a picnic again, but then any change of routine is definitely a major sport here."

In the same letter he reported that "M.S.E. & Co. should be around here this week. Maybe I will hook up with them and skip that school teaching job. It all depends on the findings tomorrow when [Dr.] Allen looks it over." When the doctor looked at the knee the next day, he took off fifty-five cubic centimeters of blood and said he didn't know whether to be pleased or not, and made no decision. Dad wrote to Mom,

> Honestly it is amazing to feel so fine and not be able to do anything but hang around a hospital. Wish now that they had sent me home in the first place, for the time factor has surely fooled me. . . . This place is beautiful and has such possibilities that I wish you and the kids could be here with me to see and enjoy it. . . . I can only hope that soon I may be sprung from here & get active as there is too much time for thought in a place like this and I think too much to be happy. God it is a funny world and I don't understand it. Much love. More soon. Devotedly, Jack

About this time Granny must have written Dad about the son of friends in Columbus who had just returned from overseas to a comfortable stateside job. Granny must have told Dad that he ought to do the same. He concluded his May 25 letter to her thus:

The hospital life and the crutch walking gets a little tiresome but I can't kick when so many are so terribly worse off and suffering too. Never had any pain here and life has been very beautiful except for boredom and inactivity to which I am not accustomed. As to being shipped home I have as yet no reason to feel that it will happen although it would be good since I can't do troop duty for from 60 to 90 days. I shall keep you posted. Much love to everyone and thanks for all the mail. Jack

On May 28 he wrote to say that "things are on the upswing." The knee gave up another forty-five cubic centimeters of old blood, bringing the total to 190. It had returned to normal size and Dad had taken a few steps on it. The crutches would go the next day, and then on Monday the doctor would assess the situation. Dad had heard from Jim Bellah, John Dilley, who took over the battalion when Dad was hit, and Pete McCarley, commander of the First Battalion of the Sixtieth since Ft. Bragg and Dad's "best buddy." A recent visitor to chat with the boys in the hospital was "Old" (a year younger than Dad) Zeke Bonura, who from 1934 to 1940 played first base and batted .307 for the White Sox, Senators, and Giants.

On May 31, still uncertain about his next assignment, Dad wrote to Colonel Joseph Teece, who had been executive officer of the Sixtieth through the North African fighting until his transfer to II Corps headquarters. Dad's letter to Teece is full of compliments on the job that the colonel had done to maintain harmony in the regiment. He told Teece that he "would be especially desirous of serving under [him] in any capacity." Apparently nothing came of this request, and by June 2 Dad had seen General Eddy, who told him he would return to the Ninth Division and become executive officer of the Thirty-ninth Infantry Regiment. Apparently the teaching job was still in the works, however, because, Dad wrote, he hoped "I can lick the school teaching assignment."

Meanwhile, in Columbus Mom got a letter from the Adjutant General dated May 29, saying,

The latest report from the theater of operations states that on May 16 your husband, Lieutenant Colonel John J. Toffey, Jr., 0–335348, was still making normal improvement.

Arrangements have been made whereby you may send a message of cheer to him. The enclosed form is self-explanatory.

You have my assurance that when additional information is received regarding his condition, you will be notified immediately.

Very truly yours,

J. A. Ulio

Major General

The Adjutant General

The enclosed form provided space for a message of five words. When the words were filled in, the form was to be returned to the Adjutant General in a postage-free envelope for transmission to the wounded soldier.

In his letter of June 5, Dad repeated the news that he was returning to General Eddy's Ninth Division. He sounded ready to get back to work.

It does not seem very distant now until we shove off against our next obstacles and it should be a big and important operation that should strike a hard blow at our enemies. This here has been a great object lesson and proving ground, but of course much remains to be done if we are to get thru soon—and that is everyone's desire. Darling, in this period of lull and relaxation I have missed you more than usual, especially with so much spare time. I'd give a lot to come home, of course, but just can't feel right about it—if there is work yet to be done. You understand I know. . . . God bless you all and lots of love. Jack

When Anne wrote Dad on June 6, she filled in one further detail on the General McNair story.

Dear Dad, When I heard that your knee was worse I was sorry, but yet I thought you might come home. All is well here and we have good food. I hope you do too. At first when Mother ansered [sic] Gen. McNair's letter she spelled his name wrong. But she changed it after finding out how to spell it right. Well I must stop now for I still have to clean up my room. Your daughter, Ann.

On the subject of spelling, we note that at this time, perhaps in the spirit of sacrificing nonessentials for the war effort, Anne had dropped the final "e" from the spelling of her name. It would return.

In the week that followed, Dad went through the steps that would get him out of the hospital where he had spent the last two months. He would have to appear before a board that would assess his readiness for release. Then he would wait around while the inevitable papers were prepared and processed. Meanwhile, he had packed what he would take with him, left the rest in a footlocker in the care of Nancy Gatch, and arranged for transportation south to the Ninth Division.

While Dad was basking in the Algerian sun, the Ninth Division saw plenty of action at places like Sedjenane and Mateur before taking Bizerte as the war in Tunisia ground to a halt. Assessing the Ninth Division in combat, Ernie Pyle wrote, "They fought hard, took heavy casualties and did a fine job generally, but nobody back home knew anything about it."[4] "At noon on May 9, 1943—182 days after the North African landings and 518 days after the attack on Pearl Harbor, the American army secured its first unconditional surrender of Axis forces."[5]

Once again the rumors started. One held that everyone who had chased the Germans into surrender or out of Tunisia was going home. Wishful in their thinking, these guys had perhaps not yet figured out that there was no rotation system in effect for infantrymen. Like their fathers and uncles before them, they wouldn't get back until it was over over there. The only way for an infantryman to get home before the end of the war was to "catch the white boat"[6]—that is, be evacuated to the States because of wounds too severe to be repaired in hospitals overseas.

In mid-May the Ninth Division went west across miles of Tunisia and Algeria to its new training area at Magenta, seventy miles south of Oran and a little south of Sidi-bel-Abbes, home of the French Foreign Legion. Dad mentions visiting Sidi-bel-Abbes on his trip to see General Eddy about a job. When Ernie Pyle visited the place, he noted on a barracks wall a message from a former commander to his men: "You, Legionnaires, are soldiers made to die. I send you where you die." Pyle remarks that Legionnaires look upon the message "with reverence, almost as holy."[7]

There was nothing reverential or holy about Magenta, "a fly-specked hell-hole."[8] Here the Ninth Division trained for its next assignment, and here Dad rejoined the division as executive officer of the Thirty-ninth Infantry. Apparently General Eddy, seeing that Dad had the makings of a regimental commander, decided to give him the second spot in a regiment. The regimental commander, Colonel William Ritter, was generally regarded as a good man but perhaps too old and too cautious for combat command. Besides, he seemed to need a little help in handling some of the officers under him.[9] So, seventy-eight days after being wounded at Maknassy and seventeen days after he had predicted a sixty- to ninety-day wait until he was ready for troop duty, Dad, limping and using a cane, returned to duty in a combat-seasoned, combat-ready infantry regiment.

chapter eight

SICILY

"At last I am back in the Army and it certainly feels good," Dad wrote on June 15. "The hospital interlude was of course perfectly grand but you can['t] win or finish wars in there." Though he missed his old outfit, "life in the new outfit is pleasant from above but the talent below leaves much to be desired in comparison with those I left—sort of slow and exasperating but we'll get it whipped into shape or know why." He told us to watch the newsreels because the regiment had paraded before King George VI of England.

During most of Dad's hospitalization, Mom had been laid up with bronchitis. Feeling rotten and missing Dad, on June 11 she had written to ask him if he wasn't coming home because he didn't want to. On July 4 he replied, "Darling, I am so very distressed at your remark about if I want to come home. If you only knew how very much I do want to come home but can't see any immediate opportunity until we do a bigger job." Concerned about Mom's health, he told her to "take a trip. Go to G[reat] N[eck] or Pinehurst or White Sulphur or someplace and get healthy." He was therefore glad to hear that we were going east for the summer. A week later Dad wished that "L[esley] J M[cNair] could suddenly decide he needs me over there to build a new outfit or something."

Early in July Mom got another letter from the Adjutant General. This one said that a report from the "North African area" stated that on June 13 Dad was "still making normal improvement. Like the one a month earlier, it contained a form on which to send a five-word message.

About this time the regiment moved. At dusk on the night of July 5, as a "small new moon is creeping up," Dad wrote that he could think of nicer places to be, "although this is better than some I've been to and many I'll go to." "Plenty is cooking and may boil at any time," he wrote. In case he were not able to write for a while, Dad wished Mom a happy birthday a month in advance. A week later, while "busy and active, poised for the bell," Dad said, "Really believe I'm sort of ready for the quiet life at last—

Although wanderlust will probably catch me after we get the new car broken in." Meanwhile, however, "The boys are in good shape—hard, lean and sun-burned, and soon again you'll have news of us that will please you all I'm sure." Waiting for the bell, "watchful waiting," Dad called it, "is nerve-racking and gives too much time for thought and memories. Pray hard for time to pass and something to reunite us."

In answering a letter from Nathaniel Howard, now serving in the Office of Censorship in Washington, Dad reported that he was in a new outfit with a "boost" in jobs and "back in the groove and waiting for the gong again." He wryly remarked that it was not easy to reconcile the fact that his wife and kids seemed to be getting along without him somehow. He also feigned surprise that Nathaniel had "not placed the full power of the press behind a campaign to have Toffey of Maknassy returned home in triumph and splendor."

To Mom on July 14, Dad wrote,

Darling, Just a chance for a quick line here to tell you to watch the papers and the radio. Here we go again. And it should be all right. Feeling swell. The knee is good. The guys are ready and it looks pretty fine. Be sure to see and talk to John Dilley if you can. He can tell you plenty. Also if you keep in touch with the news you'll be posted. Wish I had time to write all the family but know you'll explain I'm pressed for time just now. Be hoping that we can clean this mess up soon and all get home before too much time passes. Tell John and Anne that I send much love and I'm awfully proud and pleased over their school year. . . . This is a hurried scrawl, but it carries all sorts of love and good thoughts and hopes and dreams. And you can be sure that more love than I can say to all my little family. Mail hasn't caught up much of late, but probably will soon. Would like to go to the Rose Bowl game this coming winter. Can you arrange it? God bless you all. Devotedly, Jack.

The bell this time would summon Dad and his outfit to Sicily, equated by the ancients with Homer's Trinacria and home of Archimedes, Empedocles, Pirandello, and the Mafia. No stranger to invasions, Sicily had at various times in its long history been trod upon by the Carthaginians, Greeks, Romans, Vandals, Ostrogoths, Byzantines, Saracens, Normans, Spaniards, Angevins, and mainland Italians. But never in history had Sicily or anywhere else in the world experienced anything like the invasion to begin on July 10, 1943, with nine Allied divisions storming ashore across a hundred-mile front.

Like Torch before it, Operation Husky, as the invasion of Sicily was called, was a British scheme to keep the Americans in the Mediterranean and away from a premature cross-channel assault on Hitler's Europe. Unlike Torch, it would use airborne troops in the initial assault. The British Eighth Army, under General Sir Bernard L. Montgomery, would land along the southeast coast and move north and east, seize the ports of Syracuse and Catania, continue across the Catania Plain, around Mt. Etna, and on to Messina. The American Seventh Army, under General Patton, would again assume a supporting role protecting the British left flank. Together the two Armies made up the Fifteenth Army Group under the command of General Sir Harold R. L. G. Alexander. Though most American field commanders liked General Alexander better than General Montgomery,[1] Alexander's decision to use the Seventh Army in a support role indicates the low regard in which Alexander held the American fighting man.

The invasion would begin with the landing of British and American airborne units behind the beaches. American troops would then land reinforced divisions at Scoglitti, Gela, and Licata. Elements of two divisions would be held on shipboard in floating reserve, and Dad's Ninth Division would remain in general reserve in North Africa.[2]

Before the invasion fleets left North Africa, General Patton told the men of the newly arrived Forty-fifth Division that battle was "the most magnificent competition in which a human being can indulge. It brings out all that is best; it removes all that is base." In the coming fight, he added, "We must not only die gallantly; we must kill devastatingly."[3] At sea the general reminded his troops that in their hands lay "the glory of American arms, the honor of the U. S. Army, and the future of the world." "See to it," he said, "that you are worthy of this great trust."[4]

On July 9, Dad, still in North Africa, wrote to Granny and Homer. Though he said he missed "the charming luxury of the grand hospital and the beautiful watering place it afforded," life in the field was good. "We are comfortable but anxious to go again—which I feel is just around the corner. In fact news should be very plentiful as you read this."

That same night, high winds and unnecessarily complicated flight plans made a mess of the airborne operations. In the British sector, twelve of twelve dozen gliders landed on their objectives, while sixty-three landed well away from their assigned targets and sixty-nine crashed in the sea.

The American paratroopers fared no better. Dropped they knew not where, small groups of men came together and tried to do something approximating the mission assigned them.

With dawn on July 10 came an "imposing and terrifying spectacle." As Samuel Eliot Morison later recorded the hyperbolic impressions of some Sicilians, "There were thousands of vessels in the roadstead; one could not see the horizon for the ships. Thousands of troops were landing every minute."[5] The Americans came out of the sea and into the scorching Sicilian sun in wool olive-drab trousers and shirts; the British wore their desert khaki shorts.

During the first day, the British moved virtually unopposed through Syracuse. At Gela in the American sector German tanks from the Hermann Goering Division launched a strong counterattack. The Americans prevailed, thanks in large measure to devastating gunfire from the ships offshore. By the end of the first day, the Americans had a lodgment two to four miles deep and fifty miles wide. They had taken four thousand prisoners while losing fifty-eight men killed, a hundred and ninety-nine wounded, and seven hundred missing. Fierce fighting continued the next day. Unable to get reinforcements ashore, the Americans armed and brought forward navy shore personnel, army cooks, clerk-typists, and supply-dump people. The Americans held, but Seventh Army casualties for the day stood at twenty-three hundred, the largest one-day figure for the entire Sicilian campaign.[6]

On the night of July 11, General Patton called for some two thousand paratroopers from the Eighty-second Airborne to drop behind the Germans facing Gela. Though American officers tried to get the word out that our C-47s would be passing overhead, as the American planes flew over, Allied anti-aircraft guns at sea and on shore opened fire. Twenty-three planes of a hundred and forty-four were shot down, and another thirty-seven were damaged. The paratroopers lost some 10 percent of their force to friendly fire.[7] An investigation was unable to fix blame. As the Eighty-second's commanding general, Matthew Ridgway, summed it up, responsibility was "so divided, so difficult to fix" that no disciplinary action should be taken. "The losses," Ridgway said, "are part of the inevitable price of war in human life."[8]

Despite the heavy fighting around Gela and the debacle of the second airborne mission, the American Seventh Army was moving forward all across its sector on or ahead of schedule. The British, too, as they moved north and east had initial success until a German division newly rushed in from France slowed them. Here General Montgomery asked for and got a shift in the boundary between his Eighth and the American Seventh Army so that Highway 124, the best inland road to Enna and the northeast, would be in his sector. General Patton saw the order to relinquish the road as an affront to his Seventh Army's combat capability. "This is a horse race in which the prestige of the U. S. Army is at stake," he said. "We must take Messina before the British."[9]

General Patton suppressed his anger about the loss of Highway 124 long enough to get from General Alexander permission to conduct a reconnaissance in force toward Agrigento. "I want you to be in Palermo in five days," Patton told General Truscott on July 18. Truscott was then a hundred miles away, in Agrigento, but his Third Division made it to Palermo in four days.[10]

Two days after the Allied landings it was clear that the Allied foothold was too strong for the invaders to be driven back into the sea. "Clausewitz has written that when it becomes evident that a war can no longer be won, you ought, with the politicians, to try and obtain an honorable ending to the affair," one Italian general had written a month earlier to his German liaison. The German wrote back: "I entirely agree, but Hitler has positively never read Clausewitz."[11]

At Bizerte, Tunisia, through the night of July 13 and the morning of July 14, the men and vehicles of Dad's Thirty-ninth Regimental Combat Team boarded nineteen landing craft, nine LSTs and ten LCIs. At 1125 hours the convoy sailed from Bizerte for Sicily. While the convoy ploughed through the Mediterranean Sea, Dad wrote again,

> Well Bastille Day came and went and so did we. And this is written through the service and facilities of the U.S. Navy, whose guest I am at the moment but will shortly leave. There is nothing to tell that can be told save that the news is good, likewise the weather. The past 24 hours have been comfortable, pleasant and restful. Meals and sleep have been super. We are therefore ready to go. Perhaps you can and have followed our moves and know what is cooking. *Life* for June 14 had some good pictures of places we've been and scenes we've seen. This one is just to let you know I'm thinking of you and John and Anne all the time and missing you terribly. Perhaps if I'm a good boy you'll pray that the normal course of events will bring me back to you very soon. It has

been an awfully long time and the volume of missing increases. God bless you all. Give my love to family and friends and write often. All my love to you. Jack

At 1030 hours on July 15 the men of the Thirty-ninth first saw the shores of Sicily and the hills rising behind beige stucco houses gleaming almost white in the hot Sicilian sun. While Colonel Ritter went to Seventh Army headquarters for orders, Dad saw to moving his men into their bivouac areas. Here they remained, cleaning equipment and writing letters until July 17, when the Third Battalion moved forward, taking 327 Italian prisoners. Dad had time to write that all was going well, and that he was safe and happy. He chatted about not having seen Saltzman or Ibold, but of course he couldn't go into the details about what he was doing or where he was doing it.

At 0530 on July 20, the Thirty-ninth began to shuttle forward. As the regiment was moving up, a German plane swooped down on the jeep in which Colonel Ritter was riding. In his scramble for cover, the colonel was injured and evacuated to North Africa. Dad took command of the regiment. On the same day, the Thirty-ninth, three battalions of Rangers, and a supporting battalion of 155s were combined to form a task force under the command of Ranger Colonel William Darby. As Darby tells it, "Though I had a command, no one could tell me where all my troops were bivouacked."[12] Whenever he asked, the answer was always "Up ahead," along the coast road.

At about 0300 near the town of Menfi, Darby got lucky. "A tired voice came from under a bridge to indicate that, at last, the 39th RCT had been found." When Darby identified himself, Dad emerged and told Darby that Italian troops were a few miles west. Darby explained their mission, but said that he had no plans for the attack and asked if Dad had any. "No, I haven't," Dad replied, "but let's have a cup of coffee and get some sleep before we attack."[13]

Two hours later Dad and Darby had the task force up and moving toward Castelvetrano, which they had secured by noon. They took Campobello that afternoon and Mazara that night. In their advances that day the First Battalion alone took 3,456 prisoners, more than the strength of the entire Thirty-ninth Regimental Combat Team. According to the Ninth Division history, this action made it possible for the Second Armored Division to sweep north and take Palermo.[14]

On July 22, the regiment paused to consolidate its positions and to distribute food to the civilian population. On July 23, Dad continued to advance the regiment against Trapani and Marsala. When the German Fifteenth Panzer Grenadiers pulled back to central Sicily, the Italians surrendered in logistically confounding numbers. The Thirty-ninth's Unit Journal shows several requests for military police to assist with the handling of the prisoners. Someone wryly suggested that Dad had caused the tide of surrenders by offering a can of C-rations and a trip to the States to any Italian who gave up.

Marsala, the guidebooks tell us, is a seacoast town noted for the production of grain and salt. It also gives its name to the sweet wine produced from local grapes. It was this last product that especially attracted the men of the Thirty-ninth as they settled in for the night. One company commander made the mistake of billeting his troops in a winery. Quickly men of the thirsty Thirty-ninth liberated and swallowed a whole lot of Marsala before its time. Dad and his battalion and company commanders let the troops have their fill, but gave no quarter the next morning as pounding headaches, upset stomachs, fuzzy tongues, and red eyes were insufficient symptoms to gain one excuse from duty. The men would sweat Marsala in the hot Sicilian sun.

Back in Columbus on a Friday in late July or early August, the mail brought Granny and Homer Dad's letter of July 9, in which he had said his outfit might be making news soon. "We're waiting for the gong. By the time you get this letter you can probably read about us in the papers." The next afternoon when Homer picked up his copy of the *Columbus Dispatch* from the front porch, there on page one was a story by Harold V. ("Hal") Boyle of the Associated Press. Boyle quotes Dad as saying, "We got in [to Marsala] last night and the Italian troops surrendered by the thousands. There is getting to be so many of them now they are cluttering up the highways and getting to be a real military traffic problem." Of course in his letter Dad had been referring to the invasion of Sicily, not action around Marsala almost two weeks later. Still, the juxtaposition of Dad's letter and Boyle's mention of him struck Homer as newsworthy. He called the *Dispatch*, and a couple of days later, it ran a piece about Homer's having receiving Dad's "prophetic" letter.

Dad's command of the Thirty-ninth Infantry was short-lived. A week after he took over from Colonel Ritter, he was replaced by Colonel Harry A. ("Paddy") Flint. A Vermonter by birth, Flint had entered the Naval

Academy, only to drop out and enter West Point. Perhaps in these matriculations lies the source of his signature saying, "Hit don't make no difference." As a polo-playing cavalryman, Flint served at Fort Huachuca and Fort Riley out west. In World War I he had gone to France with the field artillery. As a member of the West Point class of 1912, Flint had graduated three years before the supreme Allied commander in the Mediterranean. Following World War I, while surviving the reductions and seemingly endless tedium of the interwar years, he had attended all the right schools and got to know many who would become generals in the new war. One of his best friends was the commander of the Seventh Army, General Patton. Flint had previously commanded the Sixty-sixth Armored Regiment in Patton's Second Armored Division and was godfather to Patton's son.[15]

Exactly how Flint got command of the regiment is in dispute. According to one source, Flint was stuck behind one of the many desks at Allied headquarters in Algiers, assigned by General Eisenhower to serve as liaison with the French. When Flint heard of Colonel Ritter's injury, he got on a plane to Bizerte and from there crossed over to Sicily. Another account has Flint hanging around the headquarters of his old buddy George Patton waiting for a regiment when he heard Ritter has been injured.[16] Or perhaps another old friend, II Corps Commander General Bradley, having seen Flint in Tunisia and heard his fervent plea for a regiment to command, granted his wish when the Thirty-ninth became available.[17] By whichever means, the well-connected Flint got the regiment.

On July 26, the Thirty-ninth began to move eastward to the vicinity of Enna, and by the end of the day was set up in bivouac. The following morning Dad was summoned to II Corps headquarters, where he met the new regimental commander, escorted the colonel back to the regiment, and reverted to executive officer.

From almost the moment that he assumed command of the Thirty-ninth, Paddy Flint established himself as a character. The five-foot-three-inch colonel was early and often seen running around stripped to the waist, with a black scarf around his neck, a roll-your-own cigarette in his mouth, and an M-1 rifle in his hands. As a morale-building device, going against corps policy against decorating helmets, he emblazoned the helmets of the Thirty-ninth with three A's and an O with a line through the four letters. As Flint explained in a letter to "Georgie" Patton, "Stands for Anyhow, Anywhere, Anytime, Bar-Nuthin." He concludes the letter, "Bless your heart. Always your gunman, Paddy." The letter came from Thirty-ninth Infantry headquarters, which Paddy named "Suicide Ranch."[18] A year later General Patton would say of the colorful colonel, "Paddy is clearly nuts, but he fights well."[19]

On July 28 Dad wrote to Mom, "I am somewhere in Sicily and have had an extremely busy week with my boss having been injured and evacuated. I have been boss and fun it was—but a new one came yesterday and so it goes." A little later in the letter he added, "I'm sorry to have the new boss arrive as it means Ritter won't return and my chances are delayed to a degree."

Whatever else Dad may have thought, there was little time for intro-spection or sulking in one's tent. The regiment, with supporting artillery and a battalion of Goums,[20] was attached to the First Infantry Division, "the Big Red One," under the command of General Terry de la Mesa Allen—a Texan, and like Flint, Patton and Truscott, another ex–polo-playing cavalryman. His assistant division commander was General Teddy Roosevelt, the son of the rough-riding president and another old buddy of Flint's.[21] Like Flint, Roosevelt was given to leading his men from the front, "stalking about with his helmet under his arm, barking encouragement to his men." Calling General Roosevelt "perhaps the only man I've ever met who was born to combat," the correspondent Quentin Reynolds bet one of the First Division aides that Roosevelt would be killed within two weeks.[22]

In an odd and sweeping generalization, a correspondent said that the men of the First Division were ardent Dodger fans, and as long as the Dodgers were in the National League pennant race, soldiers of "The Big Red One" talked about getting home for the World Series. The Dodgers had got off to a fast start, but by early August trailed the Cardinals by thirteen and a half games. "Thank God," a division staff officer said, "now our men can stop mooning about how nice it would be to be home. . . . Now they'll get on with the war."[23]

As the Seventh Army swung eastward from Palermo toward Messina, the Germans began to execute their strategy of digging in and fighting effective delaying actions while preparing to evacuate troops and equip-ment across the Strait of Messina. As a result, the Americans' offensive in northern Sicily became a series of battles against defensive strong points. When the Germans elected to pull out of one of these, they destroyed roads and bridges leading to Messina. Roads that were unsuitable for de-molition they mined. Sometimes they booby-trapped the mines so as to kill the engineers who were trying to clear the road. Then in orchards and other off-road places into which a tired, hungry infantryman might wander in search of rest or refreshment, they planted booby traps and Bouncing Bettys—mines that when stepped on would pop up and explode about chest-high. Said one medic, "It's just sadism. It's OK to lay mines in the road where it holds up troop movements. But they lay them out in the tomato patches. We found a booby trap tied to a bunch of grapes and a Bouncing Betty on the edge of a swimming hole."[24]

As the engineers finished clearing mines and rebuilding roads and bridges, the infantry moved forward again—always on foot, with supplies following in trucks when possible, by jeep where the trucks couldn't go, and by mule in terrain where even jeeps couldn't go. Then, at the next German strong point, another battle.

One such strong point was Troina, held by elements of the German Fifteenth Panzer Grenadier Division under Generalmajor Eberhard Rodt. To the First Division with the Thirty-ninth Infantry attached fell the job of taking Troina. Intelligence reports led to the inference that the Germans would set up their next defensive line somewhere east of Troina. First Division G-2 reported that the Germans were very tired and had little ammunition, many casualties, and low morale. Troina was, in other words, "lightly held."[25] Perhaps the flamboyant Flint and his Thirty-ninth Infantry could take it by themselves. Allen told Flint to go ahead, and elements of the Thirty-ninth moved out along Highway 120, encountering little resistance, and captured Cerami by 0900 on July 31. But the Germans apparently hadn't read the American intelligence reports. The Third Battalion was soon stalled by small arms fire, while the First Battalion managed to advance about three miles and take Hill 1034. At this point Allen was apparently thinking better of the one-regiment assault and wanted to deploy his Twenty-sixth Infantry with the Thirty-ninth in a double envelopment, a maneuver that had been successful a few days earlier.[26] Flint, however, asked for another crack at dislodging the Germans from Troina.

In the afternoon of August 1, he sent two battalions against some high ground north of Highway 120. Their advance was halted by heavy enemy artillery fire, while south of the highway the First Battalion was hit with a German counterattack. As one officer put it, "The Germans thumped hell out of A and C Companies." By nightfall, the First Battalion had withdrawn, its strength reduced to three hundred men.[27] Again, although now supported by massive artillery fire, the regiment made no headway. At this point Allen added his Twenty-sixth Infantry to the assault force, giving them supporting fire from nine artillery battalions.

William C. Westmoreland, who much later would command American forces in Vietnam, was with an artillery battalion supporting the Thirty-ninth during the Troina attack. On one occasion Westmoreland went to the Thirty-ninth's command post to report that half of his guns were out of commission because of problems with their recoil mechanisms. He found Flint and Teddy Roosevelt sitting on a hillside playing mumblety-peg "like a couple of kids." Westmoreland waited for the game to end and then said to Flint, "I want to tell you that I've only got half my guns in operation now, so you can only expect half the firepower you've received before." Flint's response: "Hit don't make no difference, just fire twice as fast."[28]

While the Thirty-ninth was slugging it out with Troina's defenders, someone managed to bring the mail forward. Among the trove of letters from family and friends Dad got six from Mom, written between June 13 and 22, and a "father's day number" from Anne. He is, he says,

> Someplace in Sicily, and some place it is too. We've been plenty busy and active . . . and lots of work and not a little responsibility for yours truly, who found himself "it" for a very trying period of business. MSE has arrived in the area with the rest of his boys and they should be in the ball game 'ere long. We're getting plenty of workout here, I can assure you and the country is as rugged as any we've seen, including Tunisia. Been feeling a little rocky lately—but the knee is okay and feel better tonite. . . . Short on sleep and tired but today was a good day for us. More as soon as possible, Darling. All sorts of love to you and the kids. Jack.

The work and responsibility that made Dad "it" during the battle for Troina may have been partially explained by a wire-service article that appeared in the *Ohio State Journal* of August 4 and the *New York Times* at about the same time. According to the Associated Press, Dad, "using a transmitter set up on a jeep in the shade of an olive tree, called both infantry and artillery support for one hard-pressed American battalion engaged by small arms and mortar fire." When asked who was going in there, Dad replied, "We're sending in B Company. They are our bums, our AWOLs and bare-knuckle fighters. They're just the boys we need and they're going through and around the left flank." And, says the AP, "they did."

When heavy fire stymied an American advance, General Allen committed the Eighteenth Infantry and the Goums with not much more success.[29] For four days both sides launched company- or battalion-size attacks and counterattacks. The Americans would gain a hill or two only to be driven off by withering German fire. On August 4, the attack plan was cancelled "due to disorganization and local counterattacks."[30]

Early on August 5 the Thirty-ninth made some progress, coming to within a mile of Troina before the Germans spotted them at daylight and stopped them with small arms and machine gun and mortar fire. Flint ordered his troops to dig in and then apparently mistook an air strike for the beginning of a new assault.[31] In the midst of the fighting a German soldier wrote home, "The damned Americans fight all day and all night and shoot all the time."[32]

That same day, Lieutenant Joseph D. Swain was pulled out of combat and sent back to the States, because, as he put it in a letter to Mom dated September 28, "I was the ranking 1st Lt. in the Reg., was 30, and had 2 children." When Dad saw Swain's orders, he of course asked Swain to "phone, wire, or write" Mom. It took Swain a month to reach the States and another couple of weeks to become reacquainted with his daughters. He apologized for procrastinating and then said,

> When I left Sicily your husband was in good health and spirits. I enjoyed serving under him very much and when a vacancy occurred for commanding officer of the Regiment we all hoped he would get the promotion, but such was not the case. However, Col. Flint is a good fellow himself and I am sure Col. Toffey enjoys working with him.
>
> A superior officer who is both able and personable occurs all too infrequently for us junior officers and when we are fortunate we appreciate it "more than somewhat."

Ernie Pyle describes the end of the battle for Troina. He watched it with three officers "sitting in folding chairs under a tree outside their tent, looking at the fighting far ahead through field glasses."

> Our troops were in a bitter fight for the town of Troina, standing up like a great rock pinnacle on a hilltop a few miles ahead. That afternoon our High Command had called for an all-out air and artillery bombardment on the city. When it came it was terrific. Planes by the score

roared over and dropped their deadly loads, and as they left our artillery put down the most devastating barrage we've ever used against a single point, even outdoing any shooting we did in Tunisia. Up there in Troina a complete holocaust took place. Thru our glasses the old city seemed to fly apart. Great clouds of dust and black smoke rose into the sky until the whole horizon was leaded and fogged. Our biggest bombs exploded with such roars that we felt the concussion clear back where we were and our artillery in a great semi-circle crashed and roared like some gigantic inhuman beast that had broken loose and was out to destroy the world.

Germans by the hundreds were dying up there at the end of our binocular vision and all over the mountainous horizon the world seemed to be ending. And yet we sat there in easy chairs under a tree sipping cool drinks, relaxed and peaceful at the end of a day's work. It just didn't seem that it could be true. After a while we walked up to the officers' mess in a big tent and ate captured German steak that tasted very good indeed.[33]

When the battle-weary men of the Thirty-ninth entered Troina, they found it virtually deserted. Having for six days stymied the American advance on Messina, General Rodt's Panzer Grenadiers had pulled out during the night. A captured German operations order called on troops to save as much equipment as possible as they pulled back.

The passport to Italy is a gun. Carry as much ammunition as you can. The Italians are to be ruthlessly thrust aside. Italian heavy weapons and motor transports are to be thrown off the road if they get in the way. The only Italians allowed passage to the mainland are those under German control.[34]

As the American troops fought Germans and the Sicilian mountains, a line officer contemplated headquarters personnel comfortable in billets well to the rear as he muttered to a correspondent, "Over in North Africa they're probably saying we're having no trouble at all in clearing out Sicily. They're probably saying the same thing in Palermo, and for all I know, in New York as well."[35] From a villa near Palermo, a staff officer complained to his wife, "I don't understand what good it does soldiers on the firing line for us staff officers to live on canned rations for weeks on end."[36] And when Ernie Pyle, the GI's correspondent, turned his attention to General

Bradley, the GI's general, Hal Boyle had some fun with his fellow corre-spondent. "He's a menace. If he starts a vogue for copy on generals, the AP will send me to AFHQ, where they march them around in platoons."[37]

Having wished her a happy birthday a month before, on August 6 Dad wrote, "We are taking it a bit easy today. After going hard and steady for three weeks, really can use the rest and really could use a bit of an ocean voyage to your shores about now. But don't know of any chances for this latter except a hope." A few lines further on, though, he wrote, "Darling, all you've got to do now is get L.J.M. to order me home to instruct at Benning or something." The same day, perhaps prompted by Lieutenant Swain's departure, Dad wrote to a friend, "It seems to me that the Great White Democratic Party should start a lobby to rotate troops in and out of combat zones." He said he was looking forward to his first bath in a long time and wondered facetiously if New York had decided whether the vic-tory parade would go up or down Fifth Avenue. He closed with a reminder to keep the beer cold.

Troina secure, the Thirty-ninth moved into a bivouac area near Cerami, from where it had begun its assault a week before. Here the regiment could rest and regroup for a couple of days, and Dad could write some letters.

On August 8, realizing that "the events of the past few days" had caused him to forget Mom's birthday, Dad fired off a cable and a letter. Sicily, he admitted, was "truly a pretty place, but we can't finish it up too soon for me, and then the future is again a problem." The same day, Dad wrote me:

> Hey there, Snod. Got a couple of swell letters from you this week—
> one from Homer's office & one from G. N. Sure glad to hear of your
> enjoyable visit to Great Neck and to hear of seeing the family and espe-
> cially good old Arcenio—and the nice salt-water swim. I'll bet Canada
> turned out to be grand too. Hope Uncle Bill fixed you up with some
> fishing and that you caught plenty of them. Be sure and write me all
> about that trip. Well, I guess the newspapers have been giving you our
> news and I'm happy if you think it is good because we've really been
> bearing down. Every battle and every day brings us nearer the finish
> and nearer the chance to return to our homes and families. I'm hoping
> and praying it won't be too long now, Snod. Really had hoped to see
> Bobo win a few this season. Now I gather he has left the Brooklyns.

Hope the Reds are going better now. Guess the war has really slowed down the big leagues some. There isn't much I can tell you Snod except that the Krauts must now know they are licked and their days numbered. We've surely dealt them some punishment around Sicily and our Air Corps is making it tough for them at home I guess. World news does seem more optimistic. When you read this you should be at home again after a wonderful trip and ready to face the fall with plenty of pep. Just pray me home & we'll be all set. God bless you all. Love, Dad.

Anne also got a letter written on August 8:

This is some rugged country we are scrapping in these days and we are plenty busy and active doing it. The mountains are big and rocky and there are not very many roads. You know we get candy and cigarettes issued to us all the time in the field and the food is amazingly good. It is a wonderful thing the way our people take care of us. I certainly miss those lovely swims I used to get at 12th General. And would give a lot for a really good swim practically any place, especially Great Neck or Columbus.

With General Eddy's Ninth Division having come up, the Thirty-ninth reverted to its parent division. Now Dad and the Thirty-ninth Regimental Combat Team were fighting alongside Dad's old outfit, the Sixtieth, still led by Colonel de Rohan. The artist George Biddle spent some time with de Rohan and the Sixtieth in the vicinity of Randazzo. During a lull in the fighting, Biddle said to de Rohan, "Our boys treat the mules well. They feed them sugar from their own ration cans. Kind to the mules and kind to the babies." De Rohan replied, "Hell, they're kind to everyone. They're even kind to the Germans unless they get into a fist fight with them." Says Biddle, "I like Colonel de Rohan." The admiration was mutual. The next day, de Rohan says to Biddle, "You ought to have a medal. You're the only correspondent I've seen near the front line. They ought to know back home what we're doing. We haven't got General Roosevelt to ballyhoo for us and we haven't got a public relations outfit like the 'Fighting First.'"[38]

After Troina the men of the Thirty-ninth would have another tough fight for Randazzo. Wilbert Goldsmith, a machine-gun section leader in E Company, remembers that Ernie Pyle spent some time with the Thirty-ninth in Sicily. As the campaign drew to a close, Pyle wrote the following:

The infantry reaches a stage of exhaustion that is incomprehensible to you folks back home. . . . Soldiers pass the point of known human weariness. . . . They keep going because the other fellow does and because you can't really do anything else. . . . It's the perpetual dust choking you, the hard ground wrecking your muscles, the snatched food sitting ill on your stomach, the heat and the flies and dirty feet and the constant roar of engines and the perpetual moving and the never setting down and the go, go, go, night and day, and on through the night again. Eventually it all works itself into an emotional tapestry of one dull, dead pattern—yesterday is tomorrow and Troina is Randazzo and when will we ever stop and, God, I'm so tired.[39]

In a "cool shady grove" on August 14 Dad realized, "Just about a year ago now is when I got itchy feet about the entire proposition and let myself in for this separation." Two days later, on their anniversary, Dad wrote to Mom:

Darling—13 years ago today you hit the jackpot, or I did. And here's hoping we can do something about it before too much longer. Three swell letters from you today and good they were. I'm so delighted at the good time you are all having there [Great Neck]. This show is pretty well done up I believe and soon there will come other phases and it all adds up to the same thing—the end of war and return us to our beloved homes. Things with me are good and I'm happy in my work. What an outfit we've got. AAAO is our motto and brand. It means Anything, any time, any place, bar nothing. This gang has done one wonderful job in this operation and we are proud of ourselves and much has been accomplished in about 60 days. M.S. [Eddy] is very pleased with us. . . . Just keep happy and gay and doing things and time will get by some-how. Then we'll do all the things and places we've wanted to do and see for ages. . . . Please don't worry—keep praying for the end of this and give my love to the family and pals—and especially John and Mouse. 13 years are not long enough for me. All my love. Devotedly, Jack.

On August 17—some thirty-seven days after landing in Sicily, elements of the Third Division entered Messina, and the city surrendered to General Patton a few hours before the first British troops arrived. The battle for Sicily was over. The victory showed that the American infantryman had become "a first-class fighter."[40] Observed General Bradley,

We had learned a great deal more about fighting a war. We had conducted our first amphibious and airborne operations. We had fielded our first full-blown army. We had introduced four new divisions . . . and the Ranger battalions to combat and provided taut new leadership. . . . [Generals] Patton, Truscott, Middleton, Eddy, Gaffey, Hueber, Ridgway, Keyes and I, together with our staffs, had gained invaluable experience in battlefield management.[41]

The victory cost the Allies 5,532 killed, 14,410 wounded, and 2,869 missing.[42] They failed, however, to keep the enemy from effecting massive withdrawals of troops and equipment from Messina onto the Italian mainland. General Bradley again: "Three German divisions we had fought so bitterly in Sicily survived virtually intact. . . . They lived to fight on, taking many Allied lives before the war was over. . . . Our allowing this to happen was an abysmal tactical failure."[43]

In his letters to his family, Dad did not critique the Allies' conduct of the Sicilian campaign. The island secured, Dad and the regiment settled down to await their next assignment. "Morale in the regiment is high—personnel much improved and all looks good. . . . Chow has been pretty good of late—augmented by green stuffs and fresh meat when an unsuspecting steer inadvertently walks into a mine field." He continued to wonder if the allotments had been straightened out and were coming through okay—also the occasional money orders he sent. "The hotel and Buick fund should be well up by now." A couple of days later he wrote that he was "well and lack[s] only the sight and sound of you and kids to make me happy." He had "gotten fat and lazy and bored during the past 10 days of rest since the battle ended here." He and his men "are well rested and ready for anything at the moment." In this positive mood, he speculated, "Perhaps this job can be done this summer and early fall. It is optimistic I know but we are certain now we can lick this guy and lick him we intend to."

chapter nine

SUMMER INTERLUDES

NORTH AMERICAN

About the time the American Seventh Army invaded Sicily, Mom, Anne, and I packed up and went east to spend the summer with Dad's family at Great Neck, on Long Island's north shore. Going to Great Neck had become a routine. Homer always drove us to Union Station on North High Street. Fred, the gateman, let us go down to the platform before the train arrived. As the big steam engine rolled by, the engineer, high in the cab, waved one gauntleted hand as he pulled with the other a lever that eased the train to a halt. Conductors and porters alit and set the portable step in place as we boarded. Exciting though it was, this seemed more matter-of-fact than our boarding during the emergency stop in Pine Bluff some fourteen months earlier.

Travelers from Columbus to New York had a choice of railroads. The main line of the Pennsylvania ran east past the airport, through Ohio farmland and villages, into Pennsylvania and around Horseshoe Curve. Outside Philadelphia, trains changed from steam to electric power for a smokeless trip across New Jersey and under the Hudson River into Pennsylvania Station.

Even though the journey via the New York Central was about four hours longer, we preferred it. The Central left in the late afternoon. Somewhere between Galion and Cleveland a white-coated dining-car steward would come ringing a gong and announcing first call for dinner. A New York Central dining car was about as close we had ever been to a fancy restaurant. White tablecloths, hefty knives and forks, elegant plates, a printed menu, good food, and a solicitous waiter created an experience in our books equal to anything in Duncan Hines's. At Cleveland our train joined the main line of the New York Central System—"The Water Level Route"—because of its proximity to two of the Great Lakes, the Erie Canal, and the Mohawk and Hudson Rivers. From Albany to New York City, we would watch the river and look for our favorite landmarks: Storm King Mountain, West Point, the Bear Mountain Bridge, Sing Sing Prison, and the Palisades. There was a radio program on Saturday mornings called *Grand Central Station* that began with the announcer describing this journey, "As a bullet seeks its target, shining rails . . . are aimed at Grand Central Station." After following the Hudson for 150 miles and omitting the engine change at Harmon, the announcer had the train "flash briefly by a long red row of tenement houses south of 125th Street, dive with a roar into the two-and-a-half-mile-long tunnel beneath the swank and glitter of Park Avenue, and then Grand Central Station, crossroads of a million lives."

From here one of the family would drive us to Great Neck. Across the East River we got on a parkway that took us along a bay where the big transatlantic clipper landed. At the end of the bay was the site of the World's Fair. Then came an ugly, junky place that in later years I associated with the "ash heap" in F. Scott Fitzgerald's novel *The Great Gatsby*. Then another bay, on the south shore of which stood Fort Totten, an old coast-artillery post, and on the north, Great Neck.

At Deo's big, sprawling Victorian house overlooking Little Neck Bay, I would often sit by the radio listening to a ballgame and honing my box-score-keeping skills. Or I would field off a barn door thousands of balls that in my imagination had been hit by all my favorite Reds and a few other National Leaguers. Deo's sister, Aunt Edith, taught me to play casino, gin rummy, and various forms of solitaire. When he was around, Arcenio taught me to play blackjack and poker. Too old for military service, Arcenio had taken a job in a tool-and-die factory in New York. Whenever he could, though, he would come out to Great Neck to be with us. During the war Arcenio wore a large button that said, "I'm Filipino, not Japanese."

Below the house and past an old gristmill was a little beach. If the tide was high, if the wind kept the seaweed off the shore, and if you didn't step on a horseshoe crab as you waded into the water, the swimming was good. From the beach, as you squinted into the late afternoon sun, you could see the flag at Fort Totten and hear the retreat ceremony.

Some days we would go to Aunt Marie and Uncle Billy's place on King's Point, a spacious and comfortable stucco house set amid boxwood and gardens above Manhasset Bay. If the junky place on the way out from the city would later remind me of Fitzgerald's ash heap, I could never think of Gatsby's house without seeing Aunt Marie and Uncle Billy's. Except for net worth, Gatsby and Uncle Billy had nothing in common. Uncle Billy looked longingly at no green light on a dock across the bay. He had built his life the way he wanted it and was comfortable with it.

As darkness fell on northern Long Island, we could sense a greater proximity to war than we ever did in Columbus. Across the water the lights that once had twinkled in Queens and the Bronx were blacked out, as were the top halves of the headlights on Uncle Paul's car. Some evenings we might see searchlights groping in the night sky for a passing plane.

Seventeen miles from Great Neck was New York City. If Deo or Aunt Marie or Aunt Edith took me, we went by car. Outings with them included lunch at Schrafft's, Rose's Restaurant, or the University Club, followed by a matinee performance of some Broadway musical or once a year, maybe, a trip to Radio City Music Hall. If I went with Arcenio on his day off from the defense plant, we'd take the Long Island Railroad and subway. On midtown Manhattan excursions we would eat at Nedick's, the Automat, or one of Arcenio's favorite Chinese restaurants before going to one of the big theaters in Times Square, like the Paramount or the Roxy, to see a movie and the accompanying stage show, consisting usually of a comedian and one of the famous big bands of the day. Arcenio was partial to Tony Pastor and, secretly, I think, to Guy Lombardo, whom we saw a lot, though Arcenio pretended to scoff at "the sweetest music this side of heaven."

Other days, we'd go under the East River to Brooklyn, land of my birth, to see the Dodgers or uptown to see the Giants or the Yankees. In Brooklyn Dolph Camilli, Billy Herman, Mickey Owen, and Kirby Higbe were notable. From his diner in Hartsville, South Carolina, Bobo Newsom had come to Brooklyn, too, but, as Dad had noted in his letter, he had left again before Arcenio and I got to Ebbets Field. Up north at the Polo Grounds were the great Mel Ott, Mickey Witek, Billy Jurgess, Cliff ("Mickey Mouse") Melton, and one of my idols from the Reds, Ernie Lombardi, who was splitting the Giants' catching with Gus Mancuso. Joe Medwick, whom Dad had always admired from the St. Louis Gashouse Gang of the 1930s, spent part of the year with the Dodgers and part with the Giants. Across the river in the Bronx, though Joe DiMaggio and Tommy Henrich had gone to war, Joe Gordon, Frankie Crosetti, Charlie Keller, Bill Dickey, and Spud Chandler from the 1942 World Series were still around.

The big adventure of our summer of 1943 was a trip to Canada with Aunt Marie and Uncle Billy. Though I had traveled over a lot of American geography in the last couple of years, I had never been outside of the

United States. Going to Canada constituted foreign travel, and Canada itself represented the British Empire just north of New York. Surely I would get to see a real live Mountie.

Thus, sometime in July that summer, before Dad and the Thirty-ninth Infantry fought for Troina, our party of five boarded a New York Central train for an overnight journey to Toronto, where we changed to the Canadian National Railway's Muskoka Express and steamed farther north and deeper into the woods of Ontario. At Huntsville, on the shore of a big lake, we boarded a steamboat that would take us to an island on which stood our hotel, the Bigwin Inn. As we approached it, I thought it looked a little like the Mission Inn, in Riverside, California, where we had spent a night on our way to Fort Lewis a year and a half before.

"Big" certainly described the inn, though I would later learn that the name came not from its size but from a Chippewa chief (John Bigwin, whose name in turn seems to derive from "big wind"). The chief had hunted on the island and was probably buried there. When the inn had opened in 1920, its owner claimed that "no hotel could surpass Bigwin Inn in beauty of design, luxuriousness of appointments, excellence of service or charm of natural surroundings." It was said to be "the largest summer resort in the British Commonwealth."[1]

The main building had many guest rooms and a dining room that was said to seat 750 people. Mom said, probably with minimal hyperbole, that the entire population of Pine Bluffs, Wyoming, could be fed there at one sitting. A short walk along the lakeshore were four stone cottages. When we first arrived, we were the only residents of the cottages. Here we stayed in sylvan solitude, while up in the main building orchestras played and people walked, talked, danced, and played cards. We would walk up to the dining room for meals, which surpassed even those of the New York Central Railroad in grandeur. Waitresses in black uniforms with white aprons took our orders without writing anything down, brought plates of food, and then hovered in inconspicuous anticipation of our next wish. Aside from meals, though, and an occasional walk through the woods along the lakeshore, we stayed pretty close to our cottage.

A couple of days into our stay, we awoke to find that we were no longer alone. Overnight the other three cottages had gained occupants. As we walked past them to breakfast, it appeared that a large party had taken over all three cottages. There was some bustling about and some of the new

people eyed us rather intently as we walked by. On our return from breakfast, we heard the people talking to one another in a language that Mom
said sounded like German.

An hour or so later, having changed into our bathing suits, Mom, Anne,
and I went to the beach, Mom to write her daily letter to Dad and then
return to the book she was reading, Anne and I to dig in the sand and
splash in the lake. Soon our new neighbors began to come out of their
cottages and down to the beach. Smiles and nods were the extent of the
initial attempts at conversation. Then a sturdy, pleasant-faced woman
came over and in pretty good English introduced herself to Mom as Juliana. Juliana, it turned out, was in fact Princess Juliana of the Netherlands.
The two little girls digging in the sand were her daughters, Beatrix and
Irene, two and three years younger than Anne. Another daughter, Magriet,
seven months old, was asleep in a bassinette in the cottages under the care
of a one of the ladies-in-waiting who, with some security men, made up
the princess's entourage.

As Mom explained to Anne and me when we were back in our cottage
after lunch, Princess Juliana, her mother Queen Wilhelmina, her husband
Prince Bernard, and their two daughters had fled the Netherlands in May
1940, when their country fell before the German blitzkrieg. After a month
in London, Princess Juliana and the two girls had come to Canada, while
Queen Wilhelmina and Prince Bernard remained in Britain. Princess Juliana and her daughters had been living in Ottawa since coming to Canada,
and were now vacationing next door to us at Bigwin Inn.

In our little cottage colony and on our small beach we saw a lot of one
another. Anne had two young playmates. Older, and desperately seeking
sophistication, I would amuse myself building sand castles. Beatrix would
admire my work and top it off with a small Dutch flag. On one memorable
occasion I paddled a canoe in which my passengers were the next two
queens of the Netherlands. On shore, the security detail watched with
more anxiety than I thought the situation warranted, while Mom hoped
that her son would not cause an international incident. In moments of
greater tranquility Mom and Juliana, who were the same age, would sit on
the sand and compare notes about raising a family while their husbands
were in a war across the ocean.

On the cold, damp afternoon before we left, having said good-bye to our
friends, I walked down to the dock to watch the lake steamer *Algonquin*
make its regular stop. As the steamer pulled away from the dock and

began to wrap itself in the fog, a piper stood high in the stern playing "Will Ye No Come Back Again," Lady Caroline Nairn's lament for Bonnie Prince Charlie and the lost Jacobite cause. Of course, at the time I knew nothing about Bonnie Prince Charlie or Jacobites, and I certainly didn't know what romanticism was. Nevertheless, like William Wordsworth after hearing the solitary Highland lass singing in the field, "The music in my heart I bore / Long after it was heard no more."

SICILIAN

In Sicily, while Dad and the Thirty-ninth Regimental Combat Team adjusted to sedentary bivouac life, the Allied High Command decided to continue the war in the Mediterranean. There would be one big difference, however. As General Alexander later wrote, "The Mediterranean theatre would no longer receive the first priority of resources and its operations would become preparatory and subsidiary to the great invasion based on the United Kingdom."[2] General Marshall called the Mediterranean "a suction pump" that would draw men and materiel from the main (cross-channel) effort.[3]

On August 16, Mom and Dad's wedding anniversary, General Eisenhower decided that the next target in the Mediterranean would be Italy. Even so, the Allies were not completely sure what they wanted in Italy beyond Rome and the big airbase at Foggia. Probably they hoped for a quick and relatively easy drive north to these two objectives, followed by German withdrawal up the rest of the boot and out of Italy. Perhaps, too, they thought that once the Italians had quit the Axis, they might turn against the Germans remaining in the country. What the Allies hoped for was not what they got.

By the end of the first week in September, the British Eighth Army would cross the Strait of Messina and launch Operation Baytown in the Calabria region of the Italian mainland. Then, on September 9, executing Operation Avalanche, the American Fifth Army, commanded by General Mark Clark and including two British divisions, would hit the beaches up the Italian coast in the Bay of Salerno.

General Clark had risen meteorically from the lieutenant colonel who accompanied General McNair on his visit to Fort Dix back in 1940 to the general who became Eisenhower's deputy commander-in-chief in the

Mediterranean. A West Pointer who had been wounded while commanding a battalion in France in World War I, Clark had not yet commanded large-scale forces in combat in World War II. "Moreover," wrote General Bradley, "I had serious reservations about him personally. He seemed false somehow, too eager to impress, too hungry for the limelight, promotions and personal publicity." According to Bradley, Patton didn't trust him either. "He thought Clark was 'too damn slick' and more preoccupied with bettering his own future than winning the war."[4]

After the conquest of Sicily, the Fifth Army began to take shape as a combat force, assimilating units from General Patton's Seventh Army, which was disbanded in Sicily. Some divisions went to Britain to prepare for the cross-channel invasion. Remaining in the Mediterranean to make up General Clark's Fifth Army were the combat-tested Third, Thirty-fourth, and Forty-fifth Infantry, the First Armored, and the Eighty-second Airborne. In addition there came fresh from the States the Thirty-sixth Division, a National Guard outfit from Texas. Before the First and Ninth Divisions left Sicily for England and Normandy, two thousand officers and men from those outfits were transferred to the Third Division to bring it up to full strength.

How Dad would figure in all of this we at home did not know at the time, and his letters do not reveal how much he knew. Even before the first American soldiers entered Messina, the Thirty-ninth learned that it would shortly be trucked back to a bivouac area. With bivouac life came the inevitable training and inspections. On August 17, Dad, as executive officer, sent out a directive to battalion commanders that for the next several days there would be four hours of training, to include shooting and physical conditioning. Furthermore, every weapon was to be inspected every day. Battalion commanders would also make spot inspections of men and supplies to make sure the regiment remained combat-ready.

To understand part of Dad's job in a noncombat situation, consider this job description, written in 1990 by the grandson of Dad's once and future commanding general:

The next day the paperwork started. This was the domain of the executive officer: paperwork and more paperwork—status reports, strength reports, motor pool tool counts, arms room weapons counts, pay records, personnel updates, reports of surveys on missing equipment, requisitions for new equipment to replace that which was missing—on and on it went in a never-ending snow flurry of gibbering military attention to detail in a manner which attested, however ridiculously, that in the army no detail was too small to deserve its own separate and equal piece of paper.[5]

Nevertheless, on August 27, Dad wrote to say that he was comfortably situated. The weather was hot, but he swam in "Mare Nostrum" to cool off. The knee got stiff at times but gave him no real trouble. The routine and administrative work he was doing, sitting on boards and courts much of the day, made him wonder, "You don't know anyone who wants a good White House Aide, do you?" He told Mom to be "happy and gay—and pray for us to knock off the Jerries soon—and get a place on the curb for the parade."

The next day he was thinking about life after the war. He said he was drawn to the newspaper business and would "like to write sports for a midwestern newspaper or even the [New York] *Sun* or *Herald Trib*." "See if you can arrange that for me. Seriously, my command of the language has improved what with the austere dignity of my duties and position." The night before, he said, he had seen a "swell movie—George M. Cohan—Yankee Doodle with Jimmy Cagney doing a marvelous job." To Anne the same day he wrote, "Of course we've done many interesting, difficult and unpleasant things & seen some very strange and wonderful things and been to places you've never dreamed of. About these things I can tell you when we're all together again."

On his birthday, August 31, he spoke of a cold and minor annoyances— "Bivouac Blues and Rest Camp Retchings, as it were." Nevertheless, about the future he remained optimistic. "Surely another day nearer to reunion is the way I approach each dawn and sunset. Somehow I have hopes it can't be too long." Then he added, "Wish you'd get that White House Aide deal set up. If I get home I'll get all cleaned up and never get disheveled again. What a dude I intend to be."

About this time, a Red Cross worker named Vera Reece wrote a letter to a friend and former business associate in New Jersey:

Only last night, in the middle of Sicily, we had a long talk about Short Hills [New Jersey] with a chap named Jack Toffey. We dined with his particular group in our rounds of meeting the divisions to which we have been assigned. Feel quite flattered, too, for they are wonderful boys and it is thrilling to have them tell you, with great expression, that you're the first American girl they've seen or talked to for many, many months.[6]

Though Vera apparently did not know it, the person to whom she wrote the letter had for years been a neighbor of Dad's parents in Short Hills and knew Dad well.[7]

On September 3, the day the British invaded Italy, Dad reported that he was swimming and playing ball to keep the legs in shape. The rest of the time he was sitting on too many courts and boards. Still, "we are ready to go when they will let us hit 'em again." This letter, too, reveals more about Paddy Flint than Dad had ever said before. "This Benny Havens I work for is a marvelous character and I love and respect him. He'll make a soldier out of me yet—if he isn't careful." A little further along the letter hits a familiar chord. "Wish you could fix up some way we could get together before long, as the time has gotten very long I assure you. With me all is otherwise well, but these periods of inertia are hard on all concerned."

In the letter of September 5, the routine wears on. Dad had heard that Colonel Ritter had been around, but he hadn't seen him. General Eddy was "busy and harassed." Dad said to tell folks back home that the Red Cross does good work and that the Twelfth General Hospital held a warm spot in his heart. Also "the AAAO CT 39 is worth an occasional sock or sweater in any man's book." Of the war, he repeated,

> It can end someday it seems and we keep sweating it out and hoping for a chance to pour it on 'em ourselves. Nothing new or different and my dreams of you and home keep me reasonably happy but anxious for the day when—Don't stop hoping perhaps something can take place to ship me your way. It helps to think so.

On September 8, as the convoys carrying the Fifth Army's assault division made their way over the Mediterranean and into the Bay of Salerno, Italy surrendered. General Eisenhower gave the news to the troops who would go ashore in a few hours. Despite warnings from some officers to remain vigilant, "thoughts of a painless landing permeated the invasion force and dulled the fighting edge of many men."[8]

Dad's letter of September 9 obviously doesn't mention the invasion, about which we would have read long before we got his letter, but he did comment on Italy's surrender, and as the monotony of his situation persisted, he reflected on the past year and turned again to the inevitable financial matters and the future.

Darling—The news putting Italy out of the ball game is at least a step in the right direction. . . . To me it simply indicates possibilities for future operations against the Jerry. One year ago today we became part of Division 9 and a lot has happened to me in that year. And in another couple of weeks I will have been a Lt. Col. for a year. Today is hot and dull and boring. Court meets this PM and activity either of training value or recreational interest is nil. Any time, any thing, any place, bar nothing, except this kind of existence. Don't get anywhere since there is no place to go. Mail is in fits and starts of late. Hoping still for news on 1) the $175 money order 2) the $100 by radio before sending more by the latter method. Wish there was something thrilling to write you, but you know as much as we do—So can't tell you a thing except how much we miss you and love you and the kids. Hitler's battle is only just beginning and there is a tough fight ahead to liquidate him and his people for good and all. Say, do you feel our new car should be a Buick, Oldsmobile, Cadillac, or what? Might have a jeep on the side for a spare. The next number will be vulgar and flashy—convertible or something. Hope these are reaching you fairly fast as they bring all my love and best to everyone. Devotedly, Jack

On September 12, though, life was much better because "mail from you has been wonderful. Just about the nicest letter I ever got was your air-mail of 16 Aug.—came yesterday." To Mom's proposed approach in asking General McNair to get Dad a soft job in the States, Dad replied, "Your 'Listen, Shorty' should certainly do it—or something." More seriously, he wrote, "It has been long enough for me," though, he acknowledged, "I asked for it." Then he shifted gears, reporting that a couple of nights earlier he had dined "with Al Jolson at Div. Hq. Mess as Bus Kenny's guest." He also said that he and Pete McCarley had gone to town the other day and "among others we met and played with Louise Groody of *No, No, Nanette* fame."[9] Whether Dad or Mom had actually seen Miss Groody in the play, they surely knew her as a diminutive dancing dynamo and as the singer who eighteen years earlier had introduced to the world the show's two big hits, "Tea for Two" and "I Want to Be Happy." Now, after an accident that replaced Broadway stardom with a decade of vaudeville, radio, and summer stock, the forty-six-year-old Miss Groody was, in Dad's words, "a Red Cross gal" and "good fun."

Rubbing shoulders with celebrities notwithstanding, Dad was vexed by persistent money worries. He'd had no confirmation that Mom had received the $175 money order sent from the hospital in June, or the $100 sent by radio about August 20, or the $80 sent by radio yesterday. These "should help the Buick and hotel fund somewhat—provided they did arrive." He also continued to worry about the allotment, which should have been corrected to $398.42 retroactive to October 1942. The knee was okay, and the sinus and cold that had bothered him a week earlier were about cleared up. "Things for us are status quo and you can get bets on anything regarding our future or the world in general." He concluded, "This letter sounds dumb, but it has been interrupted frequently. Thanks for 13 lovely years and for your lovely letter about it. God bless all of you. Love, Jack."

Dad's next letter, dated September 16, bore a new return address: "Hq. -15th Infantry, APO 3." He says, "You will note . . . that my current regt'l motto is 'Can Do.' This represents about a two-year struggle to get with the 'best of the west.'" Colonel Ritter had returned to action and was commanding the Fifteenth. Dad was "very glad to be with [him] again and we'll work smoothly here—of that I am certain." Sorry to leave the Ninth Division, he called up a literary allusion again to explain that "under certain situations there my spirit was rebuked as tis said etc." More than this he did not say except that "all is well and hundreds of my old men from Maknassy are here too."

Had Dad been working on getting into the Third Division for two years? Nothing in his letters, even the speculation about jobs after the hospital, suggests that Dad is seeking transfer to another combat division. However seriously, he wrote about wanting to be transferred to a soft job somewhere—perhaps through Charlie Saltzman in Fifth Army headquarters, perhaps through Lesley J. McNair at Fort Benning or some other training facility in the States, even the far-fetched idea of serving as White House aide.

There was much to make the Third Division attractive. It was one of the best divisions in the old Regular Army. In combat in World War I it had earned its reputation as "the Rock of the Marne." The Fifteenth Infantry had fought in the War of 1812, in Mexico, in the Civil War at the same place where Dad's grandfather had won his Medal of Honor, in the

American West against the Indians, and in China in the Boxer Rebellion. It was from its long service in China that the regiment acquired its Pidgin English "Can Do" motto. Earlier in their illustrious careers Generals Marshall and Eisenhower had served in the Fifteenth. Also a part of the Third Division was the Seventh Infantry, the outfit into which Dad had been born thirty-six years earlier, with an equally long and distinguished record. Furthermore, General Truscott, under whom Dad had served in Operation Goalpost, was now commanding the division.

Coupled with these attractions, were there some negatives within the Thirty-ninth Regimental Combat Team or the Ninth Infantry Division? Who had been rebuking Dad's spirit—Paddy Flint? Manton Eddy? Under what "certain situations"? Despite the love and admiration he expressed for Paddy Flint in the September 3 letter, did Dad resent not having been given the regiment when Colonel Ritter was hurt? Did something happen during that sedentary month in bivouac after the Sicilian action? In the September 9 letter, after all, he does use Paddy Flint's AAAO motto a bit sarcastically to describe the "bivouac blues" and "rest camp retchings."

Donald Taggart, in his *History of the Third Infantry Division in World War II* (p. 184), calls the story of how Dad got into the division "epic":

His application for transfer to the 3rd from his old division—the 9th—having been disapproved, Toffey proceeded to disappear for a 48-hour period without leave. Upon his return to military control he was informed that nothing stood in the way of his transfer to the 3rd any longer.

Taggart's terse epic raises more questions. When did Dad submit the first application for transfer? Who disapproved it? Where did Dad go when and if he disappeared for forty-eight hours?[10] To whom did he plead his case? Colonel Ritter, newly appointed commanding officer of the Fifteenth Infantry? General Truscott at his Trapani headquarters? Charlie Saltzman or Bill Ibold at Fifth Army Headquarters? Or did he not plead his case anywhere? Did he just "disappear" for a while, allowing the disappearance itself to constitute reason for Flint and Eddy to include Dad in the levy of twenty-five men the Thirty-ninth was sending to the Third?

If the motivational route to the Third was circuitous, so was the geographical one. Jerry Sapiro, who would become a close friend of Dad's in the Fifteenth Infantry, recalls meeting Dad for the first time on a boat from Bizerte to Palermo. So between his letters of September 12 and 16,

Dad had gone to North Africa and back to Sicily. In Palermo Dad reported to his former bosses General Truscott at division and Colonel Ritter at regiment, drew whatever new combat gear he needed, and took command of the Second Battalion. The next day the Fifteenth Infantry boarded thirteen landing craft and sailed for Italy.

chapter ten

SOUTHERN ITALY

Dad and his new outfit missed the first battles on mainland Europe. The Salerno beaches and plain are ringed by hills and split by the Sele River. South of the Sele River, the American VI Corps under Major General Ernest J. Dawley was to drive inland and take the high ground that overlooked the Salerno plain. A shortage of landing craft forced VI Corps to use only one division in its assault. When the men of the untested Thirty-sixth Division waded ashore near the ruins of Paestum, instead of happy, noncombative Italians, they found tough, veteran German troops.

The Thirty-sixth Division fought hard to hold against strong German counterattacks. As one observer put it, "The whole operation was assuming the proportions of another Gallipoli."[1] Winston Churchill, too, thought of Gallipoli as he received reports of the battle on the Salerno beaches.[2] On September 14 he reminded General Alexander that the Battle of Suvla Bay was lost because the British commander there had remained too far away from the action to know what was going on. "Had he been on the spot, he could have saved the show."[3]

General Clark had to commit his reserves. So it was that Dad and the Fifteenth Infantry entered Italy on September 19 and moved about fifteen miles north and east to Battipaglia.

Dad's shipboard letter of September 18 largely repeats what he had written two days before about his new outfit. "Back with Ritter again and very pleased about the whole business. Life is good." He sent his love and speaks of his "pride and joy [at] being in this great outfit." But on the eve of combat, the Avoca mess and allotment matters were on his mind. He managed to get off another letter the next day just to say he was okay except for mail, which was once again slow because of the change of address. He added optimistically, "Perhaps if things continue to roll along at the present clip this business can be done before we've even dreamed. Certainly we're directing our all to this end. . . . God bless you and the kids and may it not be much longer. . . . All my love. Devotedly, Jack."

A day or so after the Third Division had come ashore and organized for the push north, General Clark relieved General Dawley as commander of VI Corps. To replace him, Clark appointed Major General John P. Lucas, who at one time had commanded the Third Division at Fort Lewis and much more recently had succeeded General Bradley as commander of II Corps in Sicily.[4]

The Third Division relieved the Thirty-sixth, which was pulled back to Army reserve to rest, refit, and reorganize after its ordeal on the beaches. From Battipaglia, the division moved north, with the Fifteenth Infantry on the division's left flank driving toward the Sabato River. The going was tougher than it had been in Sicily. Traversing more rugged mountains and deeper valleys in the fall rains and against German delaying tactics was arduous, painful, and costly.

On one stretch of mountain road near Acerno the Germans had blown five bridges in the space of 2,200 yards. Where the engineers could not create bypasses, they rebuilt the bridges. In two days, September 22–23, an engineer company rebuilt a "two-story, two-bent trestle span 80 feet long, capable of carrying 18 tons."[5] Where there were no roads, the army used mules. Mules, muleskinners, and mule equipment—pack saddles, shoes, bridles, and feed—were requisitioned in large numbers from Sicily, North Africa, and the United States. In these Italian mountains at least, the art of war had advanced so little that the extension course Dad had completed almost a decade earlier in "Care of Animals and Stable Management" didn't seem anachronistic.

On September 24 Dad managed to send a V-mail form repeating his change of address and dashing off a couple of notes: he asked Mom to inform Robert White, his old driver recuperating in a stateside hospital, that "many of the old gang are here" and to inform all concerned of the new address. Finally, he added, "Safe—well and reasonably happy. Missing you very much—and mail has been delayed—by change. Write soon and often. Much love, Jack."

A few days later, after his battalion had taken Mignano and Sperone, Dad wrote Mom the first full letter in nearly two weeks.

Darling—All goes well. I am happy in my work, in excellent condition and really soldiering again. Haven't felt as good since I left Maknassy. Ritter is doing fine and I enjoy having troops again—and swell ones they are too. My mail has been slow of late. Yours of 30 Aug, 2 &

5 Sept just caught up—Altho I had better than that before leaving APO 9. Sure wish T. Monroe[6] knew I was finally in this outfit. Still sweating out the news on allotment, $175 money orders of June—Radio $100 and radio $80 of July and August. Please advise me. Travel is a great thing, especially when it covers such vast areas as we've covered since last October & now that I'm somewhere in Italy you can realize I'm finally in Europe. . . . Rain has come upon us much of late and weather affords cold nights again. Surely ready to have L. J. or someone send for me. The knee is OK but feel the dampness and fatigue now that I'm really active again. My boss (top) now was same in Oct & Nov last. Glad to see me with him again—he said. World news is good when we get it. Am trying to get Miss G[atch] to mail some clothes home for me—also a foot locker that is stored in that area and will never catch up with me again. . . . Love to all—not much chance to write. Also God bless all and pray for the reunion. Devotedly, Jack.

In early October, as Dad pushed patrols to the high ground overlooking the Volturno River,[7] Colonel Ritter again broke his leg. This time, though, Dad didn't get the regiment. Instead, Brigadier General William Eagles, the assistant division commander, assumed command of the Fifteenth Infantry.

Late on the night of October 9, Dad found time to write again. He was pleased that letters had finally caught up with him—including one from Deo that included pictures taken during our summer at Great Neck. Of the Italian scene Dad said, "Ritter broke another leg. I am happy and enjoy my work. The country and the weather are rugged." Though pleased to be getting mail again, he could not do much about writing "as we are busy and only when I get a dry place at night can I write much or any so make this do for everyone." He was glad to hear that the $175 made it to Columbus, and hoped that he would hear similarly about the radioed amounts. He would send more when he got paid. The knee "gets stiff and tired in wet weather and rough country." Again he told Mom to "go ahead and work out a reunion." In the next sentence he said, "The going is not too bad yet and we are giving it plenty in an effort to finish it off." For some reason, his thoughts then turned to Paddy Flint: "My Benny Havens character was something—but he palled on me after a bit—and I'm happy at the change." Then he returned to thoughts of the family. "I miss you all terribly—would like a rest—a bath—a home and my family. It has been quite, at least quite, a year and may it not be so very long now. Love and God bless you all. Jack."

The next afternoon he had another chance to write. He was delighted to have received more mail, but again he couldn't answer it because he and the battalion were "busy as hell and getting more so." He had seen that Nathaniel Howard put something in the *Cleveland News* about our Canadian encounter with royalty. "So N. R. Howard is using us to sell papers," says Dad. "Well, I still want to write sports for a newspaper." Then he turned, as he so often did, to the family.

Darling, more than anything in the world I'd love to get home and see you all. Keep praying that it will truly come to pass. And now forgive the rush and the scrawl. Tell the kids I'll write when possible and give my love to everyone. I'm off on a move now and will be stepping fast for a time I fear. God bless you all, and may it be soon. Devotedly, Jack.

So busy, wet, and tired was Dad in the mountains of southern Italy that in the few letters he wrote in early October he made no mention of the World Series, which began in New York about the time that Colonel Ritter broke his leg. I, however, was as usual caught up in baseball's annual culminating event. About the time that the men of the First Division had given up on the Dodgers, I had given up on the Reds. My club finished in second place, 18 games behind the Cardinals, who would again meet the Yankees, winners of the American League pennant by fourteen games over the Washington Senators.

The Yankees had won the first game. Mort Cooper, the Cards' twenty-one-game winner, would pitch Game 2, with his brother Walker catching. Sometime before the start of the second game, the two brothers learned that their father had died suddenly at his home. For the second time in just three years, a starting pitcher in the World Series had lost his father—Bobo Newsom in 1940 just after he had pitched against the Reds, and now Mort Cooper just before he was to pitch against the Yankees. When the radio broadcast began, the announcers made much of the grief that the Cardinals' brother battery carried. Though I had no experience with the protocols of mourning, it struck me as probably unusual and certainly heroic for Mort to pitch just after learning his father had died. After all, Bobo Newsom had a few days to recover before having to pitch. But pitch Mort did, and he won, holding the Yankees to six hits and withstanding a two-run rally in the bottom of the ninth.

The Yankees won the next three games to take the series 4–1. Cooper returned to pitch well in the do-or-die Game 5, blanking the Yankees in eight of the nine innings. Spud Chandler, however, blanked the Cards for all nine innings, and Bill Dickey's home run with one on in the sixth was the game and the World Series. As I recorded the home run in my box score, I remembered Dad's reaction a year earlier to the Cards' pitching to Dickey. Thus on October 11 did the 1943 baseball season come to an end as Dad and his battalion prepared to cross the Volturno River.

The Volturno is the major river in southern Italy. After flowing southeast down the center of the boot, it meets the Calore River south of Amorosi and then swings west, meandering through the mountains for fifteen miles before breaking out onto the coastal plain at Triflisco and continuing to snake its way to the sea. So circuitous is its route that, after crossing it three times in three weeks, some GIs thought that every river in Italy was named the Volturno.[8]

Where the Third Division would cross it, the river was 150 to 200 feet wide and three to five feet deep. In October, swollen by the rain, the river ran swiftly between steep, mud-slick banks. The Fifteenth Infantry would be one of the leading units in the operation. The Second and Third Battalions would cross the river and immediately seize two small acclivities overlooking the north bank. Dad's battalion would take Monte Monticello. From there they would take Hill 435 north of Caiazzo and then move on about four miles to Monte Caruso.

The day the World Series ended, George Biddle walked into Dad's command post on Monte Castellone. Biddle, a fifty-seven-year-old artist, was embedding himself in Dad's battalion. He had been a major force in the War Department's plan to put select groups of artists into combat zones to paint war scenes. Though he led the group assigned to North Africa, he got there too late to see the fighting. In Sicily, though, he had spent some time with Dad's old Sixtieth Infantry.

George Biddle was American aristocracy. Of the Philadelphia Biddles, descended from the first families of Virginia, he counted among his school chums at Groton two Roosevelts—young Teddy, later of the Big Red One, and Franklin D., later President of the United States. In addition, Biddle's brother Francis, another Grotonian, was serving as FDR's attorney general. From Groton, George had gone on to Harvard's undergraduate and law schools, but art was what he wanted. He interrupted his art studies to serve in World War I. Though he chose and trained for the infantry, he served in France as an intelligence officer. Between the wars, Biddle, who counted among his chief influences Delacroix, Rubens, Degas, and Mary Cassatt, was well established in the school of social realism. Biddle wanted to depict war with a line outfit, he said:

> Correspondents rarely live with the troops. They can't afford to. They start out after breakfast in jeeps to gather news and long before dark they start back with their news to meet the deadline. Of course this doesn't mean that they are not as brave or braver than the average soldier and probably more romantic. But I often wonder if they are at all interested in either grand strategy or in the emotions and hopes and fears of the line troops.[9]

George Biddle would remain with Dad's Second Battalion, Fifteenth Infantry for over a month—from October 13 until November 19, 1943. His account of his time with Dad and his men runs for some seventy-two pages in his book *Artist at War*, first published in 1944. It is from these pages at least as much as from the letters of the same period that we learn a great deal about Dad as a combat commander.

In a loft of a farmhouse, Dad gives his orders for the next day's operation. Biddle watches from a bed against the wall as the shadows of the officers are thrown onto the whitewashed wall by "light from a C ration can of burning gasoline." Fleas and bedbugs reduce the romance of the scene. Dad's orders are a classic rendering of the field order as prescribed by the Infantry School at Fort Benning. E and F Companies will make the assault, while G Company continues to send out distracting dummy patrols. H Company's heavy weapons will provide fire protection for E and F Companies. Because vehicles won't be across the river for at least a day, each man will carry extra C- and K-rations. Dad says that E and F Companies will move out at 2300 hours.

Then Dad adds a postscript.

> Lately I have received reports from company and platoon commanders that they have been "pinned down," when total casualties amounted to not more than one killed and two wounded. Let me emphasize the fact that you are pinned down when you are without maneuverability; that is when to leave cover results in men being instantly killed or wounded.

"Pinned down" does not mean "under fire" and "under fire" does not mean "having located enemy fire. . . ."

Remember additionally that when you are under mortar fire it is no relief to stay where you are, and it is as safe to move forward as to the rear. You cannot tell whether the enemy's fire is long or short and you must impress upon your men that in case of doubt they must move forward. . . .

I must make another general statement, which many of you may not like and which some of you will resent my making. You have often heard our artillery criticized for not knowing the location of our own troops and for firing upon them. Often it is not possible to get the exact location of our own troops or to know exactly to what grid line of co-ordinates they have proceeded. We may, however, at the same time have definite information that the enemy are on or near that spot. In such cases it is proper for our artillery to fire. We may cause casualties among our own troops but it is more important to dislodge the enemy. In case of doubt we must maintain our fire on the enemy and in the long run this will save our own casualties. This is a statement of fact; not fiction.

I think that is all. I will repeat it again if you wish. It is essential that everyone understands his assignment. Are there any questions?[10]

Biddle was impressed. He says that Dad "spoke with the clarity of exposition of a Harvard law professor." He says that Dad had a "keen, sharp mind and tough, salty American humor." He describes Dad as "well over 6 feet and [having] the bones and conformation of a steeple-chaser rather than a race horse." He says he is not surprised to hear that Dad had been a "star football player and varsity oarsman at Cornell." Then Biddle paints the scene in words.

While he was talking I walked around behind him and watched the men's faces, serious and attentive, as once more he went over step by step every detail of the operation. Their expressions were grave and beautiful in the deeply etched and flickering light. Not overemotional or in any way showing that they would shortly go forth part or all the way to meet death, but rather with concentrated attention, as young football players often have, listening full of confidence to the coach's last words of instruction before walking out on the field.[11]

The assault companies had moved out down the mountain to the final assembly areas, and H Company was moving to the positions from which it would provide fire support, when Dad, Biddle, and the rest of battalion headquarters started down the mountain to the plain on the south side of the river under enemy artillery fire. Early in the morning they came upon three men badly wounded when their truck had hit a Teller mine. One of the wounded was yelling, "Jesus! Get me out of here! Before I bleed to death! Why don't they bring up the jeeps? Jesus! Jesus!" Dad stopped and kneeled by the young soldier. "How ya going, kid? The jeeps will be along. You warm under your blanket? Hang on, kid. Attaboy."[12]

As dawn broke, Dad, Biddle, and their party dodged artillery fire as they sprinted across a field to reach the riverbank, which was under more artillery and machine gun fire. They saw dead men lying in ditches near where the engineers were working on the bridge. They plunged into the river, Biddle clinging to one of the guy ropes that had been strung. Dad kept yelling for people to spread out so as to cross faster, but many preferred to cling to the rope in the swift current.

By 1800 on October 13, battalion headquarters had reached the base of Monte Monticello. As Biddle caught his breath, Dad remained busy.

> He directed fire from our artillery on . . . the farm buildings from which the Germans were still sniping. From time to time he reported to Regiment; took in reports on the walky-talky from our outpost elements; asked for more telephone wire and medical equipment; inquired about measures for evacuating the dead and wounded; sent back prisoners with guard detachments; called to find out whether the tank destroyers could get across the river; sent out officers and small units to locate forward O. P.'s and C. P.'s on the near slope of Hill 435. He was inexhaustible. He seemed to carry the whole battalion on his shoulders.[13]

Correspondent John Lardner dropped in on Dad's battalion about this time. Of the Volturno crossing Lardner wrote,

> There was one unit which made an incision so deep and rapid north of the river that German hopes of holding this line were doomed within a day's time. Its leader was a very young lieutenant colonel from Columbus, Ohio, named John Poffee [sic]. He was polite and gay and busy all at once when we found him in his forward post in a fold of the hillside. "Get some coffee," he called. "I need a rest. Mr. Biddle needs a rest. Who the hell doesn't?"[14]

On the night of October 14, Dad and Biddle moved into a farmhouse and there dined on locally scrounged steaks, onions, crackers, and a ten-gallon bottle of red wine. The feast was the doing of Walter Parsons, out of White Plains, New York, who had worked for Major John Dilley in the Sixtieth Infantry, had come over to the Third Division, and now was working for Dad. As the weather cleared and the evening came on, Dad and Biddle continued to work on the wine and talked about soldiers' discipline. Dad said,

> After Kasserine I was wounded. I had been all steamed up and was on my toes and could have gone through anything. I was invalided back to a hospital in Oran. It was a swell hospital and we were well looked after and had nice nurses. There were plenty of officers in the hospital. When we got better we were sent to a convalescent camp, where we leaned over bars during the day and made dates with the nurses. Then we went to a replacement base, where we did some calisthenics and leaned over more bars and made more dates with nurses. By then the keenness was working out of us, and lots of the men somehow began to think they would be more useful back in the states or doing really important work on a swivel chair in Ordnance or Quartermaster at a base center. Anyway lots of us didn't drift back to the regiment. I wonder if I had it to do all over again whether I would?

Biddle asks Dad for the moral. Says Dad,

> The moral is discipline. You get a good soldier the way you get a good football player. You drill him and drill him and drill him, until he's all steamed up and on his toes and will go right through anything. . . . And then you've got to put into them the killing instinct. Our boys aren't born with it, and they are not tops as soldiers until they get it. When they have had enough casualties they want to kill Germans. The English Eighth Army has it. But then again lots of the Eighth Army were professionals. They had been in the Near East for five or ten years. They knew what they were fighting about because they were professional soldiers. Our boys aren't professionals, and you have to condition them to enjoy killing.

Biddle agreed, "To make a good soldier you have to teach lots of things that aren't nice or pleasant." He then turns to how the American soldier is depicted by the press.

It disgusts me the way our doggies are screened up as heroes; like college boys who have made the football team and are an honor to their best girls and the family. It's a lie. They are not heroes and are not an honor to the family—not over here any more than in some other calling. Mind you, this is not a criticism of our soldiers. It is a criticism of conditions which lower the fighting efficiency of our soldiers. I wish people at home, instead of thinking of their boys in terms of football stars, would think of them in terms of miners trapped underground or suffocating to death in a ten-story fire. I wish they would think of them as cold, wet, hungry, homesick and frightened. I wish, when they think of them, they would be a little sick to their stomachs. That would give them a little better understanding of our boys' mentality. It would give a very different moral support and squeeze a little more efficiency or will to sacrifice out of our soldiers.[15]

On Sunday, October 17, General Truscott ordered Dad's battalion forward.[16] Biddle found the countryside lovely despite the rains and the tough trudging. In rough terrain, Dad arranged for forty mules to help haul equipment and rations. Then he led the battalion over Monte Melita to the Roccaromana-Statigliano-Latina road. Of this maneuver the regimental history says, "In a beautifully executed all-night march through the mountains, [Second Battalion] got behind the Germans at Statigliano." On the morning of the October 18 the battalion had stormed Hill 330, cleared the village and sent out patrols "to cut the road from there to Latina."[17] As the rest of the battalion bedded down in a grove of trees, Biddle heard the troops laughing and joking and noted, "Our soldiers do most of their grousing at the bases. They show up best when they are hungry and wet and under fire."[18]

A couple of days later, Biddle met Corporal Jo Kindlarski, who asked Biddle if it was true that he could travel anywhere he wanted to among the troops. Biddle replied that it was. Kindlarski said, "If I was in your boots now, I wouldn't be in here now. I'd be home in the States." Biddle took a liking to Captain Harmon, the commanding officer of F Company. A serious, soft-spoken young man with a growing collection of German small arms, Harmon told Biddle that he was worried about the delivery of the baby his wife was expecting back home. Biddle asked him if he liked line duty. Harmon's reply: "I don't know. I like the tactical end of it. But I don't know how much I shall enjoy nursing men all day long; seeing they oil their guns, and dry their socks, and wash out their mess kits, and dig latrines, and scrub their teeth, and keep their ears clean."

Biddle then asked Dad, "Harmon's a good officer, isn't he? He has intelligence and plenty of nerve. . . . But I love our G.I.'s. They're at their best at the front, under fire, wet to the skins. Jack, have you ever heard a G.I. grousing under fire?"

Dad answered:

> They are the backbone of the army. You can't get the best out of a division unless you get the best out of the G.I.'s. You can't win battles with red and blue pencils on 1:100,000 scale maps, or at Ft. Leavenworth. In theory it is simple but it's the experience that wins battles. That's why I think Bradley is a great soldier. He is not showy or spectacular, but he is sound, and he has come right through with the infantry. There is one thing I insist on with my staff; and that one thing I pride myself on having: co-operation. In everything else—in deportment, physical appearance, I.Q., tactical sense—I've been rated up and down; but I've always had a high rating in co-operation. It's the quality that makes a unit successful: team play.[19]

Dad added that in his father's generation the army counted in its ranks "a great lot of soldiers . . . Liggett, Craig, Drum and MacArthur. Maybe I have hero worship, and perhaps it's because I grew up to worship them through my old man. But somehow today they don't seem to stock [sic] up so high."[20]

In expressing his admiration for General Bradley, a career infantryman, Dad may have been reacting to the number of old cavalrymen under whom he served in the past year—Patton, of course, and Truscott, and Dad's "Benny Havens," Paddy Flint, among the most prominent. Of the generals in the Mediterranean, George Biddle would write a couple of weeks later, "There are four men over here of whom I have heard only high praise: Generals Bradley, Mark Clark, Terry Allen, and Lucian Truscott." And when he sketched Truscott in November, Biddle heard from Fifth Army staff officers that "the Third Infantry Division is the best division today in the theater" and that "General Truscott is responsible for the high quality of the Division."[21]

During a lull on October 21, Biddle was chatting again with Jo Kindlarski, who said he had switched from German small arms to mess-kit utensils in his collection of souvenirs. He said he planned to bring home a dozen sets for his mother to use on picnics. Biddle asked Kindlarski how many Germans he had killed. The corporal replied, "Mr. Biddle, that's one question I don't answer. You know. I might be the next one. But I'll tell you one thing. I don't bring home no more Jerry prisoners." He then told Biddle that he might write a book after the war, repeating, "If I could draw as well as you can, I'd be so far back you couldn't see me." Then, as a machine gun opened up somewhere up ahead, Dad came up to Kindlarski. "Jo," he said, "there's some Jerry snipers up there. I think we may may have a patrol surrounded. Go get 'em, Jo. Don't bring none back, neither."[22]

For almost two weeks in October Dad had been unable to get off a letter to Mom. On October 22 he wrote this:

> Darling—The most recent from you 20 Sept and one from Belle about 16 indicate all well and the $100 rec'd. Italy is a rugged spot and I'm fed up with hillside living. As I shaved a few moments ago using my helmet for a wash basin I dreamed of barber shop shaves and rum collinses downstairs at the old Deschler. One year ago we shoved off from NOB and a long year it has been—and anything that will change my locus operandi to your area will suit me fine. No doubt my change from Div. 9 to 3 didn't speed that up any—but we shall see. No news of Ritter—except that he is hospital [sic] again someplace with his other leg broken and probably sore as hell, too. I get mail less rapidly of late on account of forwarding, etc. Got one from Deo also Robt. White yest'dy. Still trying to get that letter off to the kids, but each time I try to write we get an order to do something. So it goes. Miss G. keeps me in cigarettes, candy, soap, etc. And I sleep in a bed so seldom—I mean bedding roll—that I never change my clothes. Around here it is a blanket and the ground. Rugged is no word for the condition of our troops. They are that—tired and need a rest and a clean up. The German has been resisting just enough to keep us working plenty hard and keep us on the go. It does seem that we should and could be together by Xmas but I see no hope off hand. My chief of last Nov. is as you probably know the same gentleman—see the mags. Wish I could think of something good and interesting to say but we are too active and the limitations too important. Being really with troops again is more fun than being exec, but more active. I truly like it better. Perhaps you, my dear, can work out some mammoth deal whereby I am ordered to central Ohio to count automobile parts factories or some such. Meanwhile God

bless you all and I'm praying for the day, you can surely bet on that. Tell everyone hello and much love. Jack.

Dad's first mention of the World Series came in his letter to me written the day after the above. He called the Yankees' victory an "unpleasant surprise." He mentioned to me, as he had to Mom, the first anniversary of his sailing from Norfolk. He had hoped we would be together again before now, but noted that it had been "a long tough job." While he wrote, "it is just before dark and very noisy on account of our artillery is pounding away at the Krauts and some is flying right over us with loud bangs." He said to tell Mom that he would write again as soon as he could and that he got a bath today using his helmet for a tub and got new clothes—"so really doing pretty good."

On October 25, Dad's battalion led a "vigorous and violent" attack on San Felice, taking the town by early afternoon and pushing beyond. Two days later the battalion led off against Caievola, in what Dad called "the most messed-up action I've ever been through."[23] In the course of the action the battalion was hit by friendly artillery and German 120 mm. mortar fire, taking heavy casualties. It was here that Captain Arlo Olson of F Company single-handedly wiped out a German machine-gun position and led his company in an exposed frontal assault on a hill. For his valor, Captain Olson was awarded the Medal of Honor. In recommending him, Dad wrote,

> Captain Olson's intrepidity, exemplary conduct, and demonstrated professional skill served as a model for his officers and men and enabled the company to accept casualties without weakening the desire to close with the enemy and destroy him. This spirit, instilled by Captain Olson, has never left the company.[24]

On October 28, at Dad's request, because "the people at home ought to see things like that," Biddle drew a picture of a dead American sergeant.

> The Sergeant's face was yellow and shrunken, probably from the loss of blood. He had died of suffocation from an internal lung hemorrhage on his way down from the crest of Caievola. As often in death, his face assumed a sternly beautiful expression. There was a hollow depth beneath the brow; and the upper lip was drawn tightly down, which gave his mouth a look of ascetic mysticism. It was the face of one of El Greco's saints.[25]

The next day Biddle did a portrait of Dad, and Dad wrote to Mom—on regular paper this time, not V-mail.

Darling,

Just for a change one of these to say that yesterday brought a perfectly grand windfall of letters from you all the way from Oct 1 thru 14 and practically all of these were to the new address less forwarding. So delighted with all of this grand news of you and the kids and John's football suit and game—Mouse's braces and other homely details. Never could be anything more grand than this marvelous mail you've been getting to me. Also swell letters from Dosia, Deo, and Granny— also Marge Peck—all gratefully received. I was naturally delighted to know that the moneys had arrived which did make me feel like we're in the same world. Also glad ODB [Overseas Dependents Benefit] finally came through in shape. This is big news and a boost for the Buick and hotel fund that is truly gratifying.

Today has been a nightmare of paper work—citations, letters of condolence, etc. and a desperate struggle to get caught up on some of my own paper work—sent you a cable via EFM[26] today—also one to the Beaches—Incidentally, can't you avail yourself of the EFM cable privilege now. Our cable address is of record I'm certain. The story of Anne's vacation speech is marvelous also the story of the circus and John's flat tire fixing and in fact every bit of news you sent was grand. Pride of the Yankees was a marvel. I saw it back at good old 12th Gen'l and it was truly a tear jerker and full of all sorts of nostalgia and stuff that makes you cry. Well, the going is not easy and it is a rough and rugged job, but we are getting it done. Someday will come a big break and it will crack wide open I hope.

Mr. George Biddle the eminent artist has been with me nearly three weeks and a grand job he does of battlefield scenes on the spot. You must watch for his stuff. It is wonderful and will come out at home one day ere too long. He is doing a job or so on Toffey which should be amusing to say the least. I blush to say it is after 3 P.M. and I have yet to wash and shave what with the heavy paper work we are handling today. In just a moment I intend to handle that job. You please write Marge Peck & Dosia & White telling them I will when I can but I'm plenty busy. Hope also to dash out a V-Mail or two on this day so we can see how it compares on a time basis. Things go on pretty well, but I can't be any more anxious to see you all than I now am. Perhaps something will occur someday to bring me back to you. Italy is a strange land—Mussolini was a terrific chump to think he could possibly accomplish anything with the material he had which must have neared zero in all respects—it is now below zero as to resources and facilities. I have no news of Ritter or of #9, so cannot imagine what they are doing. I gather that some of my erstwhile companions in arms do more than well at home. I'd accept even Tullahoma, Tenn. At this point, Bragg would look good and Dix or Lewis positively luxurious. Certain we are of one thing, my darling—Life in the future of the Toffeys will be a large time family affair involving no solo travel by the undersigned. I may not get off as many letters as I used to but you may also be assured that each one carries all the love and thought that can be crammed into a letter. Also each one is like an obstacle course and is almost impossible to write in the face of phones, artillery fire, questions and general harassment. Meantime and until next time—God bless you all and much love—Devotedly, Jack.

It was probably too soon for Dad to be including a letter to Captain Harmon's wife among the condolences that made up a part of the day's paperwork. Harmon had been hit by shell fragments a couple of days before up on a ridge and had died coming down the mountain on a stretcher. Harmon's death hit Biddle hard.

I hardly knew [him], but for some reason he stirred my imagination. I wondered what his home was like. I began to think about his wife. What is she doing these next few days of grace before she gets the telegram from the War Department? He had said to me: "She don't have to worry about money." Still she would be worrying, like all of them at home, about meatless days, or the gas ration, or finding someone to cut firewood or mow the lawn. I thought how much would go out of her life when the blow struck her. The wastage that lay ahead of life's ambition, of love's fulfillment, and of the child who would grow up without a father.[27]

Dad wrote by V-mail on October 30 to say that he had written and wired the day before. He repeated that he was in pretty good shape and got a bath once in a while. He wrote, "The German is fighting skillfully here and takes advantage of the rugged country, but we will in time eliminate him here as we have elsewhere. Our people are in good shape and spirits and doing a fine job." As the frequency of his letters confirmed, it was harder to find time to write than it had been in July and August. He said that Charlie Saltzman knew that he was in the area, but Dad hadn't seen him yet. "The world is a small walnut these days as people dash back and forth across and around it turning up in our area one day & yours the next." Thoughts of home led him to this:

> And keep the prayers for a speedy return going. Give my love to the kids and all our pals. I'd sure like to be trudging into the OSU stadium this P.M. to watch a good old game or even going to Loews Ohio with you all. It can't be forever now—and I hope each day something good will develop for us.

He concluded by mentioning again the footlocker full of clothes that he had been trying to get Nancy Gatch to send home from North Africa for him. He warned Mom not to worry at its arrival in Columbus, lest she think that his personal effects had been shipped home posthumously.

At the end of October, the Fifteenth was holding the heights of Monte San Angelo and Monte Caievola in the vicinity of Pietravairano. Since its arrival in Italy, the Second Battalion of the Fifteenth had lost 40 percent of its strength in battle casualties and perhaps another 30 percent in non-battle casualties. Of the battle casualties, about one-third had come in the crossing of the Volturno in mid-October.[28]

On November 1, the Fifteenth moved into Presenzano. Dad was one sentence into a letter to Mom when he was interrupted. He would not return to the letter for almost two weeks. The interruption was an attack on the battalion command post by German bombers that sent the men diving for cover. When the dust settled and the air cleared a bit, Dad lit into his staff.

> I'm God damn sick and tired of seeing these picnic gatherings out in the open. From now on I want this country-club life to bust up. There is too much preoccupation among my staff with preparing your food and making your beds. I don't give a holy God damn if none of you officers ever eat or even sleep on active campaigning. I'm sick of telling you guys to wear your helmets and carry your arms. Right now I see three of you without helmets and your small arms consist of a bunch of souvenir trench knives and toy Beretta pea-shooters. Maybe you think I'm talking crap and maybe one of these days a Kraut Minnie Werfer will fall among a lot of you, bunched up out on the lawn, scribbling V-mail letters; or a kraut patrol will walk in on you while you're

heating a cup of chocolate and picking candies out of C ration cans, with your helmets scattered around in the straw and your tommy guns hanging on bushes.

Now I want it to stop. An' when I say "stop" I mean "stop, period." I don't want any God damn Headquarters Company soldier hanging around chatting when I'm trying to telephone. An' I want more messengers where I can get at 'em. There's a war going on. Do you get me? Roger.

Says Biddle: "Jack Toffey is a good field commander. One of the best.[29]

Back home in Columbus, we awoke on the morning of November 7 to find in the pages of the *Ohio State Journal*, Columbus's morning paper, a brief article proclaiming "Columbus Man's Mortar Gets Tank." The article reads as follows:

Lt. Col. John J. Toffey, 1799 E. Long St., battalion commander of a field artillery unit in Italy, is among American artillery specialists using unheard of tactics to knock out Nazi tanks, the Associated Press reported yesterday.

Directing fire from the brush-covered side of Mt. Presenzano, Col. Toffey ordered his men to knock out two tanks hugging the base of a nearby hill. The big guns could not bring their fire down close enough but a mortar finally "laid one" right on one of the tanks from 1750 yards—described by the field artillery officers as "something to write home about, a field artillery hole-in-one."

The best account of this incident we got from Eunice Woodall, "a soldier's wife from Danville Virginia," whose husband was stationed in Marion, Ohio. She sent us a clipping from her hometown, the *Danville Register*, which carried a longer version than our paper had. After a lot of artillery fire produced only a "near hit" on one of the tanks, it began to look like the Germans could make necessary repairs and slip away after dark. "Suddenly Toffey leaped up with a yell. 'Hot dog! Direct mortar hit, one round . . . the other tank is burning.'"[30]

The mountains rising up before the Third Division in early November were even tougher obstacles than those through which the Division had just fought. Through a gap in this east–west range ran Highway 6 and a railroad line. Fourteen miles northwest up this valley lay the town of Cassino, a key feature in the German Winter Line.

On November 5, after fighting through tough German resistance just beyond Presenzano, Dad's Second Battalion began an arduous climb up Monte Cesima. As the battalion neared the summit, Dad yelled at a platoon leader, "For God's sake, Lieutenant, do you want to come out of this war alive? How often do I have to tell you guys not to attack in file formation? Spread out in squad column or platoon column formation, so your whole line can fire if a Kraut sticks his hands up." But on gaining the crest, scouts learned that the Germans had deserted their outpost on the summit. Dad and Biddle stood looking out over a beautiful valley. "You can see all the way to Rome," said Biddle somewhat hyperbolically. "Hell," said Dad, "You can see all the way into Germany."[31]

Well before they would reach either prospect or even Cassino, the regiment would have to conquer two more Italian heights—Monte Rotundo and Monte Lungo, rising to 357 and 351 meters respectively and dominating the gap just past the town of Mignano.[32] Dad's battalion drew Monte Rotundo, attacking up the southern slope. German resistance was, as usual, stubborn, and it took the Fifteenth Infantry several days to secure the mountain.

On November 11, while the Fifteenth was still battling for Monte Rotundo, General Clark presided over an Armistice Day ceremony at the opening of a military cemetery near Avellino. In his remarks he noted that once again the same Allies were fighting the same "mad dogs that were loose in 1918." He found it fitting to honor "our dead comrades who gave their all in order that the Fifth Army should succeed." He spoke of their sacrifice in securing Salerno and Naples and in crossing the Volturno, and in defense of the homes and families to save "our own land from devastation like this in Italy."

Then, sensing talk about sending home veterans of the fighting in Italy, Sicily, and North Africa, Clark said abruptly,

> We must not think about going home. None of us is going home till it's over. None of us wants to go home till it's over.
>
> It would be foolish to break up the Fifth Army after its long experience. We've got men at the front who are masters of the Germans; they're killing the Germans. Every one of us must take a pledge that we will carry on till it's over.
>
> We've caught the torch that these men have flung us, and we'll carry it to Berlin and to the great victory—a complete victory—which the United Nations deserve.

Clark presented a wreath, a volley was fired, and "echo" Taps was played. As the last notes died away, he dropped his hand from the salute and said, "That was a good ceremony."[33]

Up front on November 13, Dad was able to finish the letter he had started on November 1. "Just 12 days of interruption have transpired and it is busy we have been and working hard. . . . It is a long hard grind this business but I feel we are doing very well indeed and also I hope more than all the world that something will transpire to bring us together very soon." As if in illustration of his earlier observation about the world as a "small walnut," he told Mom that he had "been living next to and fighting side by side with" Sterling Hill, brother of the husband of Mom's cousin and in Dad's book "a fine young officer doing a grand job."

He noted, "This hurried scrawl is written under definitely adverse conditions, but it brings all my love and comes with it a prayer for our reunion soon." He wished all a merry Christmas, hoping that we might spend it together, and apologized for not having sent presents, but pointed out that "neither time nor conditions permit purchasing and mailing of same." "This is a pitiful letter," he decided, "but it at least assures you of my continued existence and strives to say I love you and miss you—in every conceivable manner. So long for now—more as soon as time permits. God bless you and keep you. Jack."

The next day Dad met a dozen young lieutenants who had just arrived as replacements. He told them how important it was that they get to know each of their men. "Remember that to get the most out of your platoon . . . you've got to get the most out of every man in it." He reminded them of the need for security. "Don't ever bivouac, or sleep, or eat, or rest, until you have your security posted." He told them that they were joining "what I believe is one of the finest overseas divisions." Nevertheless, he said, these new lieutenants will not find things as they were in training back home. "In every field here you will find less well-trained personnel and less effective equipment than what you have been used to." Finally he said:

I wish you all luck. Keep your heads up. Back there in the companies, they badly need you; and we're glad to have you with us. Remember that if I can help you I'll do it. If you ever need me, I'll try to get around to see you. Keep your eyes open and your mouth shut. Be on the alert. Best of luck to you.[34]

On November 15, the Thirty-sixth Division began to relieve the Third. The relief was completed two days later "after 59 consecutive days of offensive action against German forces employing delaying or defensive action. During this period of 59 days, the Division sustained 3,144 battle casualties and 5,446 non-battle casualties, a total loss of 8,590."[35] Battle and nonbattle casualties for the Second Battalion of the Fifteenth Infantry came to about 75 percent of the battalion's strength. Biddle thought it was a "longer period of consecutive combat duty than that of any American division in this or the last war." Dad's was the last battalion to come off the line.

After a couple of days in rear areas, George Biddle got a cable from *Life* ordering him back to the States. Before going, he returned to Dad's outfit, where, he recounts,

> I had time for a hasty bite of lunch with the Battalion Staff. It was the first time we had eaten together off a table and with a tent roof over our heads. It lent a little formality to the occasion. When I said good-by it was casual enough. In a way our acquaintance has been of the most casual kind. But we have been living all the time—that is every day and every night—very close to death. That relation breeds its own sort of intimacy. I shall probably never again see any of those faces. Yet I shall never, of course, forget them and they will never forget me, either. . . . I had been for a short time one of them. They knew I was proud of it.[36]

chapter eleven

ITALIAN INTERLUDE

As George Biddle began his journey back to the States, the men of the "Can-Do" Regiment were settling in for rest and relaxation around Statigliano and partaking of the creature comforts unavailable during their fifty-nine days in the line. They moved into walled tents. Showers were up and running by the end of the first day, and the Red Cross began dispensing coffee, doughnuts, and conversation. To speed communication with the folks at home, EFM cable services were available. On November 20, clubs for the enlisted men and officers opened. There were a movie and a band concert. And there was always equipment to be cleaned.

Dad devoted that day, a Saturday, to writing his Christmas cards. Each was a V-mail cartoon with the caption "Merry Christmas 1943 from Italy," and depicting a GI who is sticking his head up over the side of a shallow muddy foxhole. Overhead shells are bursting. Around the hole are used ration cans. The soldier is saying, "What the hell is merry about this?" We all got them, signed, "Much love, Dad."

On Sunday, November 21, the chaplains held religious services, and the Red Cross staged a vaudeville show. In the midst of Sunday's relaxation, Dad wrote Mom, "At long last a quiet letter to say we are pausing on our oars and trying to rest up." Mail had been good, he said. As he had done previously, Dad had collected all of Mom's most recent letters into a book. He said that he would catch up on his letter-writing to Anne and me as well as to those to whom he had been unable to write while in the line. The Avoca mess continued to plague him, and he told Mom to "settle it with receipts and protests, please." He said that he was about to visit "one Charley S. with a view to seeing how are chances—Charley can if it can be done." He said that George Biddle left "two days ago, so stand by to hear from him. I shall miss him terribly." He closed with bits of news about army buddies and asked about people at home from whom he had not heard in some time.

On November 21 Dad also wrote to me:

My dearest son—My first chance to answer your nice letters of September 26 and October 17. Glad to have your first hand news of World Series dope and football information. Saw good old Will Ibold in a nearby town today. He is in good shape and has a nice job. Boy it is plenty muddy around here just now and it has been cold too. We are taking it easy for the present. This is a bit of all right too as it gives me this chance to tell you how proud I am of the way you are doing things—your excellent work at school and the way in which you care for your mom and sister is grand. . . . Please give my love to all the family and friends and tell them I am dreaming of a white Christmas— and may all their Christmases be bright. To you, Snod—Love and good luck. Bless you son. Devotedly, Dad.

To Granny and Homer he wrote as well, telling them much of what he had said to Mom and me and adding that a couple of weeks ago "on a shell-swept hillside," Sterling Hill "showed up to put his cannons at my disposal. It was great to see him and we had fun in spite of conditions."

To Anne, Dad said that he had seen the pictures taken at Great Neck. He thanked Anne for her letters, telling her how much he enjoyed hearing about all she was doing. About Italy he wrote:

Italy is cold and wet just now. And I feel very sorry for these poor Italian kids who do not have proper clothing, food, or places to live. War is bad enough for everyone—but most of all it is a terrible thing for the poor kids who did nothing to cause it and only suffer from it.

Monday, November 22, brought no rain—"a gratifying change," in Dad's estimation. Its absence "helps us to refit and rejuvenate and helps my morale." Having got a bunch of letters from Mom, Dad wrote to say, "I consider you have played the Avoca deal okay—and I don't care what they say—the entire matter stinks—thanks to Mrs. J. D. P."[1] About the meeting with Charlie Saltzman, Dad said that "no big deal has been consummated," but that he would see Saltzman again. Saltzman, he says, is "Clark's boy Friday and he can be a help if anyone can."

On November 26 Dad reported a flood of mail, Mom's full of good news and "gay and bright." He said that he had done a bit of sightseeing and picked up some gloves and cameos that Mom and Anne could share as Christmas presents. Having found nothing for me, he asked Mom to get something nice in his stead. He reported also that he would soon get away for four or five days to "a very splendid place, I am told." About coming home, Dad said he felt about ready but didn't look for anything good in that connection. "Wish Charlie S. could swing a deal but am not sure he can do so." Despite "miserable weather," "the knees are not bad at present, but feel a touch old and stiff." He said that the week before he had added $100 by personal transfer to the Buick and Hotel Fund, "which should be good about now—and it is my fixed opinion that I'll be a long time even getting out of that first hotel. If you recall Atlanta you can doubtless concur." Dad mentioned having heard from both Colonel and Mrs. Ritter, and said that to the former "I was sure a jinx." He also alluded to the dispatch filed by the correspondent John Lardner in which Dad's name was misspelled. He said he would try to write again to "try to say all I feel about being away so long from you and the kids."

Dad's letter of the next day is chatty and happy, though he had "no hope of better weather—It stays miserable." He was delighted that Mom would go to Cincinnati to visit friends. However, he had heard rumors that the Queen City was about to become "bourbonless," a fact about which Dad said "something better be done." He reported again that his "lovely chum" Nancy Gatch was shipping home a footlocker full of clothes that Dad had left in Oran. He added that Miss Gatch had left the Twelfth General Hospital and was working for the Navy somewhere near Oran. He mentioned again getting away for a few days, where he would have a reunion with Charlie Saltzman. "More then of the future I trust. For now suffice it so say that I couldn't want anything more than to come home to you all. And may all your Christmases be bright. Bless you. Love. Jack."

He did not write again until December 3. He was now enjoying "a complete vacation." He had mailed a package of "trinkets" including a little cameo of the Fifteenth Infantry crest, suitable for setting in a ring. Of course, he could not say where he was, but "the song made famous by Morton Downey while somewhat overdone is accurate enough to make a visit worth while." Many officers of the Fifth Army got some time at a hotel in Sorrento, and it is perhaps to a prewar recording of "Come Back to Sorrento" by Morton Downey, "The Irish Nightingale," that Dad was referring. He reported that his "health is fair—especially since bathing a few times—Morale fair, but dominated by an ardent desire to see you and remain in said state for ever. Whether [sic] continues foul although 2 days of sunshine did slip into our lives. . . . God grant that we can share the next holiday together."

By the time he wrote on December 5, he was back with the battalion. He was delighted with his Christmas packages from Mom, Anne, and me as well as those from Granny and Homer and Deo. He especially liked the recent pictures of us all that Mom had sent him. He was trying to get copies of George Biddle's portraits. He said that the real purpose of "this darn hasty scrawl is to tell you that I have the world's most wonderful family and I miss them terribly and love them more than that."

The next day, December 6, he eschewed V-mail in favor of a long, leisurely letter on Fifteenth Infantry stationery. Though the weather remained "really gruesome," Dad had "caught up on comfort and rest and change of setting—so have no personal complaints." To Mom's mention of Dad's dropping mortar rounds onto German tanks, he said only that "we had fun with that one." He was delighted with Deo's cataract operation and "proud of her courage in having same done." He was glad that I had been enjoying Ohio State football with Homer and playing some of my own. He said he couldn't imagine Anne with braces and hoped they did the job quickly, and that his visit with Saltzman "was interrupted by his many duties and chores—hence little conversation and no results." Asked if he had come across an acquaintance from Columbus among the Red Cross people in Italy, Dad replied that he had not, though "I see plenty of other famous and infamous characters." On account of these encounters and his other noncombat experiences, "I still say that when this business is over I shall write books, plays, musical comedys [sic] etc about the whole thing—featuring the 'Wanna Leave Sicily Blues,' 'Stella the Belle a Fedalla,' etc." He apologized for not having sent more money, "but I spent same on travels, Cognac & souvenirs—can't send any until Jan. or so." He again mentioned the cameo, which he said "comes from a famous spot—the story of San Michele etc. originated there."[2]

Dad had seen the Biddle portrait and urged Mom to look up Biddle in New York. A generator supplied electricity "sometimes," but as he wrote his letter at 2200 hours, he was on candlepower. He did not know or care where the Ninth Division was because "I'm happy in my work currently." He then spoke again of "that sterling and charming character Miss Nancy Gatch" and of his former exec in the Sixtieth, John Dilley, who "would be amused to know that his former orderly Parsons is my boy now." The mention of Parsons reminded Dad of his former driver from the Sixtieth, Robert White, "a great kid and one I will be wanting to see some day," and he again mentioned Colonel Ritter—"a very right guy." Continuing his social notes, he said without elaboration,

Recently, whilst sojourning, I ran across a couple of dolls from South Orange & Great Neck respectively who . . . are suffering from the after effects of that disease of the early 30's "Titleitus." They'd rather have married the guy from Main Street, I now gather, on account of various little international matters like no money from home & the hollow shell of former greatness on the part of hubby.

Near the end of the fourth page, he closed,

Now my sweet one—this brings you all the love in the world and every wish for a gay and grand holiday for you and my two lovely children. I can't express how much I miss you and how much I'd love to be home with you now and forever. I'll be with you in Apple Blossom Time—my current theme song. God bless you all. Devotedly, Jack.

To Granny and Homer on December 6, he again said that Sterling Hill was "doing a fine job here and has been of great assistance to me on numerous occasions." He also thanked Granny and Homer "for having raised such a wonderful daughter. What a girl she is and I am so terribly proud of her, as of course you are."

He wrote to Mom again two days later on three sheets of lined paper pulled from a tablet. As he reminded her, it was during these times of relative inactivity that "I do most of my remembering and missing of you and wishing I was where I belong." Much as he would like to be home, he said, "I can't foresee anything in that direction now, but I'm sure hoping that some day I'll get there and we can make up for all the lost time we've suffered thru." The censors wouldn't let him say much at the moment, but he "sort of get[s] more satisfaction out of writing a regular letter [as opposed to V-mail] to you when time permits—[It] just gets me a little closer to you and seems more natural." Mom's description of how we had spent Thanksgiving Day prompted Dad to say, "Well, next year we'll go to Franklin Field or some such ourselves."

Word of a "visitation" the next day meant that Dad must "step up the efficiency of the command" and reminded him again, as it did in Morocco, that "Tolstoy was sure on the ball when he wrote War and Peace." After what he hoped would be a moment's interruption "to do a little plain and fancy talking of plans and arrangements," he resumed "many hours later."

I am beset with meetings etc. and dashing about to keep a welter of appointments. Beautiful moon these nites—same being completely wasted except for its lite-giving ability. Underfoot all is goo and muck. It rains some each day & or nite. Certainly feel you should get the heat on L. J. M. or somebody to bring me to my native heath [sic] for various obvious reasons before I grow too old to dream or something. . . . Now it seems like another era since I saw you all and I'm afraid the kids will be tremendous before I ever see them. Good nite and God bless you all. Devotedly, Jack.

He reverted to V-mail the next day to say that he was "punchy and punching." Though the weather was a bit better, mud remained. "Whipping the lads into shape daily keeps me busy again." The stateside bourbon shortage he found "indeed regrettable and will require you to lay in a supply of something else. How about beer and ale?" Then he added cryptically, "There's an item I dream of more than same." On Saturday night the regiment would throw "a big party featuring nearby nurses, Red Crossies and some food and beverage." Sterling Hill would attend. He asked about people back home, especially his fraternity brother and best man Sy Austin, from whom he had heard nothing. Then he concluded on the familiar theme of praying for a speedy reunion.

To me on December 9 Dad said, "This is some country—plenty rough, muddy, and wet and not any decent roads to speak of. The people haven't got much to live on, or with and are sort of bewildered and baffled by the whole business." To Anne on the same day he reiterated what he had said to her on November 21: "One thing you can sure be thankful for, Anne, is that you live in the good old USA, where kids go to school and live in nice houses and eat regularly. . . . They do not live such lives over here."

That fall, as the cold weather began to make its way into Columbus, I acquired a new job: keeping our furnace running properly. That we burned coal seemed appropriate, given the long trains of coal cars that ran along the Norfolk and Western tracks. A truck would pull up to the curb in front of our house, and a man would extend a chute from the back of the truck into the ground-level cellar window and begin to shovel coal down the chute and into our cellar coal bin. Under the tutelage of Willy, the janitor who looked after all the houses in our block, I learned to judge when the fire in the furnace needed more coal and how much to shovel in. I learned to bank the fire before bedtime so that it would last through the night. I learned how to shake down the ashes periodically and how to recognize clinkers and with long-handled tongs remove them from the bed of coals. It was at this time that I was soaking up the novels of Howard Pease, the protagonist of which was a lad in the engine room of a tramp steamer in the South Pacific. On wings of meditation, the furnace under 1799 East Long Street became the ship's boiler Tod Moran was stoking somewhere west of Tahiti.

Perhaps because I took to the sea stories of Howard Pease, Mom suggested that I read R. L. Stevenson's *Treasure Island*. Successful with that, she directed me to Charles Nordhoff and James Hall's three books about the mutiny on board *HMS Bounty* and its consequences. That year, too, Esther Forbes came out with *Johnny Tremain*, which kept me in the eighteenth century but brought me back to North America. My real favorites of the time, though, were *The Kid from Tompkinsville*, *World Series,* and *Keystone Kids*, three baseball novels by John R. Tunis.

That fall, too, Homer and I continued our Saturday ritual of going to Ohio State football games. In 1943 the Buckeyes lost more than they won. The only game I remember from that season was the legendary "fifth-quarter" game against Illinois.[3] With two scat backs the Illini ripped off long gains seemingly at will. Ohio State would then plod back on a long drive of short gains. Late in the fourth quarter, with the score tied at twenty-six, Ohio State moved the ball to the Illinois fifteen-yard line, fumbled it away and got it back. As time ran out we tried to pass into the Illinois end zone. Incomplete. Homer and I joined thirty-six thousand fans heading for the exits. As we walked to Homer's car, we heard a loud roar from inside the stadium. On the last play of the game Illinois had been offside, but the teams had left the field. Twelve minutes later, the officials brought them back to the Illinois twenty-one-yard line, whence a seventeen-year-old substitute quarterback kicked the game-winning field goal.[4] Homer, whose "exploits as a [drop] kicker at Ohio State will never be surpassed,"[5] was delighted that, for this game at least, the foot remained in football.

On December 14 Dad took up his new Parker 51 pen to write Mom on both sides of a piece of regimental stationery and a lined sheet. "Lately we have not been making news—but soon again we doubtless will. . . . Currently I have stomach ailments, a cold and an aching knee, but see no remedy at hand, and am working hard to be ready for the gong." He longed for home, noting that "each day is one nearer to the day that counts and truly I'm hoping it can be soon—as I'm getting old & broke down rapidly and am tired of everything that is foreign." Despite his aches and pains, though, Dad reported that he was "living in a building and have a fire—So we are more than reasonably comfortable," although "we eat at weird hours and I am not liking it. Evening chow at 4:30 has me hungry by bedtime."

He said he had received "copies from the 80th Division on all the Avoca stuff and am ignoring same on the assumption you've got that little matter under control. Advise." He had seen Charlie Saltzman again, and also Bill Ibold, but the visit did not go well "on account of I am not accustomed to the way of life of that half—nor do they have time to give to me when I come." Or, as another officer put it after the war, Fifth Army Headquarters at Caserta "with their comfortable trailers to live in, big command tents, mess halls in wooden buildings with dry floors and recreation facilities made me feel like a country cousin visiting his rich relatives in the big city."[6]

Dad mentioned also that a "pal," Joe Crawford, "got decorated last week. Big ceremony—Big surprise. We are pleased."[7] After closing the letter, he added another page "to continue telling you that you are the world's greatest family and it is awfully bad news to be staying away for so long. Truly L. J. and the lads are missing a bet with Toffey not on hand to assist." He "would give an awful lot to see the kids—not to mention their mom of course. Who knows one day you'll get a call to report to the Barclay or Waldorf or some such. Let us keep hoping and praying. It can come true, I feel sure."

Via V-mail Dad next wrote on Christmas Eve.

My Darling—Just about now, under what we were pleased to call normal circumstances, I would be fussing with tree lights or a tree stand or doing my last second shopping or coming home from an office party or trying to or forgetting to. As it is we are in "Sunny" Italy and busily engaged in our pastime of killing Krauts. I am still holding together fairly well though age has crept into the joints and to a degree I am less active than a year ago. . . .

This is not any kind of a letter but it brings plenty of love and thoughts of the season and of my little family in general and particular. You can keep working on L. J. or anyone else who will listen. As far as I am concerned it is time for me to see you all again but very soon too.

He noted that "we have sort of run away from our mail again" and that "writing is again a difficult problem."

The day after Christmas he wrote again, having received Mom's letters of December 3 and 4, telling of changes in Anne's braces and new shoes and of bathing the dog "and other homey details that had me wishing more than ever." He reported that he had gone to bed early the night before—around 9:30—and the night remained "fairly calm," except for a phone call from a rear headquarters. "The big boss himself sent us a couple of bottles to celebrate Xmas Eve with. Damn nice of him."

Dad was pleased that four of his "best lads" had recently earned battle-field promotions to first lieutenant, and he had great praise for the British, with whom he seemed to be working at the moment. "Our international cousins are some guys. You can quote me as saying 'There'll always be an England and then some.'"

The rain had stopped and it was a pretty day, though the mud remained ankle- to knee-deep. "In any case, Christmas comes but once a year and the next time it comes it better find Toffey and family on their ranch in Las Cruces, N.M. or some flat, hot, warm, dry place. . . . Give to John and La Mouse all sorts of love and say I hope I'll never spend another Christmas away from them."

The next day's V-mail letter strikes a quite different note:

Dearest Helen,

Please forward without delay a check in the amount of $192.01 to and payable to Staff Judge Advocate, 80th Inf. Div. at Camp Phillips, Kansas.

This must be done promptly to save me further embarrassment in this connection. An acknowledgement must be obtained by you and a copy of same forwarded to Adj. General of the Army, whose file reference is (s-16 Feb 44 ack cw-1646). A copy of this letter is being forwarded to the Adjutant General.

Please advise when this has been done. Another letter under separate cover.

Much love,
Jack
John J. Toffey, Jr.
Lt. Col. Inf.

He wrote the "separate cover" letter on December 28, beginning "Just dashed off a line to you saying pay the Avoca matter. Pay it so they will lay off me. The boys in Wash. are bothering me. Get a receipt and send a copy of same to the Adj. Gen." Later on in the letter he added, "Lay off any further advice to the Adj. General. Just pay under protest, but pay. They got us licked." In happier news Dad had learned that the Twelfth General Hospital had moved to Naples to be closer to the action. "Sunny Italy is cold and far from pleasant." Dad said he could not tell us much, but "just watch the papers and mags. If it gets done, you can bet the Best in the West does it." Nevertheless, he added, "My motto is 'Out of the theatre in time for the opening game.' I've missed too many double headers. God bless you all and this brings much love and many thoughts to all. Keep hoping and perhaps one day. . . . Devotedly, Jack."

We went to Great Neck for Christmas with Deo and Arcenio and all Dad's aunts and uncles. While we were in that part of the world, Mom met George Biddle and received from him the original of his portrait of Dad. Meanwhile, the Third Division moved to Pozzouli[8] for amphibious training, with which many of the men who had been around for a while were already familiar. We were back in Columbus, though, on January 2, when we received Dad's EFM wire of holiday greetings. The "canned" nature of the wire is apparent in the juxtaposition of sentiment and signature:

LOVING WISHES FOR CHRISTMAS AND NEW YEAR. YOU ARE MORE THAN EVER IN MY THOUGHTS AT THIS TIME. ALL MY LOVE. J. J. TOFFEY.

On January 5 he dashed off a quick V-mail to say that he was all right but busy. "Wish I had more time to write, but just at the moment it is difficult to find the chance. I keep on hoping and praying for the day when we can live, love, laugh and be happy with no problems except when to get up and eat or where to go for the weekend." With no word from Mom on her having paid the Avoca bill, Dad said that it was "imperative" that she pay it so that "they will stop bothering me." He repeated the amount and the address to which to send the payment.

In early January Mom got from General Ulio, the adjutant general, a third letter on the progress of Dad's recovery from the wound he had received ten months earlier. General Ulio wrote that "the latest report from the theater of operations states that on 13 June, 1943, your husband . . . was released from the hospital." He went on to assure her "that should further information be received regarding his condition, you will be notified immediately."

Dad started a V-mail letter on January 8 that he had to set aside after two sentences and could not finish until two days later. He was delighted with news of our trip east and our having met George Biddle. He had recently run into Harvey Allen, the "grand fellow" who had treated Dad when the Twelfth General Hospital was back in Oran. Then Dad returned to a continuing source of annoyance. "Hope you have paid Avoca matter as the Adj. Gen'l., Wash. D.C. is on me about same and may Mrs. J.D.P. have peptic ulcers. And you pay it and we'll forget that incident." George Biddle replaced General McNair for the moment as the person who "can hit on someone who will feel I'm needed where you are. What the hell is the matter—Can't these people remember Man O' War and Papa Dionne and stuff of that nature?"[9]

To Mom's question if he remembered a time they had spent at Uncle Billy's retreat in Dutchess County, Dad replied,

> Well, sort of. Yale 6, Army 0—Lassiter for Yale on a cut back— Lassiter on the kickoff—Sheridan killed—or am I remembering the wrong game & the wrong stuff. It is a very long time since that choo choo chugged out of Carolina—let us say—15 months ago. And it is sort of tough to remember beyond that. Front Royal, Virginia,[10] sort of gets my vote as a very favored spot—or maybe the Henry Grady Hotel[11] in Atlanta. . . . Miss Flo Keene of that hospital I was in will attend a Regimental hop with me come Wednesday. Miss K. is a very nice gal from Indiana and you should be sure to recall that I am telling you about her just in case you should hear from her some day.

He told Mom how much he had enjoyed a recent letter from me. "You have sure done a job with our offspring. The Xmas present picture of you and the kids is before me now and it is wonderful." He said that he had not looked up Will Ibold "for reasons of boredom to be honest with you— but perhaps I should—altho he can find me if he wants to look and I'm busier than he is."

Thinking about all the mail he owed and asking about people from whom he hadn't heard in a while turned home thoughts from abroad. "Say, ask N. R. Howard if I can make 50 or 75 bucks a week writing baseball and boxing for Cleveland's fastest growing newspaper. On the side I could do soap operas and get my drinks free by telling stories." He again ran through a list of hotels suitable for his and Mom's reunion, adding Cincinnati's Sherry-Netherland to an expanded list of those in "Baghdad on the Subway." He was sorry that the Reds let Bill Werber, their aging third baseman, get away. Then he asked Mom to order an olive drab shirt, "size 15^1/$_2$-34 or thereabouts," from Nat Luxenburg at 14 Union Square, New York, and "pay him will you please."

And now it is very late at nite and I miss you worse than ever and this dumb letter only makes me feel more so. God bless you dearest Helen and the same for all our brood—May it end soon and when it does where will we hide forever. Much love to you Darling and to all. Jack.

In the next letter, dated eleven days later, January 21, Dad again apologized for not having written, adding that he hoped that the Avoca matter was settled, having "worried [him] of late." He reported that "a young man from Cincinnati is a host of mine tonight. Perhaps he'll drop you a line." He says that he and his outfit are "Just about to make a bit of news for you all, it would seem—And perhaps if it is as good as some it will hasten the day for which we pray." Finally, he realized, "This is a very short and entirely inadequate letter to carry all I want to say, Darling. But it brings my deepest love and God's blessing to the best wife and kids in all the world. Keep praying. Sincerely, Jack."

The next day Dad and the "Best in the West" would begin to make news on the beaches of Anzio and Nettuno.

chapter twelve

ANZIO: THE CAN-DOS

When the Fifth Army halted on November 15, it had struggled for two months to gain some eighty miles of Italy. Ahead lay the Liri Valley, the gateway to Rome. But between the Fifth Army and the Liri Valley were three formidable German defensive lines. An end run around these defenses seemed like a good idea, provided it could be brought off without interfering logistically or strategically with the cross-channel invasion of France, now less than six months away. Urged on by Churchill, the High Command ordered Operation Shingle, the Anzio landings, to begin on January 22.

General Clark had doubts. He felt that "a pistol was being held at his head" because with inadequate landing craft and those available for only two days after the landing, and with no resupply or reinforcement after the landings, he was being asked to "land two divisions at a point where the juncture with the balance of Fifth Army was impossible for a long period, thereby leaving the two divisions in question out on a limb for a very long time."[1] A few days later, his resolve had stiffened. "I am trying to find ways to do it, not ways in which we cannot do it. I am convinced that we are going to do it, and that it is going to be a success."[2]

From the outset, the Third Division had been designated as the American unit in the amphibious assault. It had had more experience in amphibious landings than any other division in the theater. Indeed, so experienced had one old soldier become that with his tongue thrust deep into his cheek he warned another to be especially careful on his third, seventh, and thirteenth landings.[3] As more landing craft became available, though, General Alexander added a British division because casualties would probably be high and should not fall to one nation's troops.[4] The two divisions would form a corps under the command of General John Lucas.

The wording of the orders given to General Lucas is important. General Alexander's order was for Lucas's corps "to cut the enemy's main communications in the Colli Laziali area southeast of Rome, and to threaten the rear of XIV German Corps."[5] But as General Clark sent these orders on to General Lucas, they sounded more simple and direct. Lucas was "to seize and secure a beachhead in the vicinity of Anzio" and to "advance on Colli Laziali," about twenty miles inland. If the Anzio landing force pushed quickly off the beaches and succeeded in taking the high ground commanding Highways 6 and 7, the main German escape routes from the south, they would have carried out Alexander's orders. But Clark's orders didn't specify that Lucas was to take the Colli Laziali—only that, after securing the beachhead, he was to advance "on" them. The preposition was deliberately ambiguous. As General Brann, General Clark's G-3, explained to General Lucas, the primary goal of Lucas's corps was to get and hold the beachhead. It would be up to Lucas to decide how and when to execute the part of his orders about the Colli Laziali.[6]

General Lucas, too, had his doubts about Operation Shingle. "I am running this thing on a shoestring, and a thin little shoestring at that, he wrote. "Unless we can get what we want, the operation becomes such a desperate undertaking that it should not, in my opinion, be attempted." At a meeting on January 9, Alexander had massaged Lucas by telling him, "We have every confidence in you. That's why we picked you." Lucas, however, said he "felt like a lamb being led to slaughter but thought I was entitled to one bleat so I registered a protest against the target date as it gave too little time for rehearsal."[7]

Of the coming operation, Patton had said to Lucas, "John, there is no one in the Army I hate to see killed as much as you, but you can't get out of this alive. Of course, you might be badly wounded. No one ever blames a wounded general." And General Clark, apparently reaffirming his operational order, offered this advice to Lucas: "Don't stick your neck out, Johnny. I did at Salerno and got into trouble." To Lucas as he prepared to lead his corps, "this whole affair had a strong odor of Gallipoli and apparently the same amateur was still on the coach's bench."[8]

General Truscott, too, had reservations about Operation Shingle and expressed them to General Gruenther, Clark's chief of staff:

> I believe that you know me well enough, to know that I would not make such a point unless I actually felt strongly about it. If this is to be a "forlorn hope" or a "suicide sashay" then all I want to know is that fact—If so, I'm positive there is no outfit in the world that can do it better than me—even though I reserve right (personally) to believe we might deserve a better fate.[9]

At Clark and Lucas's insistence, a rehearsal was held January 18, four days before the real thing. It was a disaster. Forty-five amphibious vehicles were swamped, with huge losses of equipment. One artillery battery lost all of its 105s. Timing was terrible; no one landed on the right beach. Clark was furious, attributing the mess to "overwhelming mismanagement by the navy."[10] But all the participants in the rehearsal could share the blame for the prodigious foul up. Horrible as the rehearsal had been, there was no time for another.

At Pozzuoli, where the Third Division had been training, Italian opportunists sold postcards of the resort towns of Anzio and Nettuno.[11] As the invasion force boarded their ships, the main body of the Fifth Army continued to press the attack it had launched ten days earlier. In trying to cross the Rapido River, the American Thirty-sixth Division, the assault division at Salerno, was cut to pieces. Stalled by the German defenses and the Italian winter, the Fifth Army remained well south of Frosinone, an objective once considered prerequisite to the Anzio landing. As the task force sailed out into the Bay of Naples and turned south to mislead any Germans who might be watching from the air or on the beach and hadn't seen the postcards, few realized that the men who would execute Operation Shingle would be on their own for a long, long time.

But for the moment, at least, it was pleasant going for the invasion force of 354 vessels of almost every type.[12] The seas were generally calm and the winds light. A pale winter sun shone for much of the day and the temperature hovered in the mid-fifties. The convoy sailed on unmolested and apparently undetected. A little before midnight the convoy turned right to begin to approach the beaches of Anzio.[13]

Until January 1944, Anzio, about thirty miles south of Rome, was a quiet little resort town. When it was called Antium, Nero and Caligula were born there. Later, Shakespeare set some scenes from *Coriolanus* there. Much more recently, Mussolini had doffed his shirt to pitch hay and promote the agricultural benefits created by his draining of the Pontine Marshes just below the town.[14] In the intervening centuries, Romans found summer solace in the town and the refreshing waters of the Tyrrhenian Sea.

The Third Division launched its assault battalions—one each from the three regiments—at 0200. Dad's Second Battalion swung southeast to protect the right flank of the division, and thus the corps. By 0335 the Fifteenth reported that the initial phase had been successful, and by 0410 the

Third Battalion had captured some errant Germans. Still before sunrise, General Truscott and his staff were ashore and division headquarters was operational.[15] By midmorning, the Third Division had advanced three miles inland. On the flank, along the Mussolini Canal, Dad's battalion destroyed four bridges, put guards on three others, and, anticipating a German counterattack, dug in.[16]

Sometime on the first night ashore, Dad's jeep hit a mine. When Dad stopped by regimental headquarters to report the event and see if he could get another jeep, Jerome Sapiro, commanding Headquarters Company, noticed that Dad appeared calm about the incident but that the back of his field jacket was shredded. Having reported in, Dad continued on his rounds, checking on his battalion.

The Germans had in the vicinity of Anzio very few troops—perhaps a couple of battalions in garrison, some troops resting up after a stint on the Gustav Line, and some coast artillery. In response to the Fifth Army's attacks begun on January 12, the Germans had sent south most of the troops stationed near Anzio. As German Generalmajor Siegfried Westphal put it after the war, "There was nothing else in the neighborhood which could be thrown against the enemy on that same day [January 22]. The road to Rome was open. No one could have stopped a bold advance guard entering the Holy City. The breath-taking situation continued for two days after the landing."[17]

Remembering General Clark's advice about sticking his neck out, General Lucas elected to consolidate the gains of the corps and dig in. Perhaps he could have sent a mobile force speeding up the road to Rome and entered the city, but in all likelihood he could not have held it. Furthermore, he had his orders: first to establish a beachhead and then to advance on the Colli Laziali. The rest of the Fifth Army was too far south and too heavily opposed to offer relief to the troops on Anzio in the foreseeable future. Lucas had to secure his situation before he could think about pushing very far inland. A couple of miles to his immediate front, though, the towns of Campoleone and Cisterna would help to anchor the beachhead perimeter and could serve as jumping-off places for the main attack inland, whenever he chose to launch it.

On the right of VI Corps, the Third Division would move on Cisterna, while on the left the British advanced on Campoleone. On the afternoon of January 24, Dad sent patrols toward Conca across the west branch of the Mussolini Canal. About three hundred yards beyond the canal, they ran into stiff opposition. At dawn the next day, General Truscott renewed the advance in greater strength. This time Dad's battalion, supported by three tanks, crossed the canal and moved toward Feminamorta Creek.[18] They had made about a mile and a half when machine guns and armor of the Hermann Goering Panzer Division brought heavy fire to bear. American tanks and tank destroyers came up to neutralize the German guns and enable the infantry to advance. The next day Sterling Hill's Ninth Field Artillery and two other battalions laid down a barrage behind which Dad's battalion again advanced up the Conca-Cisterna road.[19] But again they were stopped well short of the town.

During a lull on January 29 Dad wrote for the first time in a week— "Just a line to let you know we are plenty busy and there is a lot going on. Haven't had much chance to write of late and hope you are hearing at sufficient interval to know that I'm okay." Of course, he did not say where he was or what he had been busy doing, but I'm sure that from the newspapers we were able to make a pretty good guess. He did tell us, "Watch the Mags—Time & Life. They may have stuff on our recent work— especially stuff by Will Lang and Bob Capa—the photog—." He reported himself as fairly well at the moment—"Have a cold, legs n.g., and generally decrepit but still in there punching O.K. for, and will do as an aged character [sic]."

Conscious of the steady buildup of German forces opposing him and reasonably sure that his beachhead was secure, General Lucas decided it was time to launch his attack on the Alban Hills. This would begin on January 29, to coincide with a renewed push by the main Fifth Army force at Cassino. Unbeknownst to the Allies, however, the Germans had planned for January 28 an attack to lance the abscess and drive the invaders into the sea. Two days before the attack was to begin, the Germans, awaiting reinforcements and bothered by Allied air strikes on supply lines, postponed the attack and rescheduled it for February 1. In the meantime the Allies took the offensive.

The Allied offensive would be a coordinated, simultaneous two-pronged attack. The British, led by the Grenadier Guards, would drive north along the Anzio-Albano Road, through Aprilia and on to Campoleone. In the American sector General Truscott would commit his entire Third Division to the task of taking Cisterna. Colonel Darby, with whom Dad had worked in Sicily, would send two of his Ranger battalions ahead of the Third Division to infiltrate and seize the town. One hour later the Seventh Regiment and the First and Second Battalions of the Fifteenth would launch the main attack, flanking the town and cutting Highway 7, the Appian Way, above and below Cisterna.

In the final stages of preparation, a jeep carrying company commanders of the Grenadier Guards to a briefing missed a turn, became lost and ran into a German outpost. When the firing stopped, three British officers were dead and maps and orders had fallen into enemy hands. Corps Headquarters decided to postpone both prongs of the attack for twenty-four hours.[20]

The idea of having the American Rangers infiltrate Cisterna was based on the assumption that the overextended Hermann Goering Division opposing the Third Division was relying on strong points between gaps along their front. In fact, however, during the twenty-four-hour delay, the Twenty-sixth Panzer Grenadier Division had moved up to solidify the German line.[21] There was no gap through which to infiltrate.

Around 0130 on January 30, the Rangers waded into the Pantano ditch and began their four-mile slog to Cisterna. Despite passing within a few feet of German sentries on the banks, the Rangers seemed to be progressing undetected. At dawn the head of the Ranger column emerged from the ditch onto the road eight hundred yards from Cisterna.[22] But they had been detected. The Germans opened up with self-propelled artillery, machine guns, mortars, and small arms. The Rangers fought back desperately and heroically, but woefully outgunned and outnumbered, they could not hold on. Of the seven hundred and sixty-seven Rangers who started out for Cisterna, only six returned.[23]

The assault regiments of the Third Division were unable to relieve the Rangers because they were having troubles of their own. On the first day of the attack they had advanced about half the distance to Cisterna but were unable to break the German defenses and take the town. In the afternoon of January 31, Dad's Second Battalion renewed the attack on Cisterna. As one of General Truscott's aides described the situation, "Boche" in red farm buildings were holding up the operation. "They had to be driven out before a new attack by Lt. Col. Toffey can jump off, but going is extremely slow."[24] Behind an artillery barrage the battalion finally fought its way a mile closer to Cisterna, wiping out some German armor in the process. But they were still a mile from Cisterna when the Germans counterattacked. The battalion held them off until ordered to pull back, so as not to go beyond the limit of their own artillery support.[25]

On February 1 it became clear that the Allied attack would not achieve its objectives. The Third Division was not going to take Cisterna. In three days of hard fighting, the Division had taken some two or three miles of territory along a seven-mile front, inflicting heavy casualties on the Germans. But it was still fifteen hundred yards from Cisterna and had taken heavy casualties. For the first time in the war, it seemed, the Third Division was going on the defensive, and it began to prepare the kinds of defenses it had been breaching so effectively in Sicily and Italy.[26]

Before we got Dad's letter, we had a chance to read about him in action. In the February 7 issue of *Time* appeared Will Lang's report of the "local, intermittent fighting in the first few days" on the beachhead. From clues in Lang's notebooks[27] it would appear that Lang accompanied Dad as he led his battalion across Bridge 8 on January 31.

> Shortly after dawn the battalion commander, burly Lieut. Colonel John Toffey, stopped his men in an abandoned farmhouse and set up his command post there. The medics took over the crude workshop and began unpacking packages and plasma bottles in the dark. The Colonel ordered most of the men into a long, smelly stable for safety, but sat himself down at the rear of the building with a portable radio. . . .
>
> There was a quick deafening scream, then a shell exploded a few feet away from the farmhouse. Dirt splattered through the stable windows on the doughboys lying in the straw and manure inside. Another shell tore open the black soil nearby. Four bundles of feathers fluttered from the hen house down to the ground. "If all they get is chickens, we've got a good day ahead," said Toffey. Three more explosions within 25 yards shook the house and stable. A wide-eyed replacement raised his head from the floor and gasped: "Them's bombs."[28]

Dad kept on the radio, now talking to Lt. Benny Reece in one of the companies up ahead. "All right, Benny, all right," Dad said. We're doing what we can. Don't get excited. Got many casualties? We'll try to get litter bearers up as soon as possible." Overhead some British Spitfires chased off a couple of German fighter-bombers that had just hit the beach. To quote Lang, "'The bastards,' snorted Toffey." Dad's supporting tanks and mortars from his heavy weapons company demolished a couple of buildings from which Germans had been firing. Just then an 88 began to zero in on the farmhouse. As Dad stood in the stable door watching the shells land about a hundred yards away, he said to Lang, "We'll get some artillery on those Krauts if we locate them." Dad then turned to look back into the farmhouse, amused that at that moment a sergeant had started to shave. Then Dad turned back to the radio. "Look, Benny," he said, "Don't get excited. We just killed you some Krauts and we'll kill you some more as soon as you tell us where they are."[29]

While with Dad, Lang jotted some other observations in his notebook. On one occasion he described Dad as "Not a man to let a weapon sit around without using it." As the battle for Cisterna wound down, Lang saw Dad as "tired but sleepless; [he] never loses aplomb or sense of humor despite rapidity of events."[30]

To defend the beachhead, the Allies had prepared three lines of defense. Along each line the defenders dug in and worked to augment their holes with whatever they could find to shore up the sides and keep the bottoms as dry as possible. The Germans in the hills and even in the upper stories of farm buildings had a virtually unobstructed view of the Allied positions. In the Third Division sector any sort of daylight movement drew enemy fire. As one soldier new to the battlefield noted, if you were wounded at night in your foxhole, you were lucky; the medics could get you out quickly and back to an aid station. If you were hit during daylight, you might have to stay in your hole until dark.[31] You didn't even dare to crawl out of your hole to relieve yourself. As replacements were advised in a Fifth Army pamphlet, "Don't excrete in your foxhole . . . put some dirt on a shovel, go on that, and throw the load out."[32] Nor were the rear areas safe from German shelling or bombing. On February 7 a German pilot, trying to escape a Spitfire, dropped his load on the Ninety-fifth Evacuation Hospital, killing twenty-eight and wounding sixty-four. Among the dead were three nurses.[33] Rather than remain in the hospital with the big red crosshairs on the roofs, some of the walking wounded preferred returning to the front line and the relative safety of their soggy foxholes.

On Saturday, February 5, General Truscott came up to the command post of the Second Battalion, Fifteenth Infantry, to award Dad a Silver Star for his actions a few days earlier in the fighting in front of Cisterna.[34] Special Order 27 of the Third Infantry Division, as it was actually written up two weeks later, said that Dad had

Courageously led his battalion in the establishment of a spearhead across the ****** ****. Completely disregarding his own safety, he personally exposed himself to machine gun and sniper fire, to inspect his companies and rearrange their disposition. He maintained his command post well forward although it was continuously pounded by heavy enemy artillery fire. His fearless leadership inspired the men of his command to the successful defense of the battalion position against enemy counter-attacks and afforded a protective buffer and screen to the division beachhead.[35]

Dad next wrote Mom on February 10, mentioning her letter of January 21, in which she told him that at long last the Avoca matter had been taken care of. "Thanks," he said, and "Sorry about it all." "Things here have been sticky and rugged," he said, but "We are doing okay. I got a Silver Star the other day which is being sent home to you—except the ribbon." Then he turned to a familiar theme:

> Perhaps we can get that reunion going ere long. It has been to dam [sic] long since that dismal Oct. day. Get Biddle going on putting me in politics, will you please. . . . I think of you all at every possible moment and never cease to dream of the day when we will again go to Crosley Field or Red Bird Stadium and thence to one of those eating joints— Milders—thence to Louisville or something and so she goes—but the Kraut don't cooperate. It is a long tough war and I know it. All my love. God bless all. Jack

On February 14 he started a long "regular letter," hoping Mom will "enjoy it better than the postage stamp type." He again asked if Mom had received the various things he had sent in December. He said that he is still punching but a little punchy himself and really sweating out a change of status. He is ready to leave the professional soldiering to others and "open a fruit stand and chicken ranch around Tucson-Phoenix or Las Cruces, after about $1500 worth of Hotel Life and a Buick. Right now sunny Italy is a place they can give back to Hannibal for my money—and soon." He then wonders "what it is the Romans do in Rome that we should do there—or something." His thoughts turned again to General McNair, who, he said, "is missing a bet by not having me come to work for him." At the same time, he was happy for the thirteen soldiers of his who hit the jackpot on the boat ride. And, he says, "There is a fighting chance that I mite [sic] get a better job—who can tell—it is a rumor and I'm sweating it out strongly." After asking about lots of old friends from college and the New York days, he wrote, "Currently my bright boys are screaming into phones in both my ears, which annoys me a touch and spoils my letter-writing touch." And so, "It is sort of time to pause in this—More if time permits—and soon. For now Blessings and thanks for being the world's best wife and keep praying for a reunion. Devotedly, Jack."

Later that same day, which he mistakenly called "14 December 44," he added a page to say that he had received Mom's letters acknowledging the arrival of the various packages. He said he had just enjoyed eating a "fresh egg I squeezed out of an unsuspecting chicken—sure was good." Around him, "Guns are still booming and things stay rugged. It is a hard racket." He took comfort in knowing that Mom would

> Keep praying for our day and that each day is nearer to it. I'm dam sure you know where I am—But it don't make much difference if I'm not where you are. So get working on that please. Geo. Biddle's stuff is good—accurate and down the alley. Well, enough for now. Lots more when I can, Darling, and please keep hoping and praying. All my love and blessings on all. Jack.

That same day he wrote a V-mail letter to Anne and me:

> Dearest Anne and John—Please forgive me for trying to write you both in one letter, but I have very little chance to write lately and so am combining this in order that you may know how much I love and miss you both and how much I thank you for your nice letters. It is a long and rugged war you may be certain and I'm sure missing you all and hoping hard for the day when we may play and enjoy our lives together. . . . Haven't much I can write about except that Italy is a dismal place and personally I can't see much about it that is any good. . . . [I] like to hope you are praying hard for the day when we'll be together once again and I'm truly hoping it won't be long—So very proud of you and pleased with you I can't begin to write all I feel on that. God bless you all. My dearest love, Dad.

Meanwhile, in Cleveland, Ohio, Dad was the subject of Nathaniel Howard's column in the *Cleveland News*. Howard, who had picked up on Will Lang's piece in *Time* the week before and added his personal recollections of Dad as a bottle-cap salesman for the Aridor Company before the war, begins the column, "Hoping that a hard-headed executive of the Widlar Co. reads this piece. He'll get a kick out of it." Seems that there was a buyer for the Widlar Company who never bought anything from Dad and never even gave him the time of day. Then one night Dad called Nat to report the Widlar buyer was at least cordial now, and though he still hadn't bought any caps, Dad knew that he would get him to someday. That evening, Howard said,

> I heard quite a lot about the bottle cap industry while [he and Dad] drove around town to cool off on a hot summer night, or spent a musical evening at somebody's piano, or kibitzed a ball game. I remember thinking the bottle cap business had its interesting side.
>
> Finally came the evening when Jack called up in panicked delight. He had sold his first order of caps to the Widlar man. We celebrated until the rosy streaks of dawn were visible over Euclid Village. I offered sincerest congratulations for a job that had taken a year or so, but canny old Jack was of the opinion that he had stumbled conversationally on some hobby that had helped to melt the sales resistance. It was a memorable night of triumph.[36]

On the same day, Will Lang had another piece in *Time*. Though Dad wasn't mentioned by name, we at home thought he was one of two lieutenant colonels mentioned in the article. We knew that Lang had been with Dad's outfit from the article the week before. One of the officers in question "peered over a the edge of a ditch and watched explosions along the near-by road. 'The Krauts really got that road bracketed. Pretty. Damn pretty,' he said with professional satisfaction." Could that have been Dad? Then, with understandable alarm we read, "A wounded lieutenant colonel sloshed down the ditch." When asked how he felt he said, "I couldn't pitch a good game of ball right now." Then, as he took off his helmet and looked at the clean hole in the front and the jagged hole in the rear, he said, "This is sure a young man's game."[37] The baseball reference made us wonder. Was this Dad? Would we be getting another telegram from the War Department?

On December 15, via V-mail, Dad asked Mom to have a photographer make a copy of Biddle's portrait of Jo Kindlarski and have it sent to his mother in Hamtramck, Michigan. He thought that what Mom had told him of my social life was "a good laugh—not unlike Penrod Schofield." He concluded, again:

Well it seems that you'd best keep working on getting me home on account I'm something of a tired lad and could truly use the change of scenery to mention nothing else involved. Deo keeps threatening to work on L.J.M. Perhaps she might do it one day. Who can tell. Fatigue creeps up and paper runs out and I got to go and visit some guys. Much love. Jack.

On February 16, the Germans launched their offensive along the axis of the Anzio-Albano Road. Their idea was that, having split the beachhead, the Germans would wipe out each part and drive the invaders into the sea. Before the attack began, however, all of the VI Corps artillery opened up on German assembly areas. At the same time German guns began pounding American and British positions, and as the artillery fire lessened, German infantry and armor moved forward. The Fifteenth Infantry was still deployed southwest of Cisterna. Dad's Second Battalion was on the regiment's left flank, occupying ground between Ponte Rotto, about a mile and three-quarters west of Cisterna, and the Conca-Cisterna Road about half a mile east of Isola Bella and the same Pantano ditch that the Rangers had used. The Germans hit the Third Division in seven places, but after a day of after heavy fighting had little to show for their efforts but a lot of casualties.

General Clark picked this time to relieve General Lucas as VI Corps commander, replacing him with the Third Division's General Truscott. To succeed Truscott in command of the Third Division, Clark elevated the assistant division commander, General John W. ("Iron Mike") O'Daniel. O'Daniel had served in Clark's company in World War I, and General Clark had pinned on O'Daniel's first and second stars in North Africa and Italy respectively.[38] In a farewell message to the division, Truscott said, "The memory of your fine spirit, your self-confidence, your devotion to duty, and your splendid discipline that brought about your many victories in the last year will be with me always and I will cherish that memory as one of my most precious possessions. . . . Good luck and Godspeed to victory to you all."[39]

On December 17, Dad took a moment to write a note to the general:

My Dear General Truscott,

I have just learned that you are leaving us for bigger things. Someone's gain is truly our loss and we shall all miss you.

Young Jack, age ten, outside an orderly room of the 329th Infantry at Camp Sherman, Ohio. Lt. Lanham, who called war a game for the young, is directly behind Dad, and Jack Sr. is to his left.

Helen and Jack on their way to or from a football game circa 1929.

General and Mrs. Toffey join their son, daughter-in-law, and grandson in this 1932 picture. While Jack Sr.'s job made him a general, his permanent Regular Army rank was colonel. The general died in 1936; his wife, "Deo," in 1963.

Mom, Anne, and I in our Columbus living room in 1943. This was in our
Christmas package to Dad that year.

Anne and I join Dad after a parade at Fort Bragg in 1942.

The question on Dad's 1943 Christmas card to me sounds like one that Bill Mauldin's Willie or Joe might ask. The drawing seems accurately to portray the campaign in Italy.

Dad wrote this V-mail to me in a moment of calm just before the start of the big offensive that would, he always hoped, bring him that much closer to coming home to us.

George Biddle's portrait of Dad in Italy. The artist spent a month with Dad's battalion.

When Lieutenant Colonel John J. Toffey, Jr., Battalion Commander of the "Can Do" Regiment of the Third Division, was shelled out of his C.P., a grass ledge on the shoulder of Monte della Costa, above Statigliano, he crawled further up the mountain among the stone outcroppings and finished his letter to Mrs. Toffey.

Above: This sketch of Dad and the caption are on page 3 of *George Biddle's War Drawings,* which the artist dedicated to Dad. They are reprinted with permission of the artist's soon. Below Dad (center) interrogates a German POW in Italy.

JANUARY 22, 1944 · U.S. THIRD INFANTRY DIVISION MADE AN ASSAULT AMPHIBIOUS LANDING IN THIS VICINITY ESTABLISHED A BEACHHEAD WHICH WAS MAINTAINED FOR FOUR MONTHS AT GREAT SACRIFICE OF HUMAN LIFE, AND WITH INDOMITABLE COURAGE. IN A VALIANT AND SANGUINARY ATTACK THE DIVISION LED AN OFFENSIVE THAT DESTROYED THE STRONG GERMAN DEFENSES AND CULMINATED IN THE LIBERATION OF ROME.

22. GENNAIO 1944 · LA TERZA DIVISIONE DI FANTERIA DEGLI STATI UNITI ESEGUÍ ASSALTO ANFIBIO E SBARCO IN QUESTO SETTORE E STABILÍ UNA TESTA DI PONTE, MANTENENDOLA CON INDOMABILE CORAGGIO PER QUATTRO MESI A COSTO E A SACRIFICIO DI MOLTE VITE UMANE IN UN VALOROSO E SANGUINANTE ATTACCO, LA DIVISIONE IN OFFENSIVA DISTRUSSE LE FORTI POSIZIONI DIFENSIVE TEDESCHE CORONANDO L'ATTACCO CON LA LIBERAZIONE DI ROMA

Above: This monument to the Third Division, between the Mussolini Canal and the outskirts of Nettuno, is a moving synopsis of the Beachhead ordeal. Right: Near Isola Bella, shell holes in the pillar punctuate the marker's message. Dad fought near this spot in February 1944 and passed by again in late May. Photos by the author, 2004.

BATTAGLIA DI
CISTERNA ANZIO APRILIA
LOCALITA' ISOLABELLA
FEMMINA MORTA
ON THIS SITE
THOUSANDS OF MEN
FOUGT AND DIED

AN DIESEM ORT
TAUSEND VON MENSCHEN
KAMPFTE UND FIELEN

IN QUESTO LUOGO
MIGLIAIA DI UOMINI
COMBATTERONO E MORIRONO

1944 1994

May I extend my sincerest congratulations, sir, and may I add my most sincere wishes for your certain success whatever comes.

I desire to take this chance of thanking you for everything you've done for me, General—and to say to you that, to me, you've always been a Soldier's Soldier. It has been an honor and a privilege to serve under your command on two occasions.

The officers and men of this organization join me in the heartiest of best wishes and prayers for your future.

I am, Sir, Most Sincerely and Respectfully,

Jack Toffey

Lt. Col., 15th Inf.[40]

Just twelve days earlier, remember, General Truscott had decorated Dad, in the process of which the two men probably reminisced about what they had been through together—loading the *Anthony* at Norfolk, radio communications on the beach above Port Lyautey, the fight for the airfield, the Volturno crossing. As one might expect in a letter from a lieutenant colonel to a major general, the stiff formality of Dad's prose smacks almost of obsequiousness. Nevertheless, Dad was, as he says twice in the text, sincere in his respect for General Truscott. His admiration of and respect for Truscott appears often in his letters home. Perhaps, too, Dad might have wanted to keep himself in Truscott's mind as the general left. Might Truscott want to bring Dad onto his staff at VI Corps headquarters?

For a couple of days, fighting along the front remained fierce. By February 20, it was clear that the Allies had held. Massed Allied artillery, sometimes firing as many as twenty shells for each one fired by the Germans, broke up advancing infantry and knocked out tanks. The Germans themselves reported that some 75 percent of the battle casualties came from the hot, jagged steel of exploding artillery shells.[41] But there were individual heroics, as well, as a rifleman here or a machine gunner there held off or drove back whole units of attackers. The records of the units on the beachhead bulge with citations of individual heroism in the face of the enemy.

Between February 16 and 20, at least 5,389 Germans were reported killed, wounded, or missing. In the same period the Allies lost 3,496 battle casualties. Another 1,637 Allied soldiers were lost to exposure, trench foot, and combat fatigue.[42]

Dad, of course, told us none of this. Instead, during a break in the action on February 21, he wrote home again to tell of "the world's most amazing and amusing incident," which had occurred the night before. Dad had received "an entire mail sack" from the Ninth Division containing packages from Mom, Deo, his aunts, and assorted friends. All was Christmas stuff sent from the states in time to reach Dad for Christmas, but apparently before the senders had his new address. "You'd have died laughing to see my dugout littered with packages and paper—hundreds of the evening visitors in to get the dope & pass the time. . . . We festooned the joint with Merry Christmas in paper letters. . . . We've got Jordan almonds, lobster, fruit cake, nuts, broth, gum, and handkerchiefs, puzzles & books for all."

He was glad also to have a new pair of colored lens glasses, a new brush and comb set, a towel, and foot powder. Of his general health he said, "It isn't too bad. I itch a little and need 17 baths and a haircut. Knees are sort of tight and strained—eyes a bit foggy—continuous cold in haid [sic]—and a big pain in the fanny about a lot of stuff but in a plenty ugly mood as to Krauts who we work over more than somewhat."

In response to something Mom had written about a friend of theirs who has an aversion to hotel rooms, Dad says, "Me, I plan to get one endowed. Eggs Benedict at 1100 hours, followed by Brandy eggnog at 1130. Bathe at 1200 hrs.—and about 1630 hrs. we might get up and take a walk."

He went on to say that he had written Charlie Saltzman requesting a change of venue, "and stating why and how. It is hard to know what if any he can do on the deal." He also mentioned again the idea of politics through George Biddle. Finally, he said, "Get the ground work laid for this future life and also get reservations in for Barclay, Ritz, Sherry N., or Waldorf—and also, seriously, buy a Jeep if they sell any. They are *good!*" He concludes with his "blessings on you all and prayers for speedy return to Love Life & and the pursuit of happiness."

Early on February 29, about forty Germans worked their way into Dad's battalion's sector, only to be captured, killed, or driven back. Then at noon, said Dad, "A German company, with machine guns and tank support, assaulted our outposts near Ponte Rotto. Control of this tiny settlement was essential to our operations and the machine gunners and riflemen lodged in the houses around it were ordered, although outnumbered, to hold at all costs."[43] Similar engagements continued until March 3, when the Germans seemed to realize that they were not going to dislodge the invaders. According to the United Press in a dispatch dated March 3,

The German 14th Army has abandoned its third major attempt to crush the Allied beachhead below Rome . . . after taking a savage, 36-hour beating from the veteran American 3rd Infantry Division and a record concentration of Allied planes and cannon.

Counting their dead in the hundreds, the [Germans] fell back to their initial jumping-off place yesterday as the Americans completed the liquidation of the 1500-yard Salient won and lost by the Germans at a staggering cost.

[Lt. Gen. Mark W.] Clark paid tribute to the American 3rd Division—the Rock of the Marne—whose doughboys smashed the last Hindenburg offensive in France in July, 1918.

The 3rd, supported by a number of other units, took on the full weight of the German attack and broke it in embittered, hand-to-hand fighting.[44]

When in early March General Alexander asked General O'Daniel to indicate on a map how much ground the Third Division had lost in the recent German attacks, O'Daniel didn't even look at the map. "Not a God Damned inch," was his reply.[45]

In his letter to Mom dated March 5, Dad acknowledges receipt of Mom's letter asking about the wounded lieutenant colonel in Lang's February 14 article. "I'm okay—Not wounded yet—That was another guy." However, he said, "'The bastards snorted Toffey' is another story." Dad reported that he is now working for "'Why aren't you shooting your Artillery,' snapped Moore." The allusion is to the later Lang article, and the Moore is Lt. Col. Roy E. Moore, who had taken command of the regiment on February 6. As Dad sees the change of assignment, "I have left 'The Best By God Battalion' and am now Exec of the Can Do's which is all right too and a great honor. It has been tough here, but it's been tough on the Kraut too."[46] Dad told us that General Truscott "has gone on and up and we are proud of him but miss him terribly."

Of the war, he wrote,

There are days and other days in this game—some good—some bad—some negative and all in all it is a terrific strain on health, mind & body. One hopes always for the decisive stroke that will put the Kraut on his back for keeps and return us to our beloved homes. . . . [This letter] gets a lot of interruptions and I am always answering a phone or

a question or something and facilities are not overly good. I am somewhat easier in the mind than I was and more confident of our ability to
kick hell out of this damn Hun. Certainly we've showed the world we
are able to stop him cold with whatever he has at his disposal and although our experienced boys are taking it on the chin we're really proud
of the 3rd Division and the 15th Inf.

The next day Dad wrote separate letters to Anne and me. Anne's begins
with "My Dear Miss Mouse." He had just received two letters from her
and was glad that she was doing so well in school. In response to something she had written him about a snowball fight, he said, "Yes, my darling, the snow ball fights that you mention are much more pleasant than
the type of fighting we are in. In fact I can't tell you about our fight very
much except to say it is surely a long tough experience and we aren't doing
too badly." Then he asked that she and all of her friends "pray very hard
we can have this old war end by the time baseball season opens."

He had received two letters from me, too, written about the same time
Anne's were. He was glad that we had had a visit from Colonel Ritter. Dad
said he was "aging a bit and [has] less hair and stiff knees, hates the German and believes we can beat his ears off before too much longer." He
told me that the Fifteenth Infantry, formerly "'the Best in the West' is now
'the Best in the World.' Ask the Krauts." He congratulated me on my good
grades in school. He wished he could tell me more but was prohibited by
censorship rules to do so. He did say that he now had the job that Colonel
Ritter originally had in mind for him. To conclude, he wrote, "I don't sleep
too much or too often and so I shall turn in now to get a bit of shut eye
before morning. And as I do, John, I send much love and good wishes to
all there and pray we may soon enjoy our lives together."

To Mom on March 8 Dad wrote that he got a kick out of the publicity
he had recently received. However, he was facetiously afraid that Will Lang
had cost him the Central Ohio vote by mentioning Great Neck as Dad's
residence and that "The Bastards" snort would cost Dad the Bible belt.
Mom was apparently still asking Dad if he was the wounded lieutenant
colonel of whom Lang had written. His answer: "If I get wounded the War
Dept. will tell you—so quit guessing on the *Time* article." Of the war effort
he wrote,

Don't have the big picture at my fingertips but surely hope that those who do are planning to lower the boom on these Krauts before too long as the war is hindering my unfinished business and is robbing the American hotels and distilleries of huge sums. What are you doing about it? Why don't they put in substitutes in this game? More when I can, my dear. All my love & bless you all. Jack.

Anne also got a letter written on March 8. In it Dad responded to something Anne, recently turned eight, had said about doubting that incumbent Governor John Bricker would be reelected. (He wasn't.) He again congratulated her on her schoolwork and was glad to know she was reading the Bible. Then, on the recurrent theme, he added, "Mousie, I have seen about enough of Italy and enough of war and I keep praying it will all be over before too much longer so that we go back to enjoying the happy days we knew and enjoyed so much." He spoke of his recent publicity and wondered if he should run for Congress or something when he got back. Then he wrote,

The war here on the beachhead is done mostly at nite and we do very little sleeping as it isn't easy to sleep in the daytime. I live in a cave-like place which is damp and makes me stoop over. I'm full of kinks and aches as a result. The German here knows he is in a fight and we seem to be getting our share of them. Thanks again for your swell letter, Mousie and lots of love to you and all your little pals and here's hoping I see you very soon indeed—And may God bless you. Dad.

Dad wrote Mom again the next day, March 9. She had told him about Nat Howard's column, and Dad was looking forward to reading it himself. He says he is all puffed up about *Time, Life,* and the *Cleveland News.* "Now ask Nat," he said, "if I can have that job writing sports for him will you?" He assessed his enemy this way: "This Kraut is not such a hot individual soldier, but his high leaders are good. If he had our doughboys and his generals he'd be a tough man—but he doesn't so he isn't. And above all he is running into the lower part of the barrel on his people." He again praised the Red Cross, mentioning that a Red Cross girl had been wounded on the beachhead. He said that Joe Crawford had a regiment of his own and that Dad had Crawford's old job, "which makes me feel pretty fancy." He closed, "All I have room for now my darling is lots of love and the repetition of our prayer that our day is soon to come, and may God bless you all. Jack."

Dad got off a letter to Granny and Homer on March 9, too. After he thanked them for writing so often, he said, "I am not as yet the Lt. Col. with the scalp wound. Strangely enough most Lt. Cols. in the 3rd Inf. Div. are sort of typical. They have to be. It has been that sort of outfit." The weather had been miserable and rainy, he said, and some days the sun shone nicely, but not for long. He said he wasn't "feeling too badly considering the climate and conditions but truly could do with a bit of a rest at home," and he hoped that "ere long a discerning eye will notice and arrange such matters for us characters." Learning that one of Mom's cousins was a Marine and another 1A, Dad said, "Well, it has been pretty well established that we can't leave these wars to the professional soldiers. There aren't enough." Then to his staunch Presbyterian in-laws he said, "It's a shame Will Lang had to put that profanity in the article. Probably cost me the church vote."

I got the next letter, written March 10 on notepaper. Enclosed was a Third Division shoulder patch I had asked for. Dad had more congratulations about the good grades Anne and I were getting. I must have told him that my neighbor and pal Monty Cook was a fan of the Marine Corps, for Dad wrote, "Well, it takes 'em all to win it—Army, Navy, & Marines, and it doesn't make much difference who shoots just so someone gets the shots off often and good enough to count." He was delighted that he had just had a shower and changed his underwear.

Yes sir, we actually have showers for our men in this area and believe me that's a treat as well as a necessity. A fellow can't appreciate his bath and his clean clothes until he goes without same for a long time—Then he gets to know what a home and modern conveniences are like and to really appreciate the things we love and enjoy in America. Damn few bathrooms in Italy so far.

He asked me to tell Mom that he wore the blue scarf she sent him and loved it very much. And he kept hoping to see an opening game, "but by golly the chances don't look good, do they." But, he said, since coming overseas he had met a lot of celebrities such as

Zeke Bonura, formerly of the White Sox, Senators & Giants. Also Martha Raye, Ella Logan, Al Jolson, Louise Groody. And right here in our regiment is a guy named Tex Austin, formerly World's Champion Cowboy—a swell person he is too. Then from the newspaper world I know Will Lang, Bob Capa, Bob Landry of *Time* & *Life*. John Lardner of *Newsweek* and a couple of other guys—H. R. Knickerbocker, Jack Thompson etc. So one meets all sorts of guys in a war no matter where it is.

This is time for bed, John, but the little note carries all sorts of love and every good wish to you and Anne and to your friends Monty and Dick [Huffman] and others. God bless you son and may I see you soon for I do miss you very much indeed. As ever, Dad.

Among the letters Dad had to write were those to the next-of-kin of men killed in action. On March 10, the same day he wrote to me, Dad wrote one of those letters of condolence to Bennie Reece's wife. Lieutenant Reece had been killed when German tanks overran G Company's position on February 29, three weeks after he had appeared with Dad in Will Lang's *Time* article. Of the young lieutenant Dad wrote:

My Dear Mrs. Reece:

I have the honor to have commanded the 2nd Battalion of this regiment during the Italian campaign and as recently as 10 days ago, your grand husband and my very good friend, Bennie Reece, was in command of our Company G when he was killed in action on [censored]. Bennie had won one battlefield promotion, was recommended for another. Also he has been recommended for the Silver Star for gallantry in action, and on the basis of the action in which he died, he has been recommended for the Distinguished Service Cross.

Bennie had won the respect and admiration of all officers and men with whom he came in contact. We are all extremely fond of him and very proud indeed of his action on all occasions. A very great leader of men and a wonderful officer, he gave everything to the effort of destroying the enemy and ending this war.

Please let me extend to you our very sincerest sympathy and regret at your extreme loss. Please also try to feel that your loss is shared in the case by every officer and soldier who has been fortunate enough to know and serve with Bennie. I realize that there is very little one can say or write at such a time to lessen the blow which you feel, but I do want you to gather what consolation you can from the fact that your husband died a hero—a truly great hero—as he directed his soldiers in a very important action against the enemy.

Unfortunately I can give you no definite dates or places at this moment, but I shall write again when it is possible to do so. Please feel free to write to me or to anyone in this regiment about Bennie and we will be glad to tell you all we can about him.

I hope that I may someday be able to call on you personally to express my feelings about your husband.

Very sincerely,

John J. Toffey, Jr.

Lt. Col. 15th Infantry

Executive Officer[47]

Lieutenant Reece left his wife, an eighteen-month-old son, a father, two brothers, and two sisters. The day before he died, Reece had written a long letter to his sister, Ione Kennedy, saying, among other things, "Say, sis. I just got some news and it's red hot! Take a look at the Feb. 7th issue of 'Time' magazine. I like my colonel swell. He's one great guy."[48]

During all this letter-writing, the Fifteenth had been off the line getting a bit of rest. One night, perhaps Sunday, March 12, some officers got together for a party in the dugout of Captain Jerome Sapiro, commanding officer of Headquarters Company. In attendance were Colonel Charles Johnson, Division Chief of Staff; Albert Connor, Division G3; Mike Hurdelbrink, S2 of the Fifteenth; Dad; and Sapiro, of course. To create the principal refreshment, Jerry Sapiro mixed medicinal alcohol and lemon powder. Sapiro, it may be recalled, had met Dad on the boat from Bizerte to Palermo back in September, and the two had become good friends. They had laughed at the call signs they used for one another outside the regular designations based on unit and job. To Dad, Sapiro, a lawyer in civilian life, was always "Legal Eagle." To Sapiro, Dad was "Deep Purple Six." The reason for the party in Sapiro's dugout was to bid Dad farewell. The next day he would leave the regiment to become executive officer of the Seventh Infantry Regiment. Sapiro thought that Dad "would have preferred staying with the Fifteenth, and had some tears in his eyes over the transfer from those that knew him and with whom he had served."

chapter thirteen

ANZIO: THE WILLING

AND ABLES

Around the palace and trailers of Fifth Army Headquarters at Caserta, Lieutenant Colonel Wiley H. O'Mohundro was restless. In thirty years in the army he had seen very little combat. At the Arzew amphibious training center in North Africa he had worked with General O'Daniel, a friend since 1918 and now Third Division commander. Before the Salerno landings he had said to O'Daniel, "For twenty-five years I have been explaining why I saw no combat in World War I; I'd hate to do so after World War II. I would like to smell a little powder in this one." He got a whiff with the Thirty-sixth Division on the beach at Salerno before returning to amphibious planning at Fifth Army Headquarters.[1]

When General Clark overheard O'Mohundro tell General Gruenther that he would like a chance to earn his colonelcy, Clark told Gruenther, "Send O'Mohundro to Anzio and tell the Corps Commander [General Truscott] to give him a regiment." Truscott called O'Daniel. In the Seventh Infantry Col. Harry Sherman would soon be moving out and up. O'Daniel made O'Mohundro executive officer of the Seventh Infantry Regiment long enough to get acquainted. A couple of weeks later, O'Mohundro replaced Sherman as regimental commander.[2]

Then there was the matter of an executive officer to help O'Mohundro—perhaps someone who had already smelled a lot of powder in the past sixteen months; perhaps someone who himself was about ready to command a regiment. At 2230 on March 13, Dad arrived at Seventh Infantry headquarters[3] to become executive officer of the regiment into which he had been born thirty-six and a half years earlier. General Truscott had recently seen Dad and, sensing that he needed a change of assignment, told General O'Daniel to make Dad "Executive Officer of the 7th Infantry as soon as it could be done."[4]

The "Cotton Balers," as the Seventh was called, had earned thirty-three battle streamers going back to 1814. They had got their nickname fighting against the British with Andrew Jackson behind the cotton bales of New Orleans in 1815. Their regimental crest bore the motto *Volens et Potens*— "Willing and able."[5]

The first we heard of Dad's new job and outfit came in his letter of March 16. At first he downplayed the matter, saying he had no special news to report and no mail except letters from Bob Redpath and Dick Kent. Then he turned to the assignment.

> Things on my new job are very normal and I haven't gotten really acquainted or in the groove as yet. There is a feeling of very sentimental pride in being in a position of responsibility in my Dad's old regi- ment—altho it is a very different regiment in thousands of ways.

Perhaps some of the excitement was dampened by the fact that he was "a very tired boy, physically, organically, and mentally—but I don't see much I can do about it." While he waited for more mail from home, he observed, "Rain has been frequent in this area and weather unpleasant over a period of nearly two months."

Three days later, on March 19, letters from Mom, Anne, and me had caught up to Dad, and he felt better. Mom had apparently received the cameo bearing the crest and motto of the Fifteenth, and Dad was delighted with his "tinted glasses by H. L. Purdy," which were "marvelous and a delight to my eyes." He mentioned the motto of his new regiment, but added, "I can't figure out if I am or not." Yet again he told Mom,

> You may pull out all the stops on anything to be worked there for my case. We are again at the stage we were in when Ritter found me in Sept.—playing 2d fiddle to a second trombone to mix my metaphors. A case of the rare and ancient once more—gives me a stifled feeling again and this time I'm sort of tired to fool around with it. . . . Tell Ritter to get me back any time now—and tell him to take it easy.

Mom had apparently read recently a *Collier's* article by the correspondent Frank Gervasi and asked Dad if he knew him. In fact, Gervasi had spent some time with the Fifteenth Infantry on the bank of the Volturno back in October about the time George Biddle turned up.[6] Dad replied, "Yeah, I know Frank Gervasi—a good man and opportunist. Will Lang, Ernie Pyle, those are the guys." Then he told us to look for Bill Mauldin's book *Mud, Men and Mules*.[7] "It is marvelous. You will love it and very true to our life."

Dad was "pleased and proud" to learn that Mom had been working as a Red Cross volunteer. "Some of my *best friends* are Red Crossies, and they are good, too." He closed on a familiar note:

> This like all of my letters of late is dumb, dull and stupid—but per- haps I'm getting that way. In any case this brings much love to you and to our darling kids and again the urgent prayer that very soon we'll all get together again and live a life of happiness. Go ahead and speak to your influential pals and start the lobby as I am truly ready. So for now again much love and prayers and blessings. Devotedly, Jack.

Two days later he wrote to both Mom and me. He was happy that mail was coming through nicely. He said that he "just got all bawled up a mo- ment ago," and wrote a letter to me that he addressed to Mom. He asked her to give it, along with his apologies, to me when it came. He repeated his on-the-job frustration: "Life is again not too good for reasons of the old and ancient or something. Frankly I can use a trip home any time at all, so get working on same." He said he was glad to hear from Mom that the papers were discussing rotation and hoped that it would start soon. Again he wished that he could pep up his letters, but there "isn't much of interest that can be said and the conditions under which I write are not all what you'd call conducive to good composition."

He thanked me for my recent letter in which I had congratulated him on his Silver Star. In return, he congratulated me on my "very grand school record." As a result of Nat Howard's column, he said, he had re- ceived a piece of fan mail from a man in Cleveland. Of his transfer to the Seventh he said,

> Well, here I am in my Dad's old regiment—The very outfit he was in when he was adjutant and captain of F Co. and I was borned [*sic*] at Ft. Wayne when they were serving in the 7th. Also I am sorry to leave the 15th Inf. to which I had become deeply attached. A great outfit, Snod—but I only had to move a short ways and the job is the same. Getting awfully tired.

Though he couldn't say much about what was going on around him, he did say, "The beachhead has nothing on it but troops and the products of war—except for some poor hungry cattle & sheep which keep getting

bumped off one way or another and sometimes eaten by military personnel." While the explanation for the death of wayward livestock was that
they had wandered into a minefield, often the only external damage was a
single neat .30-caliber hole right through the forehead.

To his recurrent pleas that Mom pull some strings or talk to her "influential pals" about getting him home, Dad added one to me. "Snod, I hope
somehow that you can arrange to get me home pretty soon so I can see
you all and enjoy life with you again. It is a long and hard war to be sure."
This was like his asking me to look into the matter of Mom's allotment
checks. And though Mom did indeed once have a letter from General
McNair, her influential resources were probably little better than those of
her not-yet-thirteen-year-old-son.

Dug in and embattled as they were, having withstood and driven back
all that the Germans could throw at them, the men of VI Corps began to
feel rather special. At home we saw a small indication of this feeling in
Dad's letter of March 26. He eschewed V-mail to write a long letter on
lined paper. At the top, under his formal return address he wrote for the
first time "The Beachhead!"

He was delighted to have received seven letters from Mom, the most
recent written on March 13. He was also pleased to be living in a trailer
"complete with bed and light which is powered by Jeep—All dug deep in
the ground." He again talked of how much he missed us and home, saying
that he "had a chance to mention my case to the C. of S. here today, and
perhaps, in time, he can arrange something for me it is hoped."[8] He had
also written recently to Charlie Saltzman and to "General B at Benning."[9]
And there was John Dilley, Dad's exec in North Africa, who was rumored
to be working for General McNair in Washington now and might be able
to "suggest a channel." But, Dad concluded, "Doubt if too much can be
expected."

Perhaps Dad's preoccupation with a change of scene resulted from general war-weariness intensified by ambivalence about life in Jack Senior's
old regiment. He missed "the gang in the grand old 'Can-Do' Inf., but
guess I'll learn to like it here—Altho things are not quite as smooth and
once more the spirit is a touch rebuked by one of the old school. We shall
try to rise above it—but it isn't easy for me as you can guess." He did say
that he had made some grand friends in the Seventh and "am proud to
know a bunch of them and hope always to keep in touch." Keeping in
touch reminded Dad that he and Fred Fisher (who had fixed our car in

Pine Bluffs, Wyoming, in the spring of 1942) had "corresponded when I had time. Now it isn't too easy, so do give him my best." Of the war Dad wrote,

> The Kraut has been keeping us alert to say the least and this isn't exactly an area of tranquility but somehow I feel we can put it on him before too terribly much longer and it is hoped the boys who planned it all have something terrific layed [*sic*] on for the not too distant future. "Time" and other news deals seem to be anxiously awaiting the western invasion and it should be fairly soon and I hope big and ugly enough to put a very definite trend on things to come.

Meanwhile, "It is still cold and damp in Italy and although it doesn't rain as much, the weather is far from pleasant I can assure you." As he finished the letter, he mentioned several officers stateside who ought to "put in a little time at this business just to ease the pressure." Once again, he apologized that "this stupid letter is a mess on a/c of many interruptions and much harassment of one nature or another." Still, "It brings all sorts of love, my Darling, and every wish for happiness and health among you all and prayers again for a speedy reunion."

I got a letter dated March 27. As the beginning of a new baseball season drew near, Dad thought that the Reds had as good a chance as anyone to beat the Cardinals, who had been hurt by the draft. Apparently I had mentioned to Dad that I might be playing shortstop on the junior high team at school. I don't recall why I thought this, unless I had just read Zane Grey's book of the same name and saw myself at that position. Dad thought I was or would soon be too big for the middle infield and repeated his recommendation that I pitch or play first base. Either way, "Hitting is the payoff. I know for I was never much good with the bat and hence no shakes as a player." After a couple of pointers on how to develop a good swing or throw, he added, "Boy, how I'd love to see the opener at Crosley Field with you. Just keep hoping we can catch some games there this season, Snod." Of the Beachhead scene he said,

> Things over here have eased a bit for us of late—but it will get tough again lots of times. We are sure of that. Being a big shot in the regiment I was born in is quite a thrill and yet a very strange feeling. Also I can tell you I'm missing the 15th Inf. more than a little bit. Get some letters

from pals in the 9th once in a while and guess they will be on the way again before too long.

Anne got a letter written the next day, March 28. Realizing that I would be thirteen in two months and that Anne was going on eight, he wondered if he would recognize us when he got home. He told Anne that the weather was a little better, he had nice quarters, and "things in general have looked up somewhat." Nevertheless, "Your Dad is awfully anxious to get home and see his family after so many months away. Perhaps a kind Lord and thoughtful commander will help all this come to pass ere long."

In Dad's letter of March 29, written on real stationery, came three enclosures. The first was the "expurgated copy" of his Silver Star citation, which Dad thought Uncle Billy Beach and others might enjoy. The second and third were sheet music. "The Dogface Soldier" Dad described as "old music but words and arrangements are by one of our guys." The other, "Stella the Belle of Fedala," was written by two Seventh Regiment lieutenants, David Murdock and Tom Marnette, after the North African landings. As the song gained fame and popularity throughout the Mediterranean, it also gained about "a million bawdy verses," says Dad. The two authors were subsequently killed in action.

Again Dad was happy to have received a lot of mail. News of Anne's and my doings prompted Dad to say to Mom, "Believe me, Darling, you've done a very wonderful job on those kids and I am so very proud of you and of them. Great work indeed." Because the sun had shone for several days in a row and he had had a bath and was getting "a touch of sleep now and again" when Kraut planes weren't buzzing the area, he felt better. "We are going along and giving it our best and hoping always for the best in all ways." Still the yearning for home, though.

> Be assured, my friend, that my mind and heart are ever full of thoughts and prayers for the day when we can do the St. Regis, Front Royal, Chicago, Palmer House, Mission Inn or what have you—and be it said that daily waiting grows more and more difficult you may be sure of that. Your new picture is hanging on the wall of my current home and it is very lovely and only helps drive me nuts even more so.

As he often did, he fired off a V-mail the next day, in part to see which would reach us first. He said he had just seen Betty Grable in *Sweet Rosie*

O'Grady, the first movie he had taken in since the previous summer in Sicily. "Pretty swell," he said, "did truly enjoy it."

To his Uncle Paul Bonner on March 30 Dad wrote, "This is some war for sure—Not just a maneuver, and there is much about it that I'll never understand, but of the fact that our Dogface Soldier Boy can and does go I am plenty certain. Get him mad and he is one tough customer."

In a letter to Granny and Homer written the same day, Dad said, "I am amused, Belle, to recall a day when you said, 'Let the professional soldiers do it.' And now in your last you are provoked at those who hide behind deferments and alibis. I am proud of your change—Point of view strikes deep and hard always."

Though we could hardly tell from Dad's letters, it was some war indeed, and he had to attend to its business. One of Dad's first acts upon joining the Seventh Infantry was to establish battle patrols. In the static situation on the beachhead in March, men stayed in their foxholes all day and then would be randomly pulled out for patrol action at night. Often patrols did not fully comprehend their orders or know more of the terrain than what they could see from their holes. Some night patrols might work their way about a hundred yards out in front of their line and think they had gone a mile.

At Dad's suggestion and under his direction, four officers and forty-five enlisted men, all volunteers, formed a special unit within the regiment to handle the bulk of the nocturnal patrols. Three fifteen-man teams were formed with an officer in charge of each. Within each team were three five-man sections led by a sergeant. One section specialized in reconnaissance, another in assault, and the third in providing a firebase. The men lived behind the lines, had hot meals, clean clothes, and a dry place to sleep, and were exempt from other duties. Fed, rested, prepared, and trucked to the front, these units were able to operate much more effectively than had been the case when night patrol was just another duty to be performed after standing all day in a wet foxhole.[10] The patrols were successful and helped to improve the morale of the men involved.

Another innovation came into being about this time. Men in a static situation, it was found, soon lost the aggressive edge that they had developed in months of steadily attacking the enemy. To maintain this edge, regiments began to stage "shoot-'em-ups." A squad would rush forward until it made contact with the enemy, fire all its ammunition, and then return to its own lines.[11] It was like scrimmaging during football practice—only with live ammunition. People could and did get hurt and killed. On March 4, the last day of the big German offensive, twenty-seven men of the Seventh were killed in action. From March 5 through 26, no more than nine men were killed on any given day, but there were only six days on which no "Cotton Baler" was killed.[12]

On April 1, after sixty-six consecutive days in the line, the regiment was relieved and went into VI Corps Reserve in an area called "The Pines" near the beach. On April 5 an order came down from division headquarters stating that Lieutenant Colonel John J. Toffey and Major Lloyd B. Ramsey were "placed on temporary duty at Hotel San Vittoria [in Sorrento] for a period of seven (7) days, travel time inclusive." Upon completion of this duty, the two officers would return to their proper stations.[13]

Not until the regiment had gone back on line did we begin to hear about Dad's sojourn in Sorrento. In his letter datelined "The Beachhead," April 14, he writes that he was glad that Mom had recently visited their friends in Cincinnati, noting coincidentally that he had just seen Bill Ibold, "As I have been 'resting' at the same area as before." He also mentioned "Big Ted Cobb," an old Cornell buddy and now an Army Air Corps major with a house in Sorrento. Dad had injured his elbow in a fall. It was not serious, but because it was his right elbow, he found it difficult to write. He talked again about rotation policy—or lack of one—and said that he had again spoken to Charlie Saltzman. "Thanks to local factors," though, he had no real expectation of immediate change. Still, he gathered that Deo is "doing a touch of rustling around in my behalf which is pretty good—seeing where she starts it." Presumably she was starting near the top with General McNair.

Meanwhile, Dad remained pleased with the Will Lang material, "but it sure gets me in trouble with the boys—who now refer to me as "Burly Jack." With improvement of the beachhead weather came the realization that "soon it will be hot malaria weather." He owed a lot of people letters that he would have to put off for a while. As he prepared to put aside the Parker 51, he wrote, "This lousey [sic] effort brings you all my love darling with a bit for the kids and family. Naturally every day does bring us nearer but it is so long and I mean we are sweating you out, as the GIs say."

I got a letter from the hospital, too. Dad forgot to date it, but it mentions having "a bum arm as a result of a fall" and "resting for a day to let the swelling go down." He also wished he could be in Crosley Field for the opener "today." Much as he would love to be home, though, "The Kraut is still fighting a real war and our side with all its Allies still has plenty of work to do before we call it quits."

The big news in the letter is that "Vesuvius was pretty active around here a few days back and I saw some of the effects of the eruption recently. Everything completely covered with gray volcanic ash—and much damage to crops and vegetation—depth of ash in many places was such that it had to be shoveled out of the roads."[14]

To Anne on April 15, Dad did not mention the hospital. He spoke of his pride in her accomplishments, citing in particular a seashell collection, Posture Week at school, and a ball game in which Anne had performed left-handed. Of Italy he told her,

> This awful war-torn country leaves very little to write about—Altho one can tell that there was once some very beautiful scenery and probably some nice places to go—although none so nice as anyplace we've ever been at home. I surely pray that this summer will find me in your area and enjoying life and happiness with you, John, and Old Mom— Michigan or Canada or Wisconsin or even the Jersey Shore would be okay, wouldn't it?

He dashed off a V-mail to Mom a couple of days later to say that he was out of the hospital and back at work. Thoughts of home he couldn't get out of his mind, "which of course doesn't keep me on the ball any better than I should be." He had recently sent Mom an extra $200, he said, and he mentioned having run into Dwight Fishwick, the surgeon, somewhere.

Another V-mail followed a couple of days later. As always, he was delighted with Mom's news of home and Anne's and my school doings. So good had mail been lately that his right shirt pocket, where he carried our letters, could hardly hold them all. Dad told Mom that he was busy again. He then told her to keep an eye out for the Ranger commander Bill Darby, "my good friend, who is home by now and who saw me very recently." About rotation Dad says, "Things are slow o/c *local* politics. Long-headed [Saltzman] does what he can for me but the mill grinds too slowly for me as I'm so anxious to see you all and could do the gov't more good after a change of scene."

Anne got another letter—this one written on April 19—in which Dad notes that two years had passed since we drove east from Ft. Lewis, and eighteen months had passed since he last saw us all. The weather was warmer now, he says, and the mosquitoes seemed as big as eagles.

We are busy again and so the days are long and nites are short as far as sleep goes. This war is costing lots of money and lots of soldiers, Mouse, and the sooner it is over the better world we shall have for the future. God bless all of you and much love to all—specially you & John & your pals. Dad.

On April 20 he began a three-page letter, "Just thought that since I'm sitting up all night or probably will, I'd best employ my time getting off a decent letter to you." Whether or not he finished would depend on "outside interests, shall we say." It was a philosophical kind of night. "It is a funny world and war, and often times I think of such weighty matters as the Avoca Mess and say to myself—Nuts!" On the other hand, Bill Darby, "when last seen about 10 days ago, stated that if he found a slot for me in his reorganized outfit, he'd holler. This would be a very swell and possible deal." He turned then to the fullest account yet of the "'spring day' affair we enjoyed at Ted Cobb's place."

It was a circus, and it was in the "Yale-Cornell" baseball game on Cobb's living room floor—sliding into third that my arm was injured—slight crack in elbow—but only stood two days in hospital to get swelling out of arm. It is okay no doubt. We sang—we drank—we laughed till we cried. Smiling Will Ibold was on hand for one of the sessions and I provided a motley gathering from the Can-Do and from the Willing and Ables. There was everything but the boat race and we gave some thought of having that, only lacked the shell.—"'Neath the war's red curse / Stands the Army nurse / She's the Rose of Old Oran . . ." or something. The theme song for the affair was the "Dog Face Soldier" sung on, off or near key at the drop of a bottle. Somehow my pal Ramsey and I eventually got a boat and came back—damn it—C'est le guerre, I guess or some such. Well it was plenty fun anyway and Cobb was a perfect peach and we did enjoy it.

This he had written despite about "600" interruptions. But he had "flailed thru it anyway and put on several deals of assorted sizes the whilst—Phones—maps, patrols, battles etc. sort of hamper the continuity of my otherwise flawless composition." The rotation matter is "a weird state of affairs, I know, but *our* local lads *on top* look differently on the policy than do some of the more lenient."

On April 24, Dad stayed with regular stationery to acknowledge again mail from home and express delight in news of Anne's and my doings. He imagined that Anne has assumed great dignity in her newly acquired glasses. Apparently Mom had mentioned to Dad a connection between someone in Columbus and Colonel O'Mohundro. "Such things are nice," said Dad, "and seem to keep the world small and bring us close together." The colonel was "a nice old gent, but not too easy to work for as he is of the old school and most exacting." Dad repeated his hope that Mom would get to meet Bill Darby, "a character, a great soldier, and my good friend."[15] In their letters both Mom and Anne had told Dad that he was prayed for in church recently. On the day after Easter, he replied, he "can always use the prayers and truly feel they help and hope[s] lots of churches and lots of people keep them ringing out for me and for all of us."

With this letter Dad enclosed a copy of the April 22 edition of *The Cotton Baler*, the two-paged, mimeographed regimental newspaper. The entire first page was devoted to the death of Medal of Honor winner Floyd K. Lindstrom, a machine gunner in H Company. After the action in November for which he was awarded the medal, Lindstrom was offered a rear-area job while awaiting shipment to the States to receive it. Instead, he stayed with the regiment, went into Anzio, and was killed on February 3.

To Granny and Homer on April 22, Dad mentioned the O'Mohundro-Columbus connection, describing his boss as "a very fine gentleman . . . considerate & nice to work with—except for a marked difference in our ages." Dad reported, "Here we are busy and not too pleasant a business it is. . . . Life gets pretty grim after a long spell of this work and my people are not much interested in rotation, it seems."

During this period Dad also wrote two letters to George Biddle. The V-mail of March 30 he pretty much repeated on regular stationery on April 24, telling Biddle he was no longer with the Can-Dos but the Seventh—"another good outfit in which my Daddy spent 13 years." "It has been plenty tough for us here I can assure you, but we have done our best and we have not done too badly. I'm pretty tired but keep punching along and hoping that some day I'll swing onto the boat myself. . . . The road to Rome is a long one and in many respects like the road to hell—inclusive of the intentions." Dad told Biddle that he still saw some of the old gang from the Fifteenth—those who were still around. He mentioned the recent trip to Sorrento. "Same was a beautiful change. I did enjoy it very much." Of the previous fall Dad said, "Those days of cold and wet we spent together were tough in many ways, George, but still the pleasantest days of the war, and we've missed you a great deal since November." But the letter was interrupted because "something appears to be cooking and it looks like a long tough nite—sleep is still scarce as it was when you were with us." To Biddle he gave the desire to get home a slightly different slant. "Surely would love to get home for a spell & see my family and kids and get a change so as to be ready for a long war if needs be."

Anne and I got letters written on April 25. To her Dad said that he was once again living in a cave, "only this is a man-made one called a 'dugout.' The days are longer now and warmer and it no longer rains very much. It will be hot very soon." He saw another school year coming to a close and noted that a year had passed since he was in the hospital in Oran—"and a very full year it has been too." To me the subject was baseball.

> Next to missing you all terribly I think that Big league ball is the one great void in my life just during these warm lazy spring days. How I'd love to see old Frank McCormick bust one off the fence with two on in the 8th and Mort Cooper hurling for those Cardinals. Maybe this year we can catch a game. Let's keep hoping for that. Why I'd go to Yankee Stadium and watch an American league game with joy the way I feel now. The Red Birds vs Toledo would even look like big stuff.

Then he asked if I could play "The Dogfaced Soldier" on the piano yet. I had better "learn it on a/c I sing it all the time." Indeed, I had learned to play it using only my right index finger, and I was ready to accompany Dad when he came home.

A V-mail to Mom on April 26 reported that Dad was glad that Deo was putting in a word somewhere. Meanwhile, "Around here there are still plenty Kraut and we have been busy with them on a full time basis." He then interrupted a fantasy about homecoming with, "What the hell am I talking about?" And he told Mom to tell the woman in Columbus who knew Colonel O'Mohundro that "he is a soldier and might make one out of me given time. We are doing all right together and he's a real product of the Old Army that knows what the Dogface Soldier thinks & does." Back in Sicily, Dad had used the same image of an old soldier making a soldier out of him in reference to that "Old Benny Havens," Paddy Flint, shortly before they parted. In closing, Dad said, "It is getting sleepy in my dugout and so good nite. But you keep praying. I've got a hope or a hunch or a dream or something and maybe Deo clicked who knows. All my love, Jack."

From April 13 through 30, the regiment occupied ground between the British Sixth Gordons and the American Thirtieth Infantry from their own Third Division. The regiment's action during this period is listed as "defensive warfare." "Contact was maintained with the enemy by aggressive patrolling. New positions were improved by installation of defensive wire and overhead cover."[16] In these actions and in just staying put, the regiment lost thirty-two men killed in those eighteen days.[17]

Some time during this period Dad went to see Captain Glenn Rathbun, M Company commander, to ask him if he wanted to go back to Fifth Army headquarters and serve as General Clark's aide. Rathbun said that he would like to talk to Major Ramsey, who had done a stint as an aide to General Alexander. To Rathbun, commissioned through ROTC at the University of Idaho, where he had played football, the job seemed to consist of "kissing the General's ass for six months," getting promoted to major, and then being sent out to a combat division as a battalion executive officer. Ramsey concurred. As Rathbun saw it, he was the senior captain in a regiment soon "to go over the top to take Rome." One of the thirteen field-grade officers in the regiment was going to get killed or wounded, and Rathbun would step right into a field-grade job. He told Dad of his decision. Dad said he was right.

On Monday, May 1, the Seventh again reverted to corps reserve in "The Pines" for rest and relaxation and training with battle sleds.[18] The battle sled was the invention of General O'Daniel. Each sled was a metal half-cylinder—originally a one-hundred-gallon water drum cut in half—mounted on runners. It was just wide enough to accommodate a prone infantryman. The idea was that a tank could pull the sled forward while the soldier was protected from shrapnel and small arms fire. A medium tank could pull twelve sleds—an infantry squad.[19]

Dad kicked off his stay in "The Pines" with a letter dated May 1. Mail was now getting from Columbus to Anzio in two weeks or less. Dad had heard from "General B at Benning," who said he would like to have Dad but apparently could not ask for him, so Charlie Saltzman was working on that from his end. Dad said that he had heard from George Biddle and from Deo, who was "bursting with pride" at Dad's being in the Seventh.

Life in "The Pines" wasn't too bad—"fresh eggs, fresh meat, beer (limited supply) and plenty candy." He said that on May 4 he had been invited to attend the "Organization Day" ceremonies marking the hundred and thirty-first anniversary of the formation of his old outfit, the Fifteenth. Again he reported his postwar plan "to undertake the writing of plays or musical comedies or some such. . . . This is truly a fertile field for all such stuff, and I have collaborators and plenty of material in mind. Oh boy!"

He was glad that Deo had been in touch with L.J.M. "I am serious when I say that failure to substitute in this line up is causing a lag in the ball game." Meanwhile, though, with Colonel O'Mohundro off for a rest, "Little Jack will pilot the 7th for a few days. That should really steam 'em all up somehow, and it helps my morale too. . . . Tomorrow I'm taking a bath for sure and putting on some clean clothes so I'll be all set to be the chief." But as always, what he really wants is "to sit in the sun and sip juleps and play with you and watch my kids grow up in the beautiful way you've raised them, darling, and have a good automobile and time to retrace some trails thru Michigan & the West & Southwest."

In 1944, the Kentucky Derby was run on May 6. If Dad had been at home, the neighbors would have come over to listen to the race on the radio and drink Dad's mint juleps. At a safe distance from the beachhead, the Naples office of *Stars and Stripes* handled enough inquiries about the Derby to open its own bookmaking operation. Some fifty officers and men bet about two hundred dollars, most of it on the morning line favorite, Stir Up. Sixteen hours later, when Ted Husing's call of the race was broadcast in Italy, bettors and bystanders alike learned that a 7–1 shot named Pensive had won the race.

Dad didn't mention the Derby in his letter of May 6. He did say his "health is fair—knee aches a bit and so does one arm and eyes are not so hot, but what the hell, I still get around more than a bit." At Mom's request, Dad had looked up a Sergeant Michael Cormanick in Company L of the Fifteenth. Apparently Mom had met his sister somewhere. Dad said that the sergeant "is a good lad in good shape complete with Silver Star." He said he would try to expedite the release of the Silver Star certificate for the sister back home. Nancy Gatch, of the Oran sojourn, "has for some time been threatening to show up around this place, which, in my opinion, is no bono for her although many of them do it seems." Rotation remained prominent in Dad's thoughts, and he prayed "that something will happen to make these people realize they are wrong here in their attitude on the subject. Only local policy prevents action and it is very difficult to comprehend."

In a letter to George Biddle a couple of days later, Dad attempted to answer a question Biddle had asked about young officers serving in Italy. Said Dad,

> The quality of young officers in this theater is of necessity the same as in any other theater. Same boys, same walks of life, same background. In my opinion, the leadership displayed by officers of field grade is always reflected in the actions of the junior officers. I do not say that the field officer leadership here has not been good at times, but I do submit that efficiency in general and combat efficiency in particular suffers when individuals remain too long and too constantly under the gun. One can become "over-golfed," stale or fatigued. Rotation— both inter- and intra-theater—was designed to prevent this condition from existing. Local policies or lack thereof have frequently caused rotation to bog down or fail to occur.

Despite the hardships of life on the beachhead, one could find vestiges of his humanity. Thirty-seven men of the Third Division became naturalized American citizens, and a Third Division first lieutenant and a second lieutenant nurse from the beachhead hospital became husband and wife.[20] And there were opportunities for amusement and diversion—especially when units were pulled back into division or corps reserve. There was the Red Cross, with coffee, doughnuts, shows, and dances. There were movies and music. Bands from American outfits as well as the pipes and drums of the Scottish battalions put on concerts whenever they could. And, of course, there were sports. The Tyrrhenian Sea offered good swimming and fishing. Someone discovered that setting off a Teller mine in the water made hook, line, and sinker unnecessary. Softball and baseball flourished.[21] In a quiet sector of the beachhead near the Mussolini Canal, so a story goes, a player was called "out" on a play at home. So close to the enemy was the ball field that a German observer disputed the umpire's call.[22] In the Forty-fifth Division sector, some GIs put on a horse race of their own. For the Anzio Derby horses from nearby farms were pressed into service, and a mare named "Six-by-six" for the occasion came home in front to garner the Derby prize—a two-pound box of chocolates. So successful was this event that two days later, while Pensive was winning the real Preakness in Baltimore, the Anzio Preakness was run for a box of candy bars and a lifetime pen.[23]

Dad did not make it to the races. He did, however, write two letters of note. One, of course, was to Mom to report that her letter written May 2 had reached him—the fastest yet. Still nothing to report about rotation or intervention, "and yet local policy here is all that prevents since plenty of opportunities and openings are given them." Dad said that he "got awarded a second Purple Heart today for hitting a mine about D + 1 last January. Very nice ceremony, too." He told Mom to be on the lookout for Colonel Roy Moore, a good friend of Dad's and "former chief in the Can Do's." He concluded by asking if money and various other things he had sent had found their way to Columbus yet.

The other letter Dad wrote that day was in response to a letter from Mrs. Pat Kennedy, sister of Bennie Reece. Mrs. Kennedy had written to thank Dad for his March 10 letter of condolence and to ask for some details of the lieutenant's death and burial. Dad tells her that "Bennie was killed instantly—never knew what hit him. It was a high velocity tank shell. Ray Steere, his executive officer, was nearest to him." Then Dad added, "Bennie was very properly and honorably buried in an American military cemetery and there was indeed a service."[24]

About the time that Dad was writing these letters, well to his south the main body of the Fifth Army and the British Eighth Army launched Operation Diadem, billed as the crowning achievement in their arduous efforts to break through the German defensive lines. Two weeks later VI Corps would mount its attack to break out of the beachhead to which it had been confined for four months.

chapter fourteen

THE ROADS TO ROME

On Friday, May 5, General Alexander visited General Truscott at his head-quarters on the beachhead. For VI Corps's breakout, General Truscott and his staff had prepared four different plans named for an incongruous as-semblage of fauna. Operation Grasshopper called for VI Corps to strike east to make the quickest possible linkup with the main body of the Fifth Army. Operation Buffalo called for an attack to the northeast against Cis-terna and then on to Valmontone,[1] cutting the German Tenth Army's es-cape route on Highway 6. Operation Turtle had VI Corps attacking along the Anzio-Rome road north through Campoleone to cut Highway 7 near Lake Albano. Operation Crawdad proposed an attack parallel to the coast northwest through Ardea and on to Rome by the shortest route.[2]

The tactical merits of the four plans aside for the moment, the choice seemed clear. Wouldn't one rather be part of something code-named Buf-falo than Grasshopper, Turtle, or Crawdad? As Winston Churchill put it in a memo dated August 8, 1943,

> Operations in which large numbers of men may lose their lives ought not to be described by code-words which imply a boastful or overconfi-dent sentiment, like "Triumphant," or, conversely, which are calculated to invest the plan with an air of despondency, such as "Woebetide". . . . They ought not to be names of a frivolous character, such as "Bunny-hug" . . . or "Ballyho."
>
> After all, the world is wide, and intelligent thought will readily sup-ply an unlimited number of well-sounding names which do not suggest the character of the operation or disparage it in any way and do not enable some widow or mother to say that her son was killed in an operation called "Bunnyhug" or "Ballyho."[3]

For General Alexander, only Operation Buffalo was likely to achieve the "worthwhile result" of putting large numbers of German troops out of the war permanently. It would do what the Anzio landing was originally supposed to accomplish.

General Clark was less sure. He thought the German Tenth Army too smart to be caught in such a trap. As he had demonstrated in planning Shingle, Clark opposed a fixed plan. He wanted his field commanders to retain some measure of flexibility to move as the situation allowed. Besides, General Clark suspected that the British wanted the glory of entering Rome first. Might Alexander be giving the Americans a subordinate role, as he had in Tunisia and Sicily? Clark wanted his Fifth Army to liberate Rome. As he said, "They more than deserved it." He wanted to lead the first army in fifteen hundred years to capture Rome from the south. And he wanted to do so before the imminent invasion of Normandy pushed everything else off the front pages of the newspapers. Finally, however, Clark agreed that Buffalo would be the way off the beachhead, but he insisted that Truscott should be free to develop other plans as well.[4]

There was much to do before "Buffalo" could begin. Units had to receive and integrate replacements to reach combat strength. Supplies had to be brought up. There were new fire missions for artillery to plot. And everything had to be done so as to keep the Germans from anticipating the exact when and where of Buffalo. And with the Germans able to shoot at anything that moved on the beachhead, preparations had to occur at night or under smoke screens. It might be the third week of May before everything was ready.

In "The Pines," the Seventh Infantry rested, refitted, and trained. Sunday, May 14, was Mother's Day, which in Dad's words "calls for a real letter to [Mom]—one that trys [sic] to tell you how proud I am of the mother of my kids and trys [sic] also to tell you what a marvelous mother you've been to those two grand creatures." From the beachhead he reported nothing "except a raucous party Friday nite including a football game after the dance featuring live tackling and blocking by many high ranking characters." He hadn't seen Nancy Gatch, who was still said to be around somewhere, nor Sterling Hill. He did eat supper with his "swell friend, young Major [Lloyd] Ramsey, who accompanied [him] on the trip to that Rest—'Ithaca in Italy' Week." Dad says he played some volleyball, got a beer ration, and is "getting fat in the gut again on a/c of my executive officer job and too much good food and bum cognac—but will lose it soon again no doubt."

About homecoming, he said, "Things are not currently hopeful. . . . It is, as I keep saying, snagged locally by a couple of gents who don't believe in it." He added, "Frankly I'm resigned on this rotation business and now feel that I'll be home when they build a bridge and we march over it. So that's the way it is and I'll stick in there and punch—but so many of my pals are shoving off—Not of my grade, however, mostly lower grades."

Of his boss, Colonel O'Mohundro, Dad said, "This old bird who runs this regt. is all right in many ways—very human—altho not highly original as to ideas and a touch old for the task. He nevertheless keeps me busy." And Dad had just heard from Robert White, his driver in North Africa, "who is still at WRGH [Walter Reed General Hospital], and I'm going to keep said letter always. What a lad he is and how I love him. 'Just a dogface soldier'—that's our official song." Then he closed,

> Well, darling, to you all I send my very deepest love and blessings and may our prayers one day be answered. Give the kids a big hug for their Dad and tell them I'm counting the hours till I can see them.
>
> The St. Regis or Pine Bluff, Wyo.—I don't care, but how long Oh Lord—How long. Devotedly, Jack

I got a letter on May 14, too. Dad apologized for not having written more frequently, but he had been busy. He was proud of my "success in baseball, grand hitting ability and interest in the game." The war "has gone on a long time and seems to be going a lot longer. I feel we ought to see our folks once in a while to keep us going." He mentioned having seen a few old friends and said that Sgt. Edgar Poinsett, who used to drive us around at Fort Dix, was now a captain in Dad's regiment. He closed, "Pray hard, John, on this Mother's Day—for me to see my mother and yours very soon. God bless you all. Love, Dad."

Dad's V-mail to Mom written the next day, May 15, started happily enough with the arrival of several letters from home. He was glad, too, that Mom had had a return visit from Cincinnati friends. The Italian weather was really heating up, especially at midday, and the flies and bugs were out in force. About rotation, "Nothing has developed here on the matter nearest our heart nor do I now feel it is likely to at once." Dad said he didn't know much about the big picture and couldn't write about it if he did. That something might be in the works was implicit in his reference to "Busy days, nerve trying days, and a constant strain to keep on the ball make it difficult to be normal. One smokes too much—drinks too much if he can get it, and sleeps too little if he can get that." Anne's and my "grand development will be a very pleasant shock to me specially if I can come home during their summer vacation and play a bit with them. . . . I won't cease to pray, darling, but I assure you we are not currently optimistic on same."

On May 17 Dad's boss got his eagles. In a memoir Colonel O'Mohundro remembers that it was the Third Division's practice to rotate officers back to the States based on their length of time overseas. He says that when he learned he was due for rotation, he turned it down because he "didn't want to let Clark down" while working for his colonelcy.[5] Obviously this recollection differs from Dad's understanding at the time.

Anne got a letter from her "beat up old father" written on the same day that O'Mohundro made colonel. Though he said he wanted "to wish [her] happiness and a good happy time as [her] school year draws to a close," the real purpose was to write, as he had on the eve of every major action from Port Lyautey through Anzio, what might become a last letter. He said he was going swimming later that day. He asked Anne to wish me a happy birthday, though he would try to get a message to me himself on the day. Of the war and the world he told his daughter,

> I've been fairly busy and expect to stay that way. It is a strange and different world, Miss Mouse, and the good old U.S.A. looks pretty good to me—but sort of remote as time goes by. Things are cooking briskly on all fronts these days and doubtless the German will sort of feel the press by mid summer and maybe commence to pinch a little. I really can assure you it couldn't be soon enough for us gents. . . . Write down a list of all the things you and John want to do and when I get home we will surely do them. I'm off on a job now, Miss Anne, but I send you much love and I would like some pictures of you—recent ones. Goodbye for now. I'm very proud of you and John. Devotedly, Dad.

On Thursday, May 18, General Truscott was ordered to report to General Clark's headquarters at 0930 the next day and to "be prepared to discuss the feasibility of continuing the 3rd Division in Operation Buffalo to take objectives 1 and 2 instead of passing the 36th Division through."[6] In their meeting Clark suggested that after taking Cisterna and Cori, VI Corps might turn northwest into the Alban Hills while the First Special Service Force finished up Buffalo by moving on Valmontone. Truscott pointed out that the First Special Service Force, six infantry battalions, wasn't large enough. Clark's suggestion strongly implies that his eyes were on Rome, not the annihilation of the German Tenth and Fourteenth Armies. Clark told Truscott that D-Day for Operation Buffalo would be two days later, May 21.[7]

The Third Division would spearhead Operation Buffalo. General Truscott thought it was by far the best division on the beachhead. Taking Cisterna in two or three days would be tough. Only the Third Division, he felt, had the esprit, the aggressiveness, and the leadership to get the job done.[8] Having failed to take the town at the end of January, the division would now get another crack at it. With the First Armored Division on its left flank and the First Special Service Force on its right, the Third would send its three regiments against Cisterna. The Thirtieth and Fifteenth would flank the town while the Seventh attacked it frontally. The Thirtieth and Fifteenth would then advance toward Cori and the hills while the Seventh secured the town.

Bad weather predicted for May 21 postponed the attack. On Saturday morning, May 20, the men of the Seventh Infantry assembled in their bivouac area to hear General O'Daniel and Colonel O'Mohundro speak. When the two had finished, the chaplains held services for all seeking "comfort and succor . . . in this transitory life."[9] That day, too, the editor of the *Cotton Baler* published his paper. In the "C. O.'s Corner" at the bottom of the front page, Colonel O'Mohundro placed this message:

The Germans have boasted they make a business of war, while other nations merely play at it. The action of the "Cotton Balers" in this and past wars can hardly be classed as "parlor games." The regiment may soon face the enemy in another "little game." If everyone makes each shot the best shot of his life it will mean business for the Bosche—BAD BUSINESS.

MAKE EVERY SHOT YOUR BEST SHOT.

Four of the letters Dad wrote on that day still exist. Two—to Anne and me—are V-mails featuring a cartoon sketch of Dad outside his bunker. Dad said it had been drawn by one of "our lads." He sent it along as another "souvenir of this place." The cartoon takes up about half the page, leaving Dad just enough room to tell us how proud he was of us and how he looked forward to seeing us. "Perhaps one day I'll make it your way," he told Anne. "Maybe one day I'll get out of here and we can really celebrate," he told me. He apologized to Granny and Homer for not having written. He had been busy, he said, and "have also been batting out the mail." He was glad to hear that a cousin of Granny's had gotten a furlough, adding, "Say, those lads at home don't do badly in that connection, do they? Well, one day I'll get one, but it is sure a long time coming." Maybe something would break by fall.

On a "beautiful Sunday" Dad also wrote to Mom. He could "hear bagpipes playing close at hand—very fine music for marching purposes—wonderful drum accompaniment, good rhythm." To Mom's news of "Kultur in Ohio," Dad said, "Get me home and I'll tell 'em about the dogface soldier if they'll ply me with enough bourbon." "Yesterday," he added, "I did a terrible thing—to wit burned all old letters. This hurt me to do, but space had become such a factor that I found it necessary to retain only yours of April and May. Hope you will forgive this, but I really had too many and had to do something about it." He told her that he was pretty well caught up on correspondence, "Don't owe many at present." As he again told Mom how much he loved her daily letters, his writing was interrupted: "Turmoil and much work have suddenly descended on me—hence I shall pause once more and go about my father's business—until it cools down a bit and I can calmly write." In the hiatus he picked up Mom's letter of May 12 describing with great humor some ball game I had played in. "I would love to catch a few innings of one of those ball games of his—and I'd like to play a few innings on your field too." Then he signed off: "Pray long and hard, my sweet, that we may very soon again be back together. I'm still doing my very best, but it ain't as good as it was and I'm a bit war weary more than somewhat. God bless you all. Devotedly, Jack."

On Sunday evening the Third Division began to move out of "The Pines" under cover of smoke. As the men of the Third Division came onto the main road, they were met by the division band playing "Dogface Soldier" and a selection of familiar martial music. The division history reports hyperbolically: "As judged from the attitudes and remarks of the passing columns, never had the men been in finer fettle; never had morale been higher."[10]

As the division began to move out, word came that Operation Buffalo would begin at 0630 hours on May 23. General Clark informed General Truscott that he would arrive at Fifth Army's Advanced Command Post on the beachhead about noon on Monday, May 22.[11] Meanwhile, General Clark found time to dine Sunday evening with Irving Berlin, of "This Is the Army" fame, who "played the new Fifth Army song he had written, a new infantry song, and other war ballads which were very good."[12]

The general also detached the two British divisions—the First and Fifth—from VI Corps and placed them under Fifth Army control.[13] The assault troops of VI Corps that would liberate Rome were now all American.

By midnight of May 21–22, the Seventh Infantry had moved into position. They dug in and camouflaged themselves and got what sleep they could. While they lay low throughout the daylight hours of May 22, Dad found time to write once again:

> My Darling—Just a line to say I got yours of 11 May and many thanks. We are busy and getting busier so don't worry if letters come scarcely or in bunches. I wrote you a long one last nite and this will have to do until I can sit still long enough to do a real one again. It seems that the Kraut is going to catch hell from all sides at any time now and may it really spell finis for him. Certainly that is one sure way we can live our lovely life again. I miss you all so very much and do hope something pops up to let me see you. It may happen and we can hope and dream.
>
> Meanwhile forgive this hurried scrawl and give my love to everyone. God bless you all and pray hard for the end of War and Peace ever after and our quick reunion. Devotedly, Jack.

During the night of May 22, General O'Daniel confirmed the D-Day and H-Hour times. "Be prepared," he said, "to push beyond final objectives on Division order. Good luck and pour it on." At 0545 on May 23, ten battalions of field artillery opened fire. Then the infantrymen moved forward. The Second Battalion started to advance along the Conca-Cisterna road. Almost immediately the leading elements reported they were "pinned down." "We have no such words in our vocabulary now," replied General O'Daniel. "You're supposed to be at the railroad track by noon. You'll get a bonus if you do, something else if you don't." To make matters worse, minefields made it impossible for tanks and tank destroyers to provide close-in fire support. Third Battalion advanced about a mile by midafternoon but was reeling from heavy casualties.[14] Though ordered to resume the attack at 1645, the battalion failed to move. Major Ramsey, the executive officer, took command and tried to rally his men for a night attack that he had to postpone because supporting armor failed to show up. Before he could start again, the Germans counterattacked. Though the Seventh Infantry made some progress the first day, it paid a high price, losing fifty-four men killed. The division counted 995 casualties, the most suffered in any single day since it went into combat in 1942.[15]

On the second day, the regiment continued its attack on Cisterna. Major Ramsey was wounded, and Captain Glenn Rathbun took over as commander of Third Battalion. As he had predicted, through the attrition of field-grade officers, Captain Rathbun had gone from company commander to battalion commander in less than two days.

By daylight on May 25, the leading elements of the Seventh were fighting through the rubble that was once Cisterna, but not until nightfall had the last of the enemy been killed, captured, or driven out. The little town had not been bought cheaply. In three days the Third Division lost about 1,400 killed or wounded. In the Seventh Infantry, 116 were killed and 556 wounded—nearly half of the division's casualties. In the three days the Third Battalion lost two battalion commanders, and Company K lost two company commanders. Of the two German divisions defending Cisterna, one was wiped out and the other reduced to half-strength.[16]

While the Seventh was mopping up in Cisterna, General Clark asked General Truscott if he had considered changing the direction of his corps's attack northwest toward Rome. Truscott said that if the Germans shifted troops into the Valmontone Gap, he would indeed consider moving the axis of his attack to the northwest. But the Germans did not.[17]

Early in the morning of May 25, in the Pontine Marshes along the coast southeast of Cisterna, a northbound patrol from II Corps met elements of a southbound task force. With that meeting, the Anzio beachhead ceased to exist. Three hours later the meeting was reenacted with General Clark present.[18] Then Clark dispatched General Donald Brann, his G-3, to tell General Truscott to change the direction of the attack. "We will capture Rome," he said."[19]

Pleased with the progress towards Valmontone, General Truscott returned to his headquarters to find General Brann awaiting him. Brann told him that Clark wanted the axis of attack changed to the northeast. Seeing nothing in the tactical situation to warrant the shift, Truscott told Brann he wanted to discuss the matter with General Clark. Impossible, Brann replied. Clark was not on the beachhead and could not be reached by radio.[20] Truscott again found himself given orders of which he did not approve. "A more complicated plan would be difficult to conceive," he said.[21] Nevertheless, he would follow these orders diligently and whole-heartedly. Indeed, by the next day, the change in the axis of attack was, to General Truscott, "an idea with which I am heartily in accord."[22]

Publicly, all this was presented as follows:

The enemy forces opposing the beachhead offensive in the Cisterna-Cori area have been decisively defeated. The Beachhead and main Fifth Army forces have joined. The overwhelming success of the current bat-tle makes it possible to continue Operation Buffalo with powerful forces and to launch a new attack along the most direct route to Rome.[23]

The part about continuing Operation Buffalo was intended to keep General Alexander happy. Clark could not ignore the plan that Alexander had approved back on May 5. To Fifteenth Army Group Headquarters, Buffalo was the name of the game. To maintain token compliance, Clark had to advance on Valmontone and Highway 6. So, while the bulk of VI Corps swung to the left to attack "along the most direct route to Rome," the Third Division, the First Special Service Force, and a task force under the command of Colonel Hamilton Howze pressed on to Valmontone.

Thus did the capture of Valmontone, the cutting of Highway 6, and the consequent trapping of the German Tenth Army become a secondary undertaking in the Italian campaign. Was Buffalo becoming Bunnyhug?

The Third Division continued past Cisterna and Cori toward Artena and Valmontone. At first, with the First Armored Division on the left flank and the First Special Service Force on the right, and with no fixed enemy defenses immediately in front of it, the division found the going pretty pleasant. So pleasant that in the opinion of one officer, "troops . . . seemed to be relaxing without helmets, arms . . . picking daisies, and enjoying the spring air. What do [they] think—that the war is over?" American fighter planes spotted a column moving along the road. Thinking they had found retreating German troops, the fighters swept in, bombing and strafing. What they had found was not a German column but the Third Division. More than a hundred men were killed or wounded by friendly fire. More than seventy were in Dad's old Second Battalion of the Fifteenth.[24]

By noon on May 27, the Seventh Infantry was close to Artena. Task Force Howze was within eight hundred yards of Highway 6 near Labico. Pleased, General O'Daniel told General Truscott that he was "convinced we could go into Rome if we had more stuff up here." Truscott told O'Daniel that before dawn the next day "Highway 6 must be . . . cut and the gap between Artena and the Alban Hills must be closed."[25]

Near Artena on May 27, Dad found time to get off a letter to Mom. He had just received one from her, and he mentioned a couple of other people from whom he had recently heard. "Things with us is [*sic*] plenty good as you may have read in the papers," he says. "In point of fact things are splendid and we are on the go again and nabbing beaucoup Kraut in the action." Splendid, too, "and a bit touching" were the Mother's Day poems Mom had sent Dad. Whether she wrote them or Anne and I had wasn't clear. He did say that he and Mom have "a couple of pretty wonderful children, haven't we?" Perhaps the poems suggested to him "The Dogface Soldier," which he predicted will be "the biggest number to come out of this war." Then he turned to the subject of regimental commanders.

This guy here commanding is another character—wow!—One of those types of whom there are too many left over in our business. Driving me nuts to be honest with you. Boy have I done some backstopping for a couple of wild hurlers in the past year. It is tough on the arteries.

That thought seemed to make him "wish 'our day' would roll around as I am really long overdue on the matter of Life, Love, and the Pursuit of happiness." He asked Mom,

Tell family and friends that I am currently too busy to do much writing, but I do love them all and would really give much to see them. It does not appear that L.J.Mc. pulled a very heavy string so far. Tell J. (Lombardi) Toffey I am most pleased with him and his baseball. Well, this ends the page, but not the ideas. You may be certain I got plenty of ideas and you figure in all of them, my love. Bless you all, Jack.

Opposing the Third Division were German troops from at least fifty different small units,[26] but they fought as if they were from a single outfit. The Hermann Goering Panzer Division also was hurrying to defend Valmontone and to keep open an escape route. In northern Italy and slated for duty in France, the division was called back when the Allied breakout began, and elements were trickling into the area. If the Third Division got to Valmontone first, it would achieve in rather short order the goal of Operation Buffalo. If the Hermann Goering Division got there in strength first, the matter would remain unresolved.

On May 28, the Seventh Infantry moved forward three battalions abreast. Even in this broad advance, however, most of the fights were small but fierce skirmishes against German machine-gun emplacements or dug-in tanks or self-propelled guns. In one such action, Colonel Frank Izenour said that the men of his First Battalion reached their objective because they "wanted that ground more than Goering's did."[27] By evening, the Seventh Infantry had taken all its objectives east of Artena.

On May 30, the Third Division, First Special Service Force, and Task Force Howze were detached from VI Corps and assigned to General Keyes's II Corps, made up of the Eighty-fifth and Eighty-eighth Infantry Divisions, which were advancing up the Italian peninsula. Thus the operation against Valmontone was no longer the responsibility of VI Corps.

On May 30, Memorial Day, General Clark presided over services at the new American cemetery outside Nettuno. Truscott was there, too. "Believe me," he wrote to his wife a couple of weeks later, "standing amid those thousands of white crosses within sound of the guns was most impressive."

In the same letter the general touched on a major theme in Dad's letters. Mrs. Truscott had told her husband she was glad he "was back on the job after a rest period" and that she disapproved of such periods "in principle." Truscott replied that these rest periods "are good and save lives in the long run." "Anyway, nothing happened while I was gone—and I was far more fit for the job as a result of the rest."[28]

On May 31 General Clark, through General Brann, issued this order to II Corps:

> After having secured the high ground North of Valmontone, blocked all traffic through Route 6 and secured that part of Colli Laziali that lies within its zone, [will] be prepared on Army Order to pursue and annihilate German forces withdrawing Northwest and will send hard hitting mobile forces under vigorous leadership via Route 6 on Ferentino to capture or destroy any enemy forces withdrawing from the fronts of Eighth Army and French Expeditionary Corps.[29]

At 1400 on May 31, the Seventh Infantry began to move forward against enemy resistance "scattered but determined" enough to kill eighteen men. Once the regiment had reached its objectives, First Battalion was attached to Task Force Howze. At 0500, June 1, the division's other two regiments began their attack. They met stiff enough resistance to require the deployment of a battalion of the Seventh.[30] During the night of June 1–2, the Fifteenth Infantry shot up German vehicles moving along Highway 6. "Shoot every goddamn vehicle that comes by there," ordered General O'Daniel.[31] That same night the Germans pulled out of Valmontone, leaving only a small rear guard. The Third Division entered the town unopposed around 1030, June 2.

That same day Colonel O'Mohundro told Dad to take the Second and Third Battalions north toward Palestrina to secure two road junctions about half a mile below the town. They were not to capture the town; they were to keep the enemy from attacking Highway 6 and cutting off elements of the Third Division. The action assigned to Dad's two battalions was described as "an aggressive defense with limited objectives."[32]

At 1650 on June 2, Dad left the regimental command post to go to the Second Battalion command post. At 1800 he called regiment to report that the Second Battalion was doing a good job and moving as well as possible while carrying combat loads over a mountain. He said that he was then going on to the Third Battalion command post. At 1935 Third Battalion was moving despite taking fire from small arms, a flak wagon, and some tank airbursts. At 2110, Second Battalion reported that artillery was falling short and that supporting tanks and tank destroyers had not yet reached the battalion. About the same time Third Battalion reported that it had four tanks with it and was moving again.[33]

At 2215 Dad reported two Mark VI and one Mark IV tanks on the Cave-Palestrina road. At 2220 Division called to say that the Seventh (minus First Battalion) would hold ground and tomorrow start moving northwest, and the French would follow and pass through the Seventh. Five minutes later regimental headquarters called Dad and told him to push on as rapidly as possible. At 2300 Dad reported Third Battalion moving slowly, now accompanied by five tanks. He said that the shoot on Palestrina looked good, that there were enemy tanks on Third Battalion's objective, and that there was still traffic on the Cave-Palestrina road.

The next day at 0320, Dad reported Second Battalion reorganizing but their exact position not known, with no change in Third Battalion's position. At 0445 Third Battalion reported German tanks holding up progress. One Mark VI in particular had been giving Third Battalion trouble. It was down in a road cut, where our tanks and tank destroyers could not bring effective fire to bear. Shortly after sunrise on June 3, Dad joined Captain

Rathbun and Lieutenant Colonel Arthur Snyder at Third Battalion's forward command post. Between 0930 and 1000, regiment ordered Third Battalion to establish a roadblock, then told Dad to have the battalion secure the road junctions by moving beyond them. Third Battalion reported to regiment that Dad, Rathbun, and Snyder were putting together a combined armor and infantry attack. Plans were solidified by 1205. Dad reported that the French had been sighted coming up. Division said that relief by the French would not occur until after dark.

Back at Fifth Army, General Clark had just visited every division commander in VI Corps, where he had found the main attack to be going well. Despite Clark's order to his commanders "to pursue relentlessly and destroy the enemy and not think of Rome," thoughts of Rome danced in lots of heads. "No one is doing any work here this afternoon," reported General Gruenther. An "unsuppressible wave of optimism and expectancy has swept through the headquarters." Public-relations officers were composing headlines for the communiqués they would soon be issuing: "Fifth Army Troops Enter Rome," "Rome Falls to Fifth Army, "Advance Elements of Fifth Army Enter Rome."[34]

All day on June 3, a thirteen-man patrol of K Company had been pinned down in a wheat field not far from the Third Battalion's forward command post. In the course of the day, the patrol lost eight men to German tank and machine-gun fire. Sometime in the afternoon they heard the Germans begin to pull out and saw a couple of American tanks moving up.[35] At 1414, half a mile south of Palestrina and well away from the euphoria sweeping through Fifth Army headquarters, Third Battalion reported to Regiment: "Lt Col. TOFFEY, Regimental Executive Officer, has been wounded—extent of injury cannot be determined—will keep you informed." At 1440, Captain Rathbun, who had risen so precipitously to command Third Battalion, called Regiment to say, "Lt Col TOFFEY, Regimental Executive Officer, is dead."

Later that afternoon, "after defeating a stubborn enemy delaying action, consisting of tanks supported by Infantry, and capturing all final objectives, the Seventh Infantry (minus the First Battalion) was completely relieved by the 3rd DIM (French) and reverted to Division Reserve."[36] The regiment would not fight again in Italy and would not see any combat again for more than two months.

chapter fifteen

THE PATHS OF GLORY

In Columbus we were unaware of what had happened, unaware that we were living in what George Biddle had called the "few days of grace" between fact and notification. In the newspapers we had been following the big Italian offensive since it began on May 23. On Wednesday, May 24, my thirteenth birthday, our morning paper proclaimed, "Allied Armies Hurled at Rome. Clark personally directs attack at beachhead." The paper called it "the greatest Allied attacking force yet thrown into battle in this war outside the Russian front."[1] We knew that Dad was somewhere in all that action and that he would write when he could, as he always did, to tell us he was okay.

On Saturday, June 3 all we knew of events in Italy was what we read in the papers under the headline "Clark Draws Noose on Remnants of 12 German Divisions": "Powerful armored and infantry forces smashed through the key German strongholds of Valmontone and Velletri in the Alban Hills before Rome, shattering the enemy's last ditch defenses and foreshadowing the beginning of the end of the battle for the Eternal City."[2] We wondered when we would hear about Dad's entry into Rome.

After reading the war news, Mom checked the week's ration calendar in the paper. Stamp A-11 was good for three gallons of gas through June 21, and a pound of waste kitchen grease and fat turned in at Kroger's meat counter would get us a two one-point red tokens and four cents.[3]

That afternoon I listened to the radio to see if Pensive would win the Belmont Stakes. He didn't, losing by half a length to a long shot aptly named Bounding Home. Our Reds were playing in Boston, where they lost 5-4. Bucky Walters pitched—my idol and cousin of the lieutenant we had met at Fort Dix.

I wrote Dad on Sunday afternoon, telling him that school was winding down. We would be having exams that week and commencement the next. Meanwhile, as the weather warmed, we went swimming a lot. A favorite spot was the Bath Club, on Nelson Road about a mile north of where we lived. Membership in the club was restricted to anyone who had the price of admission. Sometimes Homer would take us to the Country Club, but a trip there—about three times as far out East Broad Street—put a strain on Homer's weekly gasoline ration. I also told Dad I had a couple of possible jobs lined up for the summer. In a letter to Dad a couple of days earlier, Granny had said that I needed to be away from Mom and "have some work to do at regular hours."

One of the jobs I mentioned to Dad was leading ponies at the zoo, but the zoo was miles away across town, out the Scioto River Road and past the roadside monument to Chief Leatherlips. I liked Leatherlips.[4] In my imagination I lumped him together with all those exotic people Homer knew and used to tell us about—Al Jennings, O. Henry, James Thurber, Oley Speaks, Jesse Owens, Jack Wilce, and Chic Harley. In the reality of 1944 a daily round-trip to the zoo was out of the question. The other job possibility I mentioned was working on a farm, but an agricultural job wasn't any more likely than the job at the zoo. We would be going to Great Neck in early July.

As I reached the bottom of the V-mail page, I didn't mention Bucky Walters's having lost to Boston the day before. All I said was that the Reds were occupying second or third place in the National League standings. It was the last letter I wrote to Dad.

Anne also wrote a newsy letter to Dad on June 4:

> Dear Dad, We had examinations at school, and I think I did pretty well. We get out on Wednesday. We are going swimming today and are going to take a picnic supper. Last night the next door neighbor girl came over to spend the night. We got candy and cookies from the kitchen and ate them in bed. One school day I have to announce a poem in French. It goes "Nous allons reciter une petite ryme qui s'appelle 'J'ai dix doigts.'" I hope we are going East this summer, if so I hope we can go with you. Lots of love, Anne.

Monday's paper announced that the day before, "Amid kisses and tears from hysterical Romans, 5th Army tanks and infantry fought a four-hour battle . . . against German armor five miles from the heart of the city." Four paragraphs later, "Smiling, brown-eyed girls brought bouquets of flowers to dust-covered riflemen who were crawling up a sloping field of wild barley and poppies to scout German positions flanking the heavily mined airport at Centocelle." And four paragraphs after that we saw that "infantry units . . . commanded by Lt. Col. Frank Izenour . . . and Lt. Col. Joseph Crawford . . . were in the forefront of the spectacular drive from the Valmontone area."[5]

Thus it was that the Allies entered Rome 275 days after landing on the Italian mainland. In those 275 days, General Clark's Fifth Army had 124,917 casualties. Of the 20,389 dead, 11,292 were Americans.[6] From Anzio to Rome in a little over four months, the Seventh Infantry Regiment sustained more than 3,000 casualties, the equivalent of the entire regiment's strength. Of these, 729 were killed.[7]

On Monday Granny wrote to Dad again. "Well," she began, "we see you captured Rome. What a thrilling experience! Our concern is for your safety—that is about all we are thinking about. We hope now the government will see fit to let you come home for your much needed rest. Suppose they could not spare you before this."

On Tuesday, the Allies crossed the English Channel and landed on the beaches of Normandy. The war in Italy went into the recesses of the papers and the minds of all the Americans not immediately or emotionally connected to it. George Biddle remembered Italy, though, and wrote Dad on Wednesday:

> Dear Jack: Pecker up. Yesterday we—I guess that means you—rolled into Rome. Today the invasion. This morning I worked on a big painting of the Troina bombing. In the afternoon I mowed and raked an acre of rank grass. This evening letters to you, Manhart, Jo Kindlarski. Do sit down, Jack, & write one short word about the run into Rome. It left me restless and envious. I wanted to be with you.
>
> I go down to Mexico for a year to do a mural in the Department of Education. I spoke to Don Longwell of *Life* and told him when I get back I want to be sent out to the Pacific to do some close-ups of Hirohito and Tojo. He said "O.K." My book [*Artist at War*] comes out in 2 weeks. In a sense you're the hero. I'll send you a copy. Don't sue me. Love to the boys. Your friend George Biddle

News of the Normandy landings brought to Columbus a solemn excitement that had not attended the campaigns we had been following for so long. Churches held special services. We went to one that afternoon at Trinity Church downtown. We sang the version of "Eternal Father Strong to Save" that had verses for those in peril on the land, on the sea, and in the air.

Certainly the Normandy landings meant the start of another front and, presumably, another step towards the ending of the war in Europe. But by June 6, 1944, Dad had been overseas for just over nineteen months, and had already been on the continent of Europe for eight and a half months. We had worried him through two assault and two follow-up landings on foreign soil and some two hundred days in frontline engagement with the enemy on two continents. We were certainly aware of the implications of the new fighting in France. On the service flags in the front windows of houses in our neighborhood and around the country a lot of blue stars would change to gold. The daily casualty lists in the three Columbus papers would grow longer. But Dad wasn't in Normandy; he was somewhere in or around Rome, and, as Granny had put it, his safety was all we were thinking about.

Dad's letter of May 27 probably reached us around the time we learned of the liberation of Rome and the Normandy landings. Getting a letter always brought relief. It was easy to forget about the time it took for the letter to travel from Italy to Columbus and take receipt of the letter as evidence that Dad was okay on the day you got the letter.

There was a lot to do in Columbus that spring. Friends and I would climb through the forsythia bushes up the embankment of the Norfolk and Western tracks and let a northbound coal train or southbound string of empties flatten pennies that we had put on the tracks. Or we might wander north along Alum Creek, watching patient, silent fishermen and stooping to scoop up crawdads from the shallows.

On Saturdays my classmates and I might attend the matinee double feature with newsreel and serial at the Drexel Theater. Sometimes girls we knew were there. Too young to date, we just congregated. After the movie, we moved a few doors along Main Street to the soda fountain at Wentz's Drug Store, where chocolate-cherry or lemon-lime phosphates were the drinks of choice, and where the latest issue of *Baseball Magazine* provided a comfort zone away from the complexities of intergender conversation. In good weather I could ride my bike to the theater. But good weather also meant outings with Homer. Amid Ohio State baseball games and track meets that spring we took in the intersquad football game. And there would be an occasional trip out to Red Bird Stadium to watch the Cardinals' local Triple-A farm club. It was that spring at Red Bird Stadium that I saw my first night game.

Dad's letter telling of his entry into Rome should have arrived around June 15. Sometimes, though, mail from overseas was delayed or lost somewhere en route. As June wore on, we should have heard something. In the absence of a letter from Dad, though, there was nothing we could do—no one to call—to check on him. We went on doing what we had been doing since October 1942: we waited.

On a hot Friday afternoon in the middle of June, we decided to go to the Bath Club for a swim. I rode my bike. Mom drove Anne and her friend Joanie in our blue transcontinental Plymouth. At the pool Mom sat in the sun reading and chatting with friends. Anne and her friend splashed daintily while off the low board my friends and I performed endless repetitions of the cannonball. Around 6:00 o'clock, we gathered our gear for the return trip. Just in front of Mom and our car, I pedaled into Nelson Road, across the northbound traffic and toward the curb of the southbound lane. Somewhere in this maneuver, I was hit by a car. As she waited to pull out into traffic, Mom saw her son struck and knocked off his bike, hit the pavement, and lie motionless. I remember coming to under the car that had hit me. I could hear a siren and see the ambulance coming down the street. People were crouching beside me. Mom was somewhere among them.

My injuries were not particularly serious, as it turned out. I had a cut on my head and a concussion that kept me in the hospital overnight for observation, and assorted other scrapes, bumps, and bruises where the car, the bike, or the pavement of Nelson Road had made an impression. Mom probably had a far worse time seeing the accident than I did participating in it. I was still a bit fuzzy, I guess, when I went home the next day, and the doctor told Mom to keep me quiet for a few days.

I was still keeping quiet in my room on the third floor on Sunday morning, June 25. I happened to be looking out my window when I saw Homer drive up and park his Oldsmobile in front of the house. It was unusual for Homer to appear here on a Sunday morning. He was usually at church. I watched him get out of the car, come around, and open the door for Granny. They stood together for a minute before Homer turned and started up the walk to our front door with Granny a step or two behind. Something about this scene didn't seem right. When I got to the living room, I saw Mom and Granny and Homer standing there. No one was saying anything. Mom handed me the telegram Homer had given her, and as I started to read it, she put both arms around me.

THE SECRETARY OF WAR DESIRES ME TO EXPRESS HIS DEEP REGRET THAT
YOUR HUSBAND LIEUTENANT COLONEL JOHN J TOFFEY JR WAS KILLED IN
ACTION ON THREE JUNE IN ITALY LETTER FOLLOWS.
    ULIO THE ADJUTANT GENERAL

That was it. No pair of officers wearing Class A uniforms and appropriately somber faces expressing the thanks of a grateful nation. Instead there was Homer, bearing to our house the burden of the terrible telegram as he had brought word of Dad's having been wounded fourteen months earlier. Homer because, when Dad left us in Fayetteville, we didn't have a house of our own, and Homer's address was as close as we could come to permanence.

In May and June letters traveled between Dad and us in about ten days. Early in the war, it seems, theater commanders had reported casualties to the War Department by radio or cable, but errors in transmission ran as high as 25 percent. By the time Dad was killed, theater commanders were preparing a punch card for each casualty. After the cards were checked, they were flown to the adjutant general in Washington, reaching him within eight days. He could then report to the next of kin two days later.[8] At least so the theory went. It had taken twenty-two days for the adjutant general to get his telegram to us.

Mom and Granny and Homer had to attend to grim logistical matters of their own. Sometime that Sunday they started making the phone calls to all the relatives and friends too close to learn of Dad's death in the papers. Mom, of course, called Deo to break the news that her son was dead. Deo in turn would tell her sisters and brothers and their spouses. Then she would begin to notify all her army friends. Mom would call our Cincinnati friends, while Granny and Homer took care of all their relatives in Columbus and beyond.

Monday's *Columbus Citizen* gave its front page to the imminent capture of Cherbourg and the stampede to nominate Thomas Dewey at the Republican National Convention. Dad's death was noted on page 8 under the headline "Col. John Toffey Killed in Action." The article went on to give a brief biographical sketch, including military history and family. The *Ohio State Journal* that morning used as a subhead to Dad's obituary, "Africa, Sicily, Anzio Campaign Veteran Wore 2 Purple Hearts and Silver Star." The *Dispatch* included Dad's obituary in a summary article about six Columbus men killed from Burma to Britain and six more wounded in Italy.

Under the headline "Colonel Toffey Dies in Fighting in Italy," the *New York Times* ran the subhead "Jersey Resident Was Third of Name to Serve in Wars." The *Newark Evening News* ran the obituary and mentioned the three generations of John Toffeys to have gone to war. In Cleveland, Nat Howard mentioned Dad's death at the end of his column. And on they went, all reporting pretty much the same facts with varying emphasis to suit local readership.

The mailman who had brought Dad's letters to us now began to bring the letters of condolence. One of the first was the one from the adjutant general confirming what he had said in the telegram. He added that there was no additional information he could give at the time because "reports of this nature contain only the briefest of details as they are prepared under battle conditions and the means of transmission are limited." Dad's boss, Colonel O'Mohundro, wrote his letter long before the official telegram would reach us. From the date on the letter—June 9—the colonel must have been writing from Rome, but as he says at the beginning of the letter, "Today on the eve of what appears complete victory over the enemy in this sector, the seventh Infantry Regiment is unable to enjoy its success because of the loss of it's [*sic*] outstanding Officer, Lt. Colonel Toffey."

The letter must have lain around for some time before the colonel mailed it. Censorship regulations required that the adjutant general's telegram arrive first. From Colonel O'Mohundro we learned the first specific circumstances of Dad's death.

The Regiment had been assigned two separate missions in cleaning up the last strong points in our area, one of these missions required coordination between two battalions, and by reason of [Dad's] expert tactical knowledge, he was given command of both battalions.

He was conducting a conference with his commanders in the upper story of a farm house where he could point out terrain features, when an enemy shell pierced the wall and exploded. An officer standing next to him states that he was struck in the head by a fragment and death was instantaneous. I was notified by telephone immediately, and assigned an officer to accompany his body to our rear echelon. Burial services in a nearby cemetery were conducted by our chaplain.

His faithful orderly, "Parsons," whom he always referred to as "the old family retainer" was with him to the last.

That was essentially the story that others told as well. Arthur Snyder wrote from somewhere in Italy:

> The same shell that killed John wounded me in the hip. You will be relieved to know that Jack did not suffer—he was killed instantly. I remained with his body for some time until relief came to relieve me of command of my tanks. . . .
>
> Jack was his same old self that day at Palestrina—full of fun, & a marvelous example of courage and efficiency on the battlefield. We were having trouble with some Tiger tanks that were firing on us from high ground. They caused me heavy losses. Jack and I put on a coordinated attack which drove the Germans back. We were just reaching our objective when our forward C.P. was shelled. . . .
>
> We have felt that there will never be his like again, but we find some comfort in knowing he did not suffer. He came to his end in great glory & now rests in a grave well cared for on Anzio Beachhead.

When he told the story many years later, Glenn Rathbun remembered what happened as clearly as he had ten minutes after it happened.

> Jack had the telephone between his knees. I was on one side of him and Lt. [Harold] Wigetman [Third Battalion S-2] was on the other. Col. Snyder was just outside. . . . The barn had a tile roof but no loft. The mangers were full of my communications section. My shoulder was touching Jack's shoulder, when the tank let go his first round. The second came a few seconds later. Both were H.E. and hit in the tile roof. The three of us moved like scalded cats for the forward stone wall. All three of us sub-consciously had ourselves pre-programmed within a few minutes of entering the barn where the safest spot was. We were all on the move the instant the first shot hit. My next move was to move out the back door. It had been open but as I looked for it there was nothing but blackness. Years of dust now in the air made me think for a few seconds that the whole barn had collapsed over us. Then in a minute I saw the opening and was on my way out. The Lt. was right behind me. I saw Col. Snyder laying on the ground by his radio. He was pulling at his left hip and I could see blood oozing out the ragged hole in his pants. Col. Toffey had not come out of the door and my next move was back into the barn. By that time the dust in the air had cleared enough to let me see Jack huddled against the front wall. I moved quickly and

spoke to him. He did not move. I knew instantly he was dead or had been knocked out. I checked on him by touching his shoulder, he did not move or make a sound. His eyes were open but seeing nothing. I knew then I had lost another friend. I turned to the mangers to find three EMs dead and four wounded to some degree. I called Capt. Flynn and he got the medics on their way. I peeked around the corner of the barn at the tank. He was gone, having only left his calling card. The medics arrived and laid Jack on a stretcher, covering him with a GI blanket. This they put on a jeep (his own) and his driver slowly drove him away. I stood there quietly, letting a few tears run down my cheeks.

From Hugh MacDiarmid in Cincinnati we learned another detail. Ned Blackwood, operator of the Standard Oil station we had patronized there, had been on Anzio with the Seventh Infantry. He was standing "less than five feet" from Dad "when it happened."

Benny Reece's sister wrote, too. She enclosed a picture of the young lieutenant's infant son and copies of Dad's letters to her family at the time of Reece's death. To Mom she offered this sympathetic understanding:

> Altho we loved Ben dearly, don't think that I don't realize that it's so much worse, in a way, for one to lose their husband. It'll be harder too, to overcome the empty-gone sort of feeling. For with a loving husband with you to help you it's just easier to bear our sorrows. But there's always One who can help us when *everything* else fails.

Mark Clark wrote to express his "sadness and sympathy" at Dad's death "in action during the intense Fifth Army offensive which resulted in the capture of Rome."

> Colonel Toffey represented the finest type of American combat leader. Throughout his overseas service he continuously distinguished himself as an extraordinarily able commander of fighting troops. In Tunisia, in Sicily, during the gruelling winter campaign here in Italy last year and throughout the hardships of the Anzio Beachhead period his performance was always outstanding and he was a mainstay of his regiment. After he was wounded in Tunisia he took active steps to get back into a fighting outfit so that he could have another crack at the Boche.

I have heard from many sources how much he was admired and beloved by the troops he so successfully led in battle up to the moment when he gave his life at the front sharing their dangers as he carried out his combat duties. I know also how much his close friends thought of him, including Charlie Saltzman, Bill Ibold, and other members of my staff, and how much his loss has meant to them.

Please accept my deepest sympathy to yourself and your two children. I would appreciate it if you would convey my sympathy also to Jack's mother.

When Colonel Joe Crawford returned to the States, he wrote, too, touching on a theme recurrent in Dad's letters.

Three days before he was killed I saw him after having joined another division and being absent for some time. In conversation, he told me that he would like to get home and see you for a while, and then he would be ready to fight again. He looked well but very tired when I saw him.

My regiment was fighting next to Jack's when he was killed. The shock of his loss almost made me lose my nerve, and I can imagine what a blow it must have been to you.

If I can do anything for you or for his children please call on me. He was awfully proud of you all.

Robert White, still recuperating in Veterans Hospitals, wrote, as did Walter Parsons. Parsons, in fact, wrote often from France and Germany as the Seventh Infantry fought on. When he returned to the States a year later, he came to call bringing a duffel bag full of souvenirs, and then remained in correspondence with us for several years.

George Biddle, whom we would see again later that summer, sent along to Mom letters he had received about Dad, as well as letters that men of the Fifteenth Infantry had written to him when they learned of Dad's death. Jo Kindlarski, who took no prisoners and collected German mess gear for his mother's picnic table, said, "We had quite a few Bn. Commanders since Col. Toffey. But there wasn't or will be one like him. I sure would like to see him read your book & everyone says the same thing." Jack Woods described Dad's death this way:

He was in the forward CP when a tank threw a few rounds into the CP house—after the first one hit they were lying on the floor and a later round exploded and a fragment hit Jack in the back of the head and killed him instantly. He was never conscious before he died nor did he know what hit him. We were thankful that he didn't suffer. This all happened on the way into Rome probably 20 miles south. Parsons, his orderly, took him back to Anzio where he was buried.

These accounts tell the story as I grew up with it. Only in recent years has another version of Dad's death come to light. In it, Dad went forward to make a personal reconnaissance, taking with him a radio operator and a Sherman tank, which followed fifty to a hundred yards behind. From a vantage point upstairs in a farmhouse, Dad spotted a German observation post in a nearby house. He had the radioman tell the tank to fire on the enemy position, but the tanker mistook the house Dad was in for the one the Germans were in and opened fire, killing Dad and the radio operator. Russell W. Cloer, in whose memoir this version appears, calls it "fact" and the other "for consumption by the family and the public."[9] In his memoir, Isadore Valenti, a medic in K Company, recalls seeing Dad and a red-haired first lieutenant dead in the ruins of a stone house. He says he was told that the two officers had gone "forward to coordinate the actions of the 2nd and 3rd Battalions."[10] Valenti's account, like Cloer's, seems to separate Dad and the other officer from Rathbun, Snyder, Blackwood, and others at the battalion command post. Neither Rathbun nor Snyder mentions another officer being killed by the shell that killed Dad, but Nathan White, in his regimental history, says that Dad and First Lieutenant John Raney were killed by the same shell.[11]

Colonel Ashton Manhart, who had commanded the Fifteenth when Biddle was with it in the fall of 1943, wrote to Biddle as well.

Today I am mailing to Mrs. Toffey the copy of "An American Artist's Story"[12] which you gave to Jack last fall and which I had borrowed. I shall also be compelled to write a note of sympathy, which I don't relish. Jack prized the book highly and his going was the worst thing for me in this war when going is such a commonplace thing. He was a fine man and an exceptional leader. I shall always feel that perhaps he was kept overseas a little longer than his odds allowed.

With the borrowed copy of *An American Artist's Story* came Colonel Manhart's note of condolence to Mom. He said that Dad had prized the book because of the great admiration that existed between Dad and Biddle. Then he added,

My expression of sympathy is belated and perhaps superfluous. I thought Jack was one of the finest men I'd even known and the feeling was equal in the hearts of all the men in the 15th Infantry. He served his country well and we're told that's the highest expression of a soldier.

As his friend, I shall offer to you any help that might ever be necessary.

From Fifth Army Headquarters Charlie Saltzman wrote to Biddle, too:

I share fully your sorrow at the loss of Jack Toffey. I have known him well for ten years, and although I had seen relatively little of him in recent years, he was the kind of friend with whom that made no difference. After long absences one could always pick it up right where we had left it. I gather from people who served with him in combat, including yourself, that he was a superlatively good battalion commander from every point of view.

To Mom, Saltzman wrote,

You know how much those of us who knew and loved him share your loss. When I wrote before I tried to tell you how great a loss it is to the army, for it is clear that he approached the ideal as a fighting commander. Can't you imagine how, when the going was toughest and everyone was tense, he could ease them off by some priceless little remark here and there as he went around doing his job superbly. What a guy! Everyone who knew him in action says he was magnificent.

In November 1944, Biddle published a collection of his war drawings. He devotes the last quarter of the preface to Dad.

Compensations for war's sterility are the adventures, the comradeship, the flashes of heroism—moments that stand out as stars falling from a darkened sky. One such impact was my brief acquaintance with Lieutenant Colonel John J. Toffey, Jr., Commanding Officer of the Second

Battalion of the Fifteenth regiment. It would be prosaic to say that his mind was brilliant, his presence sunshine or a clap of thunder on a summer's day, his gorgeous shining physique a source of imparted energy. He singled moments from war's drab scrap-heap and left them with me, etched sharply and in clear profile. As when he stood over that dying shadow, among the night's rocks above the Volturno, and whispered into it: "The stretchers are coming up, kid. Hang on. Atta-boy." As he ran toward Captain Bergdorf who was staggering toward us, the blood streaming down his neck: "Easy, Bergy, easy. Lay your head against the bedding-roll. For Christ's sake, Sergeant, open a first-aid kit." As he barked to Corporal Kindlarski: "I think we have the machine-gun nest surrounded up there among the rocks, Jo, go get 'em—and don't bring 'em back." But mostly I remember his warmth and intelligent curiosity about life, as we sat in some peasant's hut eating pig-meat and C-ration crackers with red wine, the gasoline flickering from the can.

He had been wounded at Maknassy and after the long hospitalization insisted on coming back to the regiment. Once he said to me: "If I had to do it again, I wonder if I wouldn't look for a swivel chair?" Even he was getting tired. From the Anzio beachhead came a letter: "I sure need a rest. Don't they ever put subs into this ball game?" I wrote him on the day he should have entered Rome. I said: "God, I wish I were with you. And, Jack, keep your spirits up."

Two days previously he had been instantly killed, without pain. There is no better way to die. But I wish more of us older men could get killed in this war. Not his generation. Not Jack.

I think the boys of the Second Battalion of the "Can Do" Regiment—Eisenhower's and Mark Clark's old Regiment—would approve my dedicating these random sketches to the living memory of Lieutenant Colonel John J. Toffey, Jr.[13]

Anne and I got letters too, beautiful and touching expressions of love and sympathy from aunts and an occasional uncle. Uncle Billy and Aunt Marie Beach were salmon fishing in Canada when the telegram came. Uncle Billy's letter to me dated June 27 summed things up.

Dear John,

You have had a great sorrow come to you and a loss you will never forget. You are now the man of the family and you will have to assume the responsibilities that will be hard for one of your age. Just remember what your father would have had you do. Don't forget what your mother has been through and her great sorrow.

I am writing you as a young man for though you have not reached that age you must endeavor to live up to it. Always remember Johnny that you will have me to come to and don't hesitate to call on me for advice or when you think I can be of help to you in any way. I will see you before long in Great Neck and we can have a heart to heart talk.

I just can't tell you my feelings but my heart is with you all.

Affectionately,

"Uncle Billy"

N.B. Throw your shoulders back and keep your head in the air.

And there came expressions of condolence from classmates and friends, many of these no doubt mandated and even dictated by parents. I especially liked one letter from the father of a friend.

Dear John:

A letter like this takes a good many cigarets burned down to the stub and a lot of thought; it's a hard letter to write.

But it's just an effort of an outsider to tell you that you had a pretty grand Dad, and that I know that you feel his loss very, very deeply. It's an easy thing to say he died a hero for his country, and that statement goes for so many grand fellows these days that it has become a set phrase that doesn't mean a whole lot to outsiders. But when it hits close to you, your grief is just as great had he been hit by a street car, or died of pneumonia at home.

I guess the best thing to do is to remember him as he was in life, and try to and be the kind of man he would want you to be. That's a big order, and it will take a lot of doing, as he was a man's man.

About a week before your accident I talked to a Canal Winchester officer—home on a short leave—who knew your Dad, and didn't have a chance to tell you about it. Anyway, he said your Dad was one of the best officers he ever knew, and that his men idolized him. He said that Col. Toffey never asked a man to do a thing that he wouldn't do himself, and that his soldiers knew it, and respected him highly for it. I asked him, "Why is it Col. Toffey has been in action for so long without a rest?" His answer was: "He's too good a man to spare. They don't turn out officers like the colonel in 90 days."

So you see, you've got quite a reputation to live up to. And I know it won't be too hard for you, as you have a good start. I know that your Dad would be tremendously proud of you if he knew how fine you have been in recent days, bearing up under your trouble.

Two other letters written in the spring of 1944 are revealing as well, though they were not written to Mom or to us in Columbus. On June 28, three days after we got the telegram, General Truscott wrote as follows:

Lieut. General L. J. McNair
Headquarters, Army Ground Forces
Washington, D.C.
Dear General McNair:

You have probably heard that young Jack Toffey was killed in action near Valmontone, Italy, on June 3rd. He was a gallant soldier and I feel a distinct personal loss. I considered him one of the finest officers I have ever known.

You will recall that he commanded a battalion in the 60th Infantry in my landing at Port Lyautey. He remained in the 9th Division until the end of the Sicilian campaign when he transferred to the 3rd Division. He commanded a battalion in the 15th Infantry with distinction until shortly before I received your letter of April 8th, when he was made Executive Officer of the 7th Infantry, which he was at the time of his death. Toffey commanded a battalion in action longer than any other battalion commander in this theater.

When I received your letter of April 8th I went out to see Toffey and found him to be in excellent spirits. I had known previously that he was somewhat depressed and I realized that he needed a change in assignment. It was for that reason that he was made executive Officer of the 7th Infantry as soon as it could be done. I saw him frequently and valued his friendship highly. I hope that you will extend to his mother and wife my deepest sympathy.

My headquarters was relieved by IV Corps on the 11th of June near Torquina. We are now in the Naples area awaiting the next step. While the siege on the beachhead was long and, at times, a bit difficult, it was productive of many lessons. You would have been proud, indeed, of the development there in our artillery technique. Our troops distinguished themselves in the final attack from the beach. While all of the Divisions were good, the 3rd, 1st Armored, and the 36th deserve special attention. The operation by which the 36th captured Velletri and the Colli Laziali is almost a classic.

I trust you are well. With best regards always, I am

Sincerely,

L. K. Truscott, Jr.

Major general, U. S. Army

Commanding

So General McNair did at least inquire about Dad. This the lieutenant general did through the chain of command by asking the major general, who had seen Dad and reassigned him as executive officer of the Seventh before he got McNair's letter. On July 1, General McNair got off a quick note to General Truscott thanking him for his letter about Dad, which McNair said he would promptly forward to Deo, knowing she "will be comforted very greatly by your kind words and thoughtfulness." He went on to say, rather surprisingly, "I was interested in young Jack rather particularly because he and my youngster grew up together and entered West Point as classmates."[14]

Meanwhile, in Columbus, Mom continued to deal with the aftermath of Dad's death. Along with the letters of condolence came citations posthumously awarding Dad a Purple Heart (his third) and an Oak Leaf Cluster to his Silver Star (his second). Then came what the Army Services Forces called "personal effects," the first of which was in the form of a check for $14.17. Then in Dad's metal footlocker came his Combat Infantry Badge and other decorations, a magnifying class, a pen and pencil set, a Hermann Goering Division armband, a pair of civilian shoes, a souvenir map of Sicily, some photos in a folder, scarves, his OD blouse and "pink" trousers, and a trench coat. And finally there came a glasses case "damaged, apparently by bloodstain." Before sending the case, a lieutenant wrote to ask if Mom wanted it, saying, "It is our desire to refrain from sending any article which would be distressing; at the same time, we do not feel justified in removing the item without your consent."

And there were other matters to attend to as well. There were pensions due to Mom, Anne, and me as surviving next of kin. From the Social Security Administration Mom learned that she would receive $21.91 a month as Dad's widow, Anne would get $14.61, and I would get $14.60. I didn't understand why Anne was entitled to a penny more than I was, unless it was because I might be able to get a job sooner. The Veterans Administration added another $78.00 for Mom, $22.80 for me, and $22.00 for Anne. Though these amounts would change in time, the three of us would begin our new husbandless, fatherless life compensated with $174.72 a month. To receive this money Mom had to fill out countless forms and provide documentation of Dad's military service and his death. Even a little bank near Fort Dix where Mom and Dad had kept a joint account required similar documentation before it could drop Dad's name from the account.

But Mom wanted and perhaps needed something to do. What might she do with her love of the written and spoken word, her sense of humor, her flare for the dramatic? Teach. She wrote to Dr. Samuel Shellabarger,[15] headmaster of the Columbus School for Girls, seeking a position teaching English. Dr. Shellabarger had nothing at the time, he said, but thought something might open later in the summer. It did, and in September Mom found herself employed for the first time in her life, teaching freshman and sophomore girls in the school that she had attended and Anne was attending.

As the aftermath wore on, there was the matter of "Disposition of World War II Armed Forces Dead," as a pamphlet from the War Department put it. The pamphlet explained that there were four options, three of which applied to us: "The remains be interred in a permanent American military cemetery overseas; The remains be returned to the United States, or any possession or territory thereof, for interment by next of kin in a private cemetery; The remains be returned to the United States for interment in a national cemetery." If none of these was satisfactory, next of kin could submit a specific desire to the Quartermaster General.

Though the decision was technically Mom's, she felt strongly that Deo should have a say in the matter. Probably the decision came down to a choice between the first and third options. When Jack Senior died in 1936, he was buried at Arlington National Cemetery with honors befitting his rank. Deo would join him there when her time came. To bring Dad's body back and have it buried there with the same honors must have been a compelling option. However, back then, the quick return of flag-draped, ice-packed caskets by plane to Dover Air Force Base was many years in the future; it might be years before bodies would be coming home. To have Dad's body brought home for eventual burial at Arlington would have meant for all the family a revival of all the grief that had attended the War Department telegram.

Meanwhile, there was some question whether the temporary cemetery would become a permanent facility under the jurisdiction and supervision of the United States government. If so, then Deo and Mom would leave Dad's remains there. If not, he would come back to Arlington. At last assurance came, and the two women who loved him agreed that Dad would lie near where he first had been buried—in the military cemetery at Nettuno, once part of the Anzio beachhead. As one visitor described the place:

> The Cemetery is situated in a quiet spot within a half mile of the town and within a mile of the sea. Immediately to the north is an olive grove and in the distance the Alban Hills. Immediately to the South, there is another grove of olives and in the distance the towns of Anzio and Nettuno.
>
> The scene at the beautiful level field of the Cemetery, with the fertile plains and distant hills, is like that of Southern California. There is no sense of strangeness—only peace. . . .
>
> The Cemetery is in large grass plots, the greenest I have even seen. Around its walls are the olive groves and hazel and myrtle trees and in season the rambler rose. Jack's grave is the second grave from the graveled walk near the center of the Cemetery and in full sight of the Flag.[16]

This cemetery, then, replaced the one that General Truscott had visited on Memorial Day 1944 and spoken of in the letter to his wife. To that same cemetery a year later, on Memorial Day 1945, the war in Europe over for less than a month, Truscott returned to attend services. Bill Mauldin went, too, and described what he saw and heard there that day. Among the VIPs in a row of chairs directly in front of the speakers' platform sat several members of the Senate Armed Services Committee.

> When Truscott spoke, he turned away from the visitors and addressed himself to the corpses he had commanded here. It was the most moving gesture I ever saw. It came from a hard-boiled old man who was incapable of planned dramatics. The general's remarks were brief and extemporaneous. He apologized to the dead men for their presence here. He said everybody tells leaders it is not their fault that men get killed in war, but that every leader knows in his heart this is not altogether true. He said he hoped anybody here through any mistake of

his would forgive him, but he realized that was asking a lot under the circumstances. One of the Senator's cigars went out; he bent to relight it, then thought better of it. Truscott said he would not speak about the glorious dead because he didn't see much glory in getting killed in your late teens or early twenties. He promised that if in the future he ran into anybody, especially old men, who thought death in battle was glorious, he would straighten them out. He said he thought that was the least he could do.[17]

The most grimly ironic of all the papers connected with Dad's death is a memo that General Clark wrote to General Gruenther, his chief of staff, on June 7, 1944—four days after Dad was killed. The first paragraph reads as follows:

> In talking with Truscott this afternoon, he told me of Toffey's death, Hightower's[18] serious wound and the disabilities of many of our key battle-trained officers. I wish you would have prepared a memorandum to corps commanders telling them to give me the names of a reasonable number of officers who have had long and successful battle experience—those who are natural-born leaders and who will make the general officers of the next war.[19] Tell them in the memorandum that I intend communicating with General Marshall and General McNair to the effect that these men should be returned home—each one guaranteed a promotion and an assignment to an appropriate training job. In other words, I am sending them home because they are too valuable to risk in further combat.[20]

I can almost hear Dad's reaction when the order came down from Army to Corps to Division to Regiment. "It's about goddamn time they substituted in this game."

All these years later, it seems as though life in the summer of 1944 was a lot like life before Dad's death, only without the letters. It was still Mom, Anne, and I, just as it had been for the almost twenty months that Dad was overseas. While he was away, I hadn't thought seriously about Dad's not coming home. Mom, on the other hand, must have been unable to put from her mind for very long the image of the dreadful telegram. Still, she kept her fear from Anne and me, just as she and Dad had kept from us their prewar worries about making it through the Depression.

After a trip east to be with Dad's family, we returned to Columbus to start the new school year. In her new teaching job, Mom was teaching girls whom I was seeing socially. How I hoped that she would not entertain her pupils with cute anecdotes or snapshots of my infancy. Between Mom's salary and the government pensions, we were getting along. Mom began to have gentlemen callers.

One of these was a distant cousin of Dad's. Learned and witty, with an explosive laugh, he owned and directed a small boarding school in Connecticut. Though he was some seventeen years older than Mom, she saw in him, I think, a secure world of ideas and books. When they married in 1946, we said good-bye to Columbus.

That fall I went to Exeter, as Dad had. As the train began to carry me away, Mom trotted along the platform and called out her parting words. "If you have a stomach ache, don't let them give you a laxative!"

In Exeter's butt rooms I learned to smoke and play bridge. In her classrooms I sat in awe and occasional trepidation before the men who taught me the stuff of secondary education. Later I realized how much I admired them. Many men on the Exeter faculty had been there when Dad was, but I don't recall any of them ever saying, "I knew your father when he was here."

One master, however, did have a story about Dad. In early June 1944, Robert Bates arrived on the beach at Nettuno and was in the Third Division's rear area when Dad's body was brought back. The mood at division headquarters was somber enough that Bates asked why and who. An Exeter graduate, Bates left the army a lieutenant colonel and returned to Exeter to teach in 1946, the year I arrived. While looking over a student list one day, he saw my name. It sounded familiar. Then he recalled the scene two years earlier. While I was at Exeter, he never told me, though he did tell one of my classmates. Not until we met at a reunion many years later did the story come out.[1]

In February of my upper-middle (junior) year, my sister Barbara was born. In my senior year, the man who handled matters of college entrance told me that I was going to Yale. I would not be alone. About two-thirds of the graduating class would go to Harvard, Yale, or Princeton. It seemed like a good time to be going to college.

In the summer of 1950, however, two events of consequence occurred. First the Democratic People's Republic of Korea invaded the Republic of Korea, and the United Nations authorized the use of military force against the northern invader. Second, my stepfather got up one morning and left my mother.

I returned to college that fall even more confused than I would normally have been at that age. The draft loomed. I decided I would go on my terms. These included dropping out of college at midyear, enlisting in the army, and going to Officer Candidate School. After processing at Governors Island, I was told I would be called up sometime in the spring. Meanwhile, Mom had decided we would return to Columbus. A Mayflower van picked up our belongings, and Mom, Anne, Barbara, and I set out on the well-beaten path in a maroon Ford that had replaced the venerable blue Plymouth.

Home this time was a red-brick townhouse on East Broad Street just west of an early strip mall. Anne, who had skipped a grade or two, returned to the Columbus School for Girls as a junior. On my twentieth birthday I was sworn into the army and sent to basic training in the Third Armored Division at Fort Knox, Kentucky.

In a memory softened by time, basic training wasn't bad. We marched, did pushups and squat jumps, fired basic infantry weapons, laughed a lot, and went to Louisville when we got weekend passes. After basic and a couple of weeks of Leadership School, I was off to OCS at Fort Benning.

In choosing the infantry as my branch, I was unconscious of Dad's admonition in a 1943 letter to Mom that I "stay the hell out of the army" in general and the infantry in particular. I felt that I was maintaining the tradition of my father, grandfather, and great-grandfather. Besides, I already knew the words to "Far Above the Chattahoochee." Tough as it was, the training in the 160 days it took to make my classmates and me officers and gentlemen was the best I had in the army.

We graduated on June 19, 1952. In my new Class A khakis and with the lacquer still on my gold bars, I gave a dollar to the first enlisted person to salute me and went home on leave. Here I bought my first car, a green 1948 Dodge coupe, in which I drove to Fort Dix and my first commissioned assignment: cadre in the Thirty-ninth Infantry Regiment, Ninth Infantry Division, now a basic training outfit. The coincidence of my assignment meant little to me at the time, but the return address on my letters to Mom must have brought back to her unpleasant memories of the anxiety she had felt in July and August 1943.

If my being in the Thirty-ninth Infantry at Fort Dix caused Mom anguish, how must she have felt at my being ordered to the Far East? Home on leave, I reminded her that as the sole surviving son of someone killed in the recent war, I was not to go into combat. She did not let me know how worried she was as she put me on the plane that would take me to Fort Lewis, Washington, and on to what my orders called FECOM, for Far East Command. I arrived at the Camp Drake Replacement Depot, outside of Tokyo, and was immediately shipped out to the army's chemical, biological, and radiological school at Eta Jima, an island in the Inland Sea near Hiroshima.

Then one night I was on a troopship bound for Pusan, South Korea. Next a train took us north to Seoul, where we were assigned to our new units and trucked forward. I missed Dad's old Third Division, alighting instead at the headquarters of a 4.2-inch mortar battalion under Eighth Army control. One morning, while trying to remember what I had ever learned about fire missions and the care and cleaning of the 4.2-inch mortar, I was told to report to the battalion commander. "You're not supposed to be here," he said. "There's a truck going south right after chow. Be on it."

So ended my time at the front. Back through the pipeline I went to Camp Drake, where I remained as cadre. A hitch as permanent party in a replacement depot is not a foundation on which to build a military career.

But then, for a noncombatant infantryman, not much else is, either. My time up, I reverted to civilian life.

As a twenty-three-year-old ex-army officer, I was pretty sure I was too sophisticated to go back to being a sophomore in college. Instead, in the basement of a Columbus bank, I microfilmed thousands of canceled checks. When the management told me that soon they'd promote me to repossessing people's furniture, I enrolled at Ohio State, bringing with me most of my Yale credits and picking up more for having been a second lieutenant. At Ohio State I became an English major, and Homer and I resumed our ritual on autumn Saturdays.

Anne had graduated from CSG while I was overseas and had followed her mother and grandmother to Wells College. Two years later, she dropped out to marry the man she had picked out six years earlier. The wedding was in Great Neck, the honeymoon in Europe. Thus did Anne first visit Dad's grave in Nettuno.

In my last year at Ohio State I was told by an especially erudite professor that I should go to graduate school—where he had gone, of course, and where after a year of Anglo-Saxon, Middle English, Chaucer, and other heady seminars, I decided to take a break from formal studies.

As I wondered what to do next, I again overlooked Dad's recommendation to Mom that I go into law or medicine. Teaching seemed good, though. Perhaps I hadn't yet found a snappy comeback to those who asked, "What does majoring in English prepare you for except teaching?" Mom, of course, had been teaching, and from her Anne and I had inherited a love of literature. Furthermore, outside of Homer and my great-uncles, the men with whom I had most closely associated since Dad had gone overseas were teachers.

Kent School, in Connecticut, hired me to teach English and help coach football. In my first year I taught to four sections of sophomores a survey of British literature in which we read Chaucer in the original, and the football team was undefeated. That spring my roommate, a rookie math teacher, described vividly a beautiful girl he had seen in town. She was, it turned out, the local kindergarten teacher and the daughter of one of the town's most respected families. I contrived to meet her, and in the summer of 1958 Irene and I married.

A year and a half earlier Mom had married a Columbus attorney, and she and Barbara now lived in his charming country house on the edge of Canal Winchester, thirteen miles southeast of Columbus. Mom seemed happy and comfortably secure as the wife of a successful attorney and country squire. On a trip to Europe she got to see Dad's grave.

After years in the academic world, Anne and her husband bought property on Maine's Penobscot Bay. Here over the years they built the house in which they would spend their summers and to which they eventually retired.

In the 1950s and early 1960s, the older generation died. While I was at Fort Knox, Granny died in Columbus. Uncle Billy preceded Aunt Marie to Brooklyn's Greenwood Cemetery. In 1962, Homer died and was buried beside Granny in Columbus's Greenlawn Cemetery. The legendary Woody Hayes, Homer's admired friend and Ohio State football coach, served as a pallbearer. Deo had been able to visit her son's grave shortly after the war. When she died in 1963, we buried her next to Jack Senior in Arlington National Cemetery. After Deo's death, Arcenio made one trip to his native Philippines before settling among numerous cousins, nieces, and nephews in New York City. He continued to visit Anne and me and our families, doting on our children as he had on us a generation earlier. He died in 1982.

Irene and I lived on at Kent, where I taught and coached, and where our first three children were born. Unaccustomed as I was to staying put, after seven good years at the school, I left to take a job at the Columbus Academy. Though I had moved a lot in my life, Irene never had. In taking her to Columbus, I was removing her by a long day's drive from the town in which she had always lived.

Two months after we arrived, our fourth child was born. At the Academy I worked among men whose student I had been twenty years earlier. Two more cases of the six-year itch marked my professional career. The first brought us back east, this time an hour's drive up the lovely Housatonic River valley from Kent. The second did not necessitate family deracination. In 1982, on a recruiting mission to Saudi Arabia, I was able to stop over in Rome long enough to visit Dad's grave. In 1995, after twenty years on the last job, I retired, and Irene and I remained in the house from which our children had gone off to colleges, careers, and parenthood.

In January 1987, Mom's husband died, and she moved into a retirement home in Columbus. Here, with the opera broadcasts and an everregenerating supply of taped books, she spent the last nine years of her life as comfortably as her age and health would permit. Having lived to meet some of her great-grandchildren, she died suddenly in February 1996. In Union Grove Cemetery, just outside Canal Winchester, her remains are next to her last husband's. Still, as she talked to Anne and me during her last years, the times she always recalled with greatest happiness were the years with Dad.

NOTES

CHAPTER 1. THE FIRST LETTER

1. The staff of Lane Libraries, Hamilton, Ohio, has graciously recalled these details for me.

2. All quotations pertaining to Hershberger's death are from the *Cincinnati Inquirer*, August 3, 1940.

3. The national statistics in this paragraph are from Doris Kearns Goodwin, *No Ordinary Time* (New York, 1995), 42–43.

4. Chester Wilmot, *The Struggle for Europe* (New York, 1952), 31–32.

5. *Cincinnati Inquirer*, August 3, 1940.

6. Frank E. Vandiver, *Illustrious Americans: John J. Pershing* (Morristown, N.J., 1967), 228.

7. *New York Times*, August 8, 1940.

8. *Jersey City Journal*, November 13, 1934.

CHAPTER 2. YOUNG JACK

1. Documents pertaining to Jack Senior's service, unless otherwise noted, are from the New Jersey State Archives and the New Jersey Adjutant General's office.

2. M. Blumenson, *Patton: The Man Behind the Legend, 1885–1945* (New York, 1985), 62.

3. Quoted from an unsigned summary of Jack Senior's service record attached to a letter from William N. Beach to Frank H. Smith dated July 22, 1932, in the New Jersey State Archives.

4. Ernie Pyle, *Home Country* (New York, 1947), 14.

5. Descriptions of Exeter in 1925 drawn from H. D. Curwen, ed., *Exeter Remembered* (Exeter, 1965).

6. CMTC material from Donald Kingston, *Forgotten Summers* (San Francisco, 1995).

7. Porter Sargent Staff. *Handbook of Independent Schools* 1927, 130, and *Cheshire Academy Alumni Magazine*, Summer 2000.

8. College quotations from the Wells College *Cardinal* 1930, 35; courtesy of the Wells College Alumni Office. "A Little Hut in Hoboken," words by Arthur Schwartz, music by Herman Hupfield, from *The Little Show*, 1929. Song background courtesy of the Hoboken Public Library. Hupfield, of course, did better with something called *As Time Goes By*.

9. Apparently the Wilson Company acquired the rights to the painting and used it to promote their line of athletic equipment. In their version the fishing rod has given way to a couple of Wilson balls. On the advertising flyer, local purveyors of Wilson products could put their names and addresses beneath the picture.

10. Wedding details from accounts in the *Columbus Citizen*, August 18, 1930, and *New York Evening Post*, August 25, 1930.

11. Sources for information about Jack Senior's appointment from various issues of the *New York Times* and correspondence from the New Jersey State Archives.

12. Information on Dad's National Guard service from the New Jersey Adjutant General's office.

CHAPTER 3. FORT DIX AND THE FORTY-FOURTH DIVISION

1. For example, in Boston on September 11, 1940. Quoted, among other places, in William Langer and S. Everett Gleason, *The Undeclared War of 1940– 1941* (Gloucester, 1968), 202.

2. *New York Times*, September 14, 1940.

3. Ibid., September 21, 1940.

4. Langer and Gleason, *Undeclared War*, 20.

5. Accounts of training at Ft. Dix from various reports in the *New York Times*, September and October 1940.

6. *New York Times*, October 8, 1940.

7. K. R. Greenfield, R. R. Palmer, and B. I. Wiley, *The Army Ground Forces: The Organization of Combat Troops* (Washington, 1947), 1, 48.

8. *New York Times*, July 17, 1941.

9. Letter to his "Grandma," while "On Picket near the Rappahanock [sic]," Dec. 27, 1862. Typed copy of this and other of John's letters in the possession of the author.

10. Letter to his parents dated April 17, 1865.

11. Letter to his "Grandma," dated July 11, 1865.

12. Report dated August 16, 1941. Carbon copy in the possession of the author.

13. Copy of McCormick's script provided by the McCormick Research Center, Wheaton, Illinois.

14. Langer and Gleason, *Undeclared War*, 743.

15. Issue of September 15, 1941.

16. Drum quoted in *New York Times*, October 4, 1941.

17. See C. R. Gabel, *The U.S. Army GHQ Maneuvers of 1941* (Washington, 1992).

18. *New York Times*, October 9, 1940.

19. Quoted in Greenfield, Palmer, and Wiley, *Army Ground Forces*, 46.

20. Letter dated December 30, 1941. Original in the possession of the author.

CHAPTER 4. COAST TO COAST, 1942

1. Duncan Hines, *Adventures in Good Eating* (Bowling Green, 1941), 127. According to Hines, breakfasts at the hotel cost between thirty-five and sixty cents, lunches forty cents and up, and dinners eighty cents and up.

2. Jack A. Marshall, who as a new second lieutenant was in the regiment thus transferred, in conversation with the author, May 2, 2003.

3. References to General Eddy in this chapter are from H. G. Phillips's excellent biography *The Making of a Professional: Manton S. Eddy USA* (Westport, 2000).

4. *Logistics in World War II: Final Report of the Army Service Forces* (Washington, 1948), 15.

5. Hines, *Adventures*, 45. Meal prices were a little steeper than at the Irvin Cobb, though. Breakfast was a dollar, lunch $1.50, dinner $1.75.

6. Fred Fisher's biography in a letter from his son to the author dated November 14, 2002.

7. See Phillips, *Making of a Professional*.

8. Ibid., 79.

9. Diary of General Truscott's aide, Truscott Papers, Box 18, George C. Marshall Foundation Library, Lexington, Va.

10. F. Gervasi, *The Violent Decade* (New York, 1989), 354.

11. Phillips, *Making of a Professional*, 83.

12. J. Wellard, *General George S. Patton, Jr.: Man Under Mars* (New York, 1946), 53.

13. Phillips, *Making of a Professional*, 84.

14. Lieutenant Colonel and Mrs. Richard Kent in conversation with the author, May 6, 2003.

1. R. Charles, *Troopships of World War II* (Washington, n.d.), 142. Photocopy of the page provided by Merwin "Whitey" Andell, who, as a member of the Sixtieth Infantry, sailed to North Africa on her. "Tombstone Annie" provided by Alphonse Zenka in conversation with the author, May 4, 2000.

2. Aide's Diary, Truscott Papers, Box 18, George C. Marshall Foundation, Lexington, Va.

3. D. S. Freeman, *Lee's Lieutenants* (New York, 1944), 1: xxix–xxx.

4. In a 1977 interview, General T. J. Conway, who as a lieutenant colonel participated in Operation Goalpost, suggested that the name alludes to the polo-playing days of Generals Truscott and Patton. See Army War College Senior Officers Debriefing Program, Conversation between General T. J. Conway and Col. Robert F. Esslin, Jr., Sept. 29, 1977, U.S. Army Military History Institute, Carlisle Barracks, Pa., 34.

5. Samuel Eliot Morison, *Operations in North African Waters October 1942–June 1943* (Edison, N.J., 2001), 33.

6. George Howe, *Northwest Africa: Seizing the Initiative in the West* (Washington, 1957), 158.

7. Lucian K. Truscott Jr., *Command Missions* (New York, 1954), 119.

8. Howe, *Northwest Africa*, 170, 173.

9. Dad's memo, dated 3 December 1942, Truscott Papers, Box 9, Folder 4, George C. Marshall Foundation, Lexington, Va.

10. Truscott, *Command Missions*, 534–535.

11. B. H. Liddell Hart, ed., *The Rommel Papers* (New York, 1953), 345.

12. Hans Von Luck, *Panzer Commander* (New York, 1989), 103–104.

13. Aljean Harmetz, *Round Up the Usual Suspects* (New York, 1992), 12. "The Army's got Casablanca—and so have Warner Brothers," one ad proclaimed (263). The Office of War Information barred the showing of the film to American troops in North Africa for fear of offending the Vichy French in the area (283–284).

14. Alfredo Vaiani, letter to the author dated March 20, 2000.

15. Dad's notes are in his copy of *The Army Officer's Notebook*. Property of the author.

16. Eleanor "Bumpy" Stevenson and Pete Martin, *I Knew Your Soldier* (Washington, 1944), 172–173.

17. Dad's driver, Robert White, whom we shall hear from shortly. Is this Walters the lieutenant we had met in the Officers Club at Fort Dix, the cousin of my hero Bucky Walters? That Dad refers to him only by his last name seems to suggest that we would know him.

18. Doris Kearns Goodwin, *No Ordinary Time* (New York, 1995), 405.

CHAPTER 6. TUNISIA

1. W. Thornton, "One Man's View of World War II," unpublished manuscript, Veterans Survey Collection, U.S. Army Military History Institute, Carlisle Barracks, Pa.

2. Lucian K. Truscott Jr., *Command Missions* (New York, 1990), 172–173.

3. Letter dated May 10, 1943, in possession of the author.

4. George Howe, *Northwest Africa: Seizing the Initiative in the West* (Washington, 1957), 519–520.

5. Ibid., 545.

6. Ibid., 549.

7. E. Lusk, "Personal Experience in the Battle of Maknassy in Tunisia," unpublished manuscript. Copy given by Lieutenant Colonel Lusk to the author.

8. "Der Kampf um den Maknassy-Pass," German recollection of the action by veterans of the *Kampfstaffel*, a copy given to the author by Lieutenant Colonel H. G. Phillips.

9. Rudolph Lang, "Report of the fighting of Kampfgruppe Lang in Tunisia," Historical Division, U.S. Army, Europe, 1947. U.S. Army Military History Institute, Carlisle Barracks, Pa.

10. Alfred Arens, Report of the fightings [*sic*] at Maknassy Pass in March / April 1943. Typescript provided by Lieutenant Colonel H. G. Phillips.

11. Lusk's account. See also "History of the 3rd Battalion, 60th Infantry, Maknassy Campaign, March 23–April 9, 1943," National Archives and Records Administration, College Park, Md. Record Group 407: 309 – INF (60) – 0.3.

12. Alphonse Zenka in conversation with the author, May 4, 2000.

13. Ernie Pyle, "Exhaustion," filed "Before Mateur." Clipped from an unidentified, undated newspaper.

14. General Omar Bradley, *A Soldier's Story* (New York, 1951), 64–65.

CHAPTER 7. ALGERIAN INTERLUDE

1. Northwestern University Medical School *Quarterly Bulletin* 27 (Summer 1953), 169.

2. Perhaps the general referred to is General John W. (Iron Mike) O'Daniel, who at the time was commanding the amphibious training center at Arzew, Algeria.

3. Ibold and Saltzman were with Fifth Army headquarters. Activated in December 1942 under the command of Lieutenant General Mark W. Clark, Fifth Army would not come into its own as a fighting unit until the invasion of Italy in September 1943.

4. Ernie Pyle, *Brave Men* (New York, 1944), 396.

5. General Omar Bradley, *A Soldier's Story* (New York, 1951), 97.

6. Ernie Pyle, *Here Is Your War* (New York, 1943), 264.

7. Ibid., 203.

8. Henry G. Phillips, *The Making of a Professional* (Westport, 2000), 117.

9. Ibid.

CHAPTER 8. SICILY

1. Carlo D'Este, *Bitter Victory: The Battle for Sicily, 1943* (New York, 1988), 346.

2. Samuel Eliot Morison, *Sicily, Salerno, Anzio* (Edison, N.J., 2001), 28. See also A. J. Birtle, *The U.S. Army Campaigns of World War II: Sicily* (Washington, 1999).

3. Quoted in Martin Blumenson, *Patton: The Man Behind the Legend, 1885–1945* (New York, 1985), 195.

4. Ibid.

5. Morison, *Sicily*, 70.

6. Birtle, *Army Campaigns*, 14.

7. Ibid., 14–15.

8. R. Wallace, et al., *The Italian Campaign* (Alexandria, 1978), 26.

9. Blumenson, *Patton*, 202.

10. Morison, *Sicily*, 181.

11. Ibid., 52.

12. W. O. Darby and W. Baumer, *Darby's Rangers: We Led the Way* (San Rafael, 1980), 104–105.

13. Ibid., 105.

14. J. Mittelman, *Eight Stars to Victory* (Washington, 1948), 127.

15. H. H. Semmes, *Portrait of Patton* (New York, 1955), 85, 187.

16. H. G. Phillips, *The Making of a Professional* (Westport, 2000), 122.

17. D'Este, *Bitter Victory*, 452.

18. Semmes, *Portrait*, 169.

19. Martin Blumenson, *The Patton Papers, 1940–1945* (Boston, 1974), 487.

20. The Goums (properly Goumiers) were Berber tribesmen from North Africa who had originally been recruited by the French and were led by French officers. The men of the Thirty-ninth had seen a bit of the Goums in the brief struggle against the French and later against the Germans in Tunisia, and had liked what they had seen. Black-eyed, with black beards and shaved heads, they wore tan turbans and black and brown Arab dress, sometimes over French-issue uniforms. Some were barefoot; others had developed a liking for German boots.

The Goums quickly lived up to their reputation as tough, primitive fighters. With good reason, Germans feared them. So did women. Around such fighters there naturally grew a mythology, according to which if a Goum drew his sword, he could not return it to its scabbard until it had tasted blood. It was also widely held that Goums were paid according to the number of enemy ears they brought back from battle. American officers were another source of supplemental income, paying ten or twenty dollars for German Luger pistols, which the Goums easily took off the Germans they slaughtered in their nocturnal forays. Among the believers of this mythology was the American soldier who wanted to buy a pair of German boots. The next morning his Goum supplier brought him a pair—with the legs still in them.

21. Army War College Senior Officers Oral History Program Project 78–4, General William C. Westmoreland interviewed by Col. D. G. Cameron and Lt. Col. R. E. Funderburk, 1978, U.S. Army Military History Institute, Carlisle Barracks, Pa., 104.

22. Quentin Reynolds, *The Curtain Rises* (New York, 1944), 214.

23. Ibid., 217.

24. George Biddle, *Artist at War* (Viking, 1944), 109.

25. A. Garland and H. M. Smyth, *Sicily and the Surrender of Italy* (Washington, 2002), 330.

26. Ibid., 336.

27. Ibid., 337.

28. Cameron and Funderburk interview, 105.

29. D'Este, *Bitter Victory*, 457–458.

30. H. A. Flint, "Operations, Thirty-ninth Infantry, 13 July to 15 August 1943," National Archives and Records Administration, College Park, Md. Record Group 407: 309 – INF (39) – 0.3, p. 3.

31. Garland and Smyth, *Sicily*, 345.

32. *New York Times*, August 5, 1943.

33. Ernie Pyle, "Our Men Get Nervous When the General Pins on Medals," newspaper column, n.d., courtesy of the Ernie Pyle State Historical Site, Dana, Ind.

34. Richard Tregaskis, *Invasion Diary* (New York, 1944), 73–74.

35. Reynolds, *The Curtain Rises*, 210.

36. B. S. Carter, letter dated July 27, 1943. United States Military Academy Library, West Point, N.Y., Library Special Collections.

37. Quoted in Benjamin Dickson, "A G-2 Journal: Algiers to the Elbe," unpublished ms., USMA Library Special Collections, 91.

38. Biddle, *Artist at War*, 103–104.

39. Pyle, "That War Weariness Really Gets You Down and Rest's the Only Cure," column, n.d., courtesy of the Ernie Pyle State Historical Site.

40. Garland and Smyth, *Sicily*, 417–418.

41. Omar N. Bradley and Clay Blair, *A General's Life* (New York, 1983), 200.

42. These are Bradley's figures (ibid.). Carlo D'Este has them slightly lower (*Bitter Victory*, 598). Garland and Smyth give total Allied casualties as 19,245 (*Sicily*, 417).

43. Bradley and Blair, *A General's Life*, 198.

CHAPTER 9. SUMMER INTERLUDES

1. D. G. McTaggart, "Bigwin Inn's greatest years were superb," *Muskoka Sun*, July 5, 1990, 33. According to McTaggart, in 1937 a room with bath cost $6 per person per day, American plan. Ibid., July 12, 1990, 33.

2. Written by General Alexander in 1947. Quoted in Martin Blumenson, *Salerno to Cassino* (Washington, 1993), 4.

3. Robert Wallace, *The Italian Campaign* (Alexandria, 1978), 19.

4. Omar Bradley and Clay Blair, *A General's Life* (New York, 1983), 203–204.

5. Lucian K. Truscott IV, *Rules of the Road* (New York, 1990), 196.

6. "Small Talk of the Town," *Newark Evening News*, September 30.

7. Ibid.

8. Blumenson, *Salerno to Cassino*, 56.

9. Louise Groody was already a star of the American musical stage when she played the lead in *No, No, Nanette* in 1925. That show, which made $2.5 million for Harry Frazee, far more than he got for sending Babe Ruth from Boston to the Yankees, opened on West Forty-sixth Street two years after the house that the Babe built opened in the Bronx. For more on the Babe and *No, No, Nanette*, see Dan Shaughnessy, *The Curse of the Bambino* (New York, 1990).

10. Apparently Dad's "disappearance" was not unauthorized. Thirty-ninth Infantry records during this period do not list him as being absent—with or without leave. See Morning Reports, Hq. Co., Thirty-ninth Infantry Regiment, NARA National Personnel Records Center, St. Louis, Mo.

CHAPTER 10. SOUTHERN ITALY

1. Quentin Reynolds, *The Curtain Rises* (New York, 1944), 319.

2. Winston Churchill, *Closing the Ring* (Boston, 1951), 142.

3. Ibid., 143.

4. Martin Blumenson, *Salerno to Cassino* (Washington, 1969), 158.

5. Ibid., 87.

6. Colonel Thomas A. Monroe was an old family friend. He had commanded the Fifteenth when it went into French Morocco. According to Robert McFarland's *History of the Fifteenth Infantry in World War II*, Monroe "may well have been the most senior officer in the entire U.S. Army at the rank of colonel. He may have incurred the wrath of General Marshall by taking a staff job instead of going to the Infantry School in 1932. When General Truscott took over the Third Division in March 1943, he said Monroe was too old and too overweight for combat, and sent him back to the states" (321).

7. The movements of the Fifteenth from its landing at Salerno to the Volturno River drawn from McFarland's history of the regiment.

8. Leslie W. Bailey, *Through Hell and High Water* (New York, 1994), 131.

9. George Biddle, *Artist at War* (New York, 1944), 178.

10. Ibid., 169.

11. Ibid.

12. Ibid., 170.

13. Ibid., 174.

14. J. Lardner, "Crossing the Volturno," *Newsweek*, October 25, 1943.

15. Biddle, *Artist at War*, 176–177.

16. Lucien K. Truscott Jr., Diary, October 17, 1943, George C. Marshall Foundation, Box 18, Folder 3.

17. McFarland, *Fifteenth Regiment*, 83.

18. Biddle, *Artist at War*, 184.

19. Ibid., 192.

20. Ibid., 194.

21. Ibid., 225, 227. Biddle's encomium of the four generals suggests that he had not heard from Bradley or Patton on the subject.

22. Ibid., 197.

23. Ibid., 204.

24. D. G. Taggart, *History of the Third Infantry Division in World War II* (Washington, 1947), 95.

25. Biddle, *Artist at War*, 207–208.

26. EFM stands for Expeditionary Forces Message. Introduced to British and later American troops in World War I, EFM offered canned messages at a reduced rate. The sender could select up to three stock phrases or sentences, each of which had a code number. The numbers were then transmitted. On the receiving end, the message was translated and sent on to the recipient by mail rather than by messenger.

27. Biddle, *Artist at War*, 206.

28. McFarland, *Fifteenth Regiment*, 101–102.

29. Biddle, *Artist at War*, 212–213.

30. *Danville Register*, November 12, 1943.

31. Biddle, *Artist at War*, 219.

32. This is obviously a different Mignano from the one through which the battalion passed a month and a half earlier.

33. Richard Tregaskis, *Invasion Diary* (New York, 1944), 192–193.

34. Biddle, *Artist at War*, 229–230.

35. K. R. Greenfield, R. R. Palmer, and B. I. Wiley, *The Army Ground Forces: The Organization of Ground Combat Troops* (Washington, 1947), 483n.

36. Biddle, *Artist at War*, 238.

CHAPTER 11. ITALIAN INTERLUDE

1. Mrs. J. D. P. is Mrs. Joseph Dorch Patch, wife of the major general who commanded the Eightieth Division when Dad was with it at Camp Forrest in the summer of 1942.

2. The "famous spot" is the isle of Capri, which lies just off Sorrento. Dad is probably referring to Axel Munthe's villa, San Michele, built there in 1896, and to his book, *The Story of San Michele*, published in 1929.

3. It is apparently the only game Ohio State remembers as well. In the write-up of the 1943 football season in the athletic department archives on the Internet, the only game mentioned is the Illinois game. No mention that the week after the Illinois game, Ohio State went to Ann Arbor and was pounded by Michigan 45–7. Michigan's team was "Navy-Marine studded," including Elroy Hirsch still playing after a brilliant career at Wisconsin. Ohio State, on the other hand, was made up of "scrappy but outmanned youngsters." *New York Times*, November 21, 1943.

4. Details of the game from the *New York Times*, November 14, 1943.

5. In his senior year, Homer attempted and made all of Ohio State's points after touchdown.

6. Edmund Ball, *Staff Officer with the Fifth Army* (New York, 1958), 245. Oddly, Ball does not mention the magnificent palace that was at the center of Fifth Army Headquarters at Caserta.

7. Lieutenant Colonel Joseph B. Crawford, at various times Third Battalion commanding officer and regimental executive officer, won a Distinguished Service Cross for his action in French Morocco in November 1942 and a Silver Star for action in Sicily in July 1943. Crawford and Colonel Darby were members of the class of 1933 at West Point.

8. U.S. Army, Fifth Army, *Fifth Army History, Part IV: Cassino to Anzio* (Florence, 1945), 59.

9. Man O' War (1917–1947) was a famed race horse and sire. Papa Dionne was the father of the famed Dionne quintuplets, born May 28, 1934.

10. Front Royal was the site of "Druid Hill," the lovely home of old family friends General Beverly and Louise Browne. From the fruits of the general's orchard came an especially tasty applejack.

11. This erstwhile grand old hotel on Peachtree Street was replaced by the Westin Peachtree Plaza. Dad is recalling Mom's visit when he was at Fort Benning in early 1941.

CHAPTER 12. ANZIO: THE CAN-DOS

1. Mark W. Clark, Diary, January 2, 1944.

2. Ibid., January 8, 1944.

3. Paul Fussell, *Wartime* (Oxford, 1989), 49–50.

4. Mark W. Clark, *Calculated Risk* (New York, 1950), 254.

5. U.S. Army, Fifth Army, *Fifth Army History, Part IV: Cassino to Anzio* (Florence, 1945), 196.

6. Martin Blumenson, *Salerno to Cassino* (Washington, 1969), 356.

7. Ibid.; Blumenson, *Anzio: The Gamble That Failed* (Philadelphia, 1963), 60–62.

8. Robert Wallace, *The Italian Campaign* (Alexandria, 1978), 130–131.

9. Clark, Diary, January 19, 1944.

10. Ibid., January 18, 1944.

11. Samuel Eliot Morison, *Sicily-Salerno-Anzio* (Edison, N.J., 2001), 333.

12. Blumenson, *Salerno to Cassino*, 357.

13. Morison, *Sicily-Salerno-Anzio*, 334.

14. Donald G. Taggart, *History of the Third Infantry Division in World War II* (Washington, 1947), 105.

15. Morison, *Sicily-Salerno-Anzio*, 341.

16. Blumenson, *Salerno to Cassino*, 358.

17. Quoted in Winston S. Churchill, *Closing the Ring* (Boston, 1951), 482.

18. Robert C. McFarland, ed., *The History of the Fifteenth Regiment in World War II* (Boise, 1990), 119–120.

19. John Bowditch, *Anzio Beachhead* (Washington, 1989), 21–22.

20. Wynford Vaughan-Thomas, *Anzio* (New York, 1961), 70–71.

21. Ibid., 71; Fred Sheehan, *Anzio: Epic of Bravery* (Norman, 1994), 73.

22. Sheehan, *Anzio*, 78.

23. Bowditch, *Anzio Beachhead*, 29–30.

24. Aides' diaries, Truscott Papers, Box 18, George C. Marshall Foundation, Lexington, Va.

25. McFarland, *Fifteenth Regiment*, 126.

26. Bowditch, *Anzio Beachhead*, 35–36.

27. In the library at the United States Military Academy Special Collections, West Point, N.Y.

28. *Time*, February 7, 1944.

29. Ibid.

30. Will Lang's Notebooks, USMA Library Special Collections.

31. Taggart, *Third Infantry Division*, 126.

32. Fussell, *Wartime*, 274.

33. Sheehan, *Anzio*, 101. Sheehan goes on to say that the pilot was shot down and subsequently treated at the hospital he had just bombed.

34. Aides' Diaries, Truscott Papers, Box 18.

35. Third Infantry Division, General Order 27, dated 20 February 1944. Copy in the possession of the author.

36. N. R. Howard, "Bottle-Cap Jack," *Cleveland News*, February 14, 1944.

37. *Time*, February 14, 1943.

38. Army War College Senior Officers Debriefing Program. Conversation between General Mark Clark and LTC Forrest S. Rittgers Jr. at Charleston, SC. Oct 27, 1972, U.S. Army Military History Institute, Carlisle Barracks, Pa. Later Clark would pin on O'Daniel's third star in Korea.

39. Taggart, *Third Infantry Division*, 130.

40. Truscott Papers, Box 7, Folder 2.

41. Bowditch, *Anzio Beachhead*, 89.

42. Ibid., 87–89.

43. Taggart, *Third Infantry Division*, 133.

44. Ibid., 138.

45. Hugh A. Scott, *The Blue and White Devils: A Personal Memoir and History of the Third Infantry Division in World War II* (Nashville, 1984), 109.

46. Taggart, *Third Infantry Division*, 479, says that Dad became executive officer on March 10, but Dad put the date five days earlier.

47. Quoted from the *Carterville Tribune-News*, n.d.

48. Ibid., April 13, 1944.

CHAPTER 13. ANZIO: THE WILLING AND ABLES

1. Nathan W. White, *From Fedala to Berchtesgaden: A History of the Seventh United States Infantry in World War II* (Providence, 1947), 97. See also W. H.

O'Mohundro, "From Mules to Missiles," unpublished manuscript, U.S. Army Military History Institute, Carlisle Barracks, Pa., 48.

2. Donald W. Taggart, *History of the Third Infantry Division in World War II* (Washington, 1947), 447.

3. Unit Journal, Seventh Infantry–13 March 1944, National Archives and Records Administration (NARA), College Park, Md.13. Record Group 407: 303 – INF (7) – 0.7.

4. L. K. Truscott, letter to Lt. Gen. L. J. McNair dated 28 June 1944. Copy given to the Toffey family by Mrs. McNair.

5. White, *From Fedala to Berchtesgaden*, vii.

6. In his *The Violent Decade*, published in 1989, Gervasi says he was with the Second Battalion of the Seventh Infantry, but later identifies the regimental commander as General William Eagles, who acted as commanding officer of the Fifteenth from October 6 to October 20. He also mentions a Captain Andrew Leaming of Headquarters Company. Leaming, too, was with the Fifteenth, not the Seventh. Biddle, in *Artist at War*, confirms that Gervasi was with him at the Fifteenth.

7. The actual title of Mauldin's book, published in Italy in 1944, is *Mud, Mules and Mountains*.

8. Colonel Charles Johnson, Division Chief of Staff, who had attended the farewell party when Dad left the Fifteenth a couple of weeks earlier.

9. Major General Charles Hartwell Bonesteel, USMA '08. Bonesteel had served with Jack Senior in the Philippines, on the Mexican border, and in the office of the Chief of Infantry in Washington. He had been commanding U.S. forces in Iceland when in the fall of 1943 when he was appointed commandant of the Infantry School at Fort Benning, Georgia.

10. White, *From Fedala to Berchtesgaden*, 98. The idea of a special force designated for battle-patrol work was expressed in the "Comments and Lessons Learned" section of a Fifteenth Infantry report dated 6 March 1944 and signed by Lieutenant Colonel Roy E. Moore; NARA, Record Group 407: 303 – INF (15) – 0.4. See also Robert C. McFarland, *The History of the Fifteenth Regiment in World War II* (Boise, 1990), 128. While White credits Dad with the implementing the idea in the Seventh, neither Fifteenth source credits anyone with the idea.

11. Fifteenth Infantry, *Summary of Operations, March 1944*, NARA, Record Group 407: 303 – INF (15) – 0.4. Also Report of Operations, Seventh Infantry, March 1944, NARA. Record Group 407: 303 – INF (7) – 0.4.

12. White, *From Fedala to Berchtesgaden*, 296–297.

13. HQ, Third Infantry Division, AGC L/O 205, 5 April 1944. Copy given to the author by General Ramsey, March 19, 2000.

14. Dad is referring to the eruptions that began on March 18, 1944. Where he saw the destruction he describes is not clear. He does not mention the lava flows that destroyed several towns in the vicinity of Vesuvius.

15. His Rangers having been virtually wiped out, Colonel Darby had been given command of the 179th Infantry, another badly shot-up unit whose morale was sagging. Then he returned to the States to supervise Ranger training. In March 1945 he returned to Italy and was made assistant division commander of the Tenth Mountain Division. He was killed in action April 30, two days before the surrender of all German forces in Italy.

16. Report of Operations, Seventh Infantry, April 1944; NARA, Record Group 407: 303 – INF (7) – 0.4.

17. White, *From Fedala to Berchtesgaden*, 288.

18. Report of Operations May 1944, Seventh Infantry, 1; NARA, Record Group 407: 303 – INF (7) – 0.4.

19. Taggart, *Third Infantry Division*, 148.

20. Ibid., 142.

21. Lucian K. Truscott, *Command Missions* (New York, 1954), 362.

22. Mark W. Clark, *Calculated Risk* (New York, 1950), 325.

23. Bill Harr, *Combat Boots* (New York, 1952), 88–94.

24. Dad's letter to Mrs. Kennedy is quoted in its entirety in the *Cartersville Tribune*, n.d. A clipping of the article was sent to Mom by Mrs. Kennedy in a letter dated August 4, 1944.

CHAPTER 14. THE ROADS TO ROME

1. Highway 6 is the modern designation of the ancient Via Casilina, over which countless Roman legions had trod centuries ago. Despite its long and rich history as a military road, it seems to lack the cachet of the Via Appia, Highway 7. See F. Sheehan, *Anzio: Epic of Bravery* (New York, 1994), 24–25.

2. E. F. Fisher, Jr. *Cassino to the Alps* (New York, 1989), 105–106.

3. Winston S. Churchill, *Closing the Ring* (Boston, 1951), 662.

4. Clark Diary, May 8, 1944.

5. W. H. O'Mohundro, "From Mules to Missiles," unpub. Ms. U.S. Army Military History Institute, Carlisle Barracks, Pa., 56.

6. Clark Diary, May 18, 1944.

7. Fisher, *Cassino to the Alps*, 117–118.

8. Army War College Senior Officers Oral History Program, S. T. Matthews, Notes of Interview with General Truscott, April 3, 1948. U.S. Army Military History Institute, Carlisle Barracks, Pa.

9. Nathan W. White, *From Fedala to Berchtesgaden* (1947), 111.

10. D. G. Taggart, *History of the Third Infantry Division in World War II* (Washington, 1947), 149.

11. Ibid.

12. Clark Diary, May 21, 1944. Berlin's "The Fifth Army's Where My Heart Is" was added to the overseas version of *This Is the Army*. The chorus, which runs, "Not the First, not the Second, not the Third, not the Fourth, / But the Fifth Army's where my heart is," suggests that the song was not one of Mr. Berlin's best. But the staff and the rear-area troops who got to hear it probably loved it.

13. John Bowditch, *Anzio Beachhead* (Washington, 1947), 117.

14. Fisher, *Cassino to the Alps*, 133.

15. White, *From Fedala to Berchtesgaden*, 113.

16. Ibid. 117.

17. Fisher, *Cassino to the Alps*, 163.

18. Sheehan, *Anzio*, 200.

19. Fisher, *Cassino to the Alps*, 165; Clark diaries, May 25, 1944.

20. Ibid; also Matthews, interview with General Truscott.

21. Lucian K. Truscott, *Command Missions* (New York, 1959), 375–376.

22. Fisher, *Cassino to the Alps*, 166.

23. *Fifth Army History* (Florence, 1947), 5:192.

24. Fisher, *Cassino to the Alps*, 167–168. The seventy casualties in the Second Battalion, Fifteenth Infantry, are from White, *From Fedala to Berchtesgaden*, 118.

25. Fisher, *Cassino to the Alps*, 168.

26. Sheehan, *Anzio*, 206.

27. Taggart, *Third Infantry*, 176.

28. Letter dated June 15, 1944. Truscott Papers, Box 1, Folder 9, George C. Marshall Library.

29. *Fifth Army History*, 5:193.

30. Report of Operations, 3rd Infantry Division, June 1944, National Archives and Records Administration (NARA), College Park, Md. Record Group 407: 303 – 2.1.

31. Fisher, *Cassino to the Alps*, 195.

32. White, *From Fedala to Berchtesgaden*, 121.

33. These and subsequent messages from *Seventh Infantry Unit Journal* (June 2–3, 1944), 7–8. NARA Record Group 407: 303 – INF (7) – 0.7.

34. Clark Diary, June 3, 1944.

35. I. L. Valenti, *Combat Medic* (Tanentum, 1998), 52–53.

36. Report of Operations, Seventh Infantry, June 1944, 1. NARA Record Group 407: 303 – INF (7) – 0.7.

CHAPTER 15. THE PATHS OF GLORY

1. *Ohio State Journal*, May 24, 1944.

2. Ibid., June 3, 1944.

3. Ibid.

4. Sha-Te-Yah-Ron-Ya, a Wyandot chief, was called "Leatherlips" by the Whites because he never broke a promise. He was executed in 1810 on Tecumseh's order for being too friendly with the Whites.

5. *Ohio State Journal*, June 5, 1944.

6. R. H. Adelman and George Walton, *Rome Fell Today* (Boston, 1968), 260.

7. Nathan W. White, *From Fedala to Berchtesgaden*, 1947, p. 124.

8. *Logistics in World War II: Final Report of the Army Service Forces* (Washington, 1948), 111–112.

9. Russell Cloer, "Infantry Replacement: The Story of My Three Years as an Infantry Officer in World War II," unpublished manuscript, 1998, 81–82. Copy on file at the USAMHI, Carlisle, Pa.

10. Isadore Valenti, *Combat Medic* (Tanentum, Pa., 1998), 54–55.

11. White, *From Fedala to Berchtesgaden*, 121.

12. George Biddle, *An American Artist's Story* (Boston, 1939). The copy Colonel Manhart returned bears the inscription, "To Jack Toffey—For the pleasant times we have had together and hoping that he and his staff won't forget me entirely. George Biddle—November, 1943."

13. George Biddle, *George Biddle's War Drawings* (New York, 1944), 2.

14. General McNair was killed less than a month after writing this note. He had again gone overseas, this time to Normandy, to see in combat the men for whose training in the States he was responsible. He was killed when American bombers dropped their loads short of their targets. Two weeks later his son Douglas, a major serving as chief of staff of the Seventy-seventh Division in the Pacific, was killed in action. About the time that General McNair was killed, "Paddy" Flint was killed in action in France when he stuck his head up and a German put a bullet through it. Both General McNair and Colonel Flint were buried in France on July 26. Wrote General Patton in his *War as I Knew It*, "Paddy would have

been pleased with his funeral. We had a special coffin made for him and he was carried to his grave on a mechanized cavalry half-track. He had an Army Commander, three Corps Commanders, an Army Chief of Staff and a Deputy Chief of Staff and all the cavalrymen around headquarters for his pallbearers. General McNair's funeral, on the other hand, was, for security reasons, a smaller affair. Only Bradley, [Courtney] Hodges, myself, [MG E. R.] Quesada, and his personal aide were present" (95).

15. Shellabarger caused a bit of a stir when he wrote such historical novels as *Captain from Castile* and *Prince of Foxes*, both of which became movies starring Tyrone Power. Shellabarger's son was killed late in the war.

16. On September 29, 1948, Dad's remains were permanently buried in Plot J, Row 4, Grave 25.

17. Bill Mauldin, *The Brass Ring* (New York, 1971), 272.

18. Colonel Louis V. Hightower, commanding First Armored Regiment, First Armored Division, was wounded on June 6, 1944, when the tank on top of which he was riding was struck by antitank fire. See General Orders # 79, Headquarters, First Armored Division, 16 August 1944, USMA Library Special Collections.

19. Those unfamiliar with variations of the military imperative should realize that General Clark's "wish" at the beginning of the sentence is in fact a command. He is telling General Gruenther to "have someone prepare a memorandum."

20. Mark Clark Papers, Box 3, Folder 7, The Citadel Archives and Museum, Charleston, South Carolina.

EPILOGUE

1. Background on Robert Bates from the 1949 *Pean*, yearbook of the Phillips Exeter Academy; Phillips Exeter *Bulletin* 43, no. 1 (Autumn 1946) and 98, no. 3 (Spring 2003); and several conversations with Bates himself.

SOURCES

BOOKS

Adelman, R. H., and George Walton. *Rome Fell Today*. Boston: Little, Brown, 1969.

Ambrose, Stephen E. *The Victors*. New York: Simon & Schuster, 1998.

Anderson, Charles R. *Algeria—French Morocco*. Washington, D.C.: Center of Military History, n.d.

———. *Tunisia*. Washington: Center of Military History, n.d.

Astor, Gerard. *The Greatest War*. Novato, Calif.: Presidio, 1999.

Atkinson, Rick. *An Army at Dawn*. New York: Henry Holt, 2002.

Ball, Edmund F. *Staff Officer with the Fifth Army*. New York: Exposition Press, 1958.

Bailey, Leslie W. *Through Hell and High Water*. New York: Vantage, 1994.

Belden, Jack. *Still Time to Die*. Philadelphia: Blakiston, 1944.

Biddle, George. *Artist at War*. New York: Viking, 1944.

———. *George Biddle's War Drawings*. New York: Hyperion, 1944.

Birtle, Andrew J. *Sicily*. Washington, D.C.: Center of Military History, n.d.

Blumenson, Martin. *Anzio: The Gamble That Failed*. Philadelphia: Lippincott, 1963.

———. *Patton: The Man Behind the Legend, 1885–1945*. New York: William Morrow, 1985.

———. *The Patton Papers, 1940–1945*. Boston: Houghton Mifflin, 1974.

———. *Salerno to Cassino*. Washington, D.C.: Center of Military History, 1969.

Bowditch, John. *Anzio Beachhead*. Washington, D.C.: Center of Military History, 1990.

Bradley, Omar N. *A Soldier's Story*. New York: Henry Holt, 1951.

Bradley, Omar N., and Clay Blair. *A General's Life*. New York: Simon & Schuster, 1983.

Brokaw, Tom. *The Greatest Generation*. New York: Random House, 1998.

Center of Military History. *From the Volturno to the Winter Line*. Washington,
D.C.: Center of Military History, 1990.

———. *Salerno: Military Operations from the Beachhead to the Volturno*.
Washington, D.C: Center of Military History, 1990.

———. *The War in the Mediterranean: A World War II Pictorial History*.
Washington, D.C.: Brassey's, 1998.

Charles, Ronald W. *Troopships of World War II*. Washington, D.C.: Army
Transportation Association, 1947.

Churchill, Winston S. *Closing the Ring*. Boston: Houghton Mifflin, 1951.

Clark, Mark W. *Calculated Risk*. New York: Harper, 1950.

Curwen, H. Darcy, ed. *Exeter Remembered*. Exeter, N.H.: The Trustees of Phillips
Exeter Academy, 1965.

Darby, William O., and William Baumer. *Darby's Rangers: We Led the Way*. San
Rafael, Calif.: Presidio, 1980.

D'Este, Carlo. *Bitter Victory*. New York: Dutton, 1988.

———. *Fatal Decision*. New York: HarperCollins, 1991.

Director, Service, Supply, Procurement; War Dept. GS. *Logistics in World War II*.
Washington, D.C.: Center of Military History, 1948.

Fisher, E. F. *Cassino to the Alps*. Washington, D.C.: Center of Military History,
1993.

Freeman, Douglas Southall. *Lee's Lieutenants*, vol. 1. New York: Scribner's, 1944.

Fussell, Paul. *Wartime*. Oxford: Oxford University Press, 1969.

Gabel, Christopher R. *The U. S. Army GHQ Maneuvers of 1941*. Washington,
D.C.: Center of Military History, 1992.

Garland, A., and H. M. Smyth. *Sicily and the Surrender of Italy*. Washington, D.C.:
Center of Military History, 2002.

Gervasi, Frank. *The Violent Decade*. New York: Norton, 1989.

Goodwin, Doris Kearns. *No Ordinary Time*. New York: Simon & Schuster, 1995.

Greene, Bob. *Once Upon a Town*. New York: HarperCollins, 2002.

Greenfield, K. R., ed. *Command Decisions*. Washington, D.C.: Center of Military
History, 1987.

Greenfield, K. R., R. R. Palmer, and B. I. Wiley. *The Army Ground Forces: The
Organization of Ground Combat Troops*. Washington, D.C.: Historical Division,
Department of the Army, 1947.

Harmetz, Aljean. *Round Up the Usual Suspects*. New York: Hyperion, 1992.

Harr, Bill. *Combat Boots*. New York: Exposition, 1952.

Hines, Duncan. *Adventures in Good Eating*. 8th ed. Bowling Green, Ky.:
Adventures in Good Eating, 1941.

Howe, George. *Northwest Africa: Seizing the Initiative in the West*. Washington, D.C.: Center of Military History, 1957.

Howze, Hamilton H. *A Cavalryman's Story*. Washington, D.C.: Smithsonian Institution Press, 1996.

Hoyt, Edwin P. *Backwater War: The Allied Campaign in Italy, 1943–1945*. Westport, Conn.: Praeger, 2002.

———. *The GI's War: American Soldiers in Europe During World War II*. New York: Da Capo, 1988.

Isabella, Lucio. *OK Boy: A Child's War Diary*. Privately printed, 2003.

Jackson, W. G. F. *The Battle for Italy*. New York: Harper & Row, 1967.

Kahn, E. J., Jr. *McNair, Educator of an Army*. Washington, D.C.: Infantry Journal, 1945.

Kelly, Orr. *Meeting the Fox*. New York: John Wiley & Sons, 2002.

King, Michael J. *William O. Darby: A Military Biography*. Hamden, Conn.: Archon, 1981.

Kingston, Donald M. *Forgotten Summers*. San Francisco: Two Decades, 1995.

Kurzman, Dan. *The Race for Rome*. New York: Doubleday, 1975.

Langer, William, and Everett Gleason. *The Undeclared War, 1940–1941*. Gloucester, Mass.: Peter Smith, 1968.

Laurie, Clayton. *Anzio*. Washington, D.C.: Center of Military History, n.d.

Liddell-Hart, B. H., ed. *The Rommel Papers*. New York: Harcourt, Brace, 1953.

Lord, Walter. *The Miracle of Dunkirk*. New York: Viking, 1982.

Manchester, William. *American Caesar: Douglas MacArthur, 1880–1964*. Boston: Little, Brown, 1978.

Mauldin, Bill. *The Brass Ring*. New York: Norton, 1971.

———. *Mud, Mules, and Mountains*. Privately printed, 1944.

———. *Up Front*. New York: Norton, 1945.

McFarland, Robert C., ed. *The History of the Fifteenth Regiment in World War II*. Boise: Glenn Rathbun, 1990.

McPherson, Milton. *The Ninety-Day Wonders*. Ft. Benning, Ga.: USAOCSAA, 2001.

Minear, Richard H. *Dr. Seuss Goes to War*. New York: New Press, 1999.

Mittelman, Joseph B. *Eight Stars to Victory*. Washington, D.C.: Ninth Infantry Division Association, 1948.

Moorehead, Alan. *Montgomery: A Biography*. New York: Coward McCann, 1946.

Morison, Samuel Eliot. *Operations in North African Waters October 1942–June 1943*. Edison, N.J.: Castle, 2001.

———. *Sicily, Salerno, Anzio*. Edison, N.J.: Castle, 2001.

Moss, James A. *Manual of Military Training*. Menasha, Wis.: George Banta, 1917.

Mowat, Farley. *And No Birds Sang*. Toronto: Little, Brown, 1979.

Myrer, Anton. *Once an Eagle*. Carlisle, Pa.: Army War College Foundation Press, 1997.

O'Connor, Richard. *Black Jack Pershing*. New York: Doubleday, 1961.

Phillips, Henry G. *The Making of a Professional*. Westport, Conn.: Greenwood, 2000.

Porter Sargent Staff. *Handbook of Independent Schools*. Boston: Porter Sargent, 1924.

Pyle, Ernie. *Brave Men*. New York: Holt, 1944.

———. *Here Is Your War*. New York: Holt, 1944.

———. *Home Country*. New York: William Sloane, 1947.

Reichler, Joseph L., ed. *The Baseball Encyclopedia*. 6th ed. New York: Macmillan, 1985.

Reynolds, Quentin. *The Curtain Rises*. New York: Random House, 1944.

Rossi, Francesco, and Silvano Casaldi. *Quei Giorni a Nettuno / Those Days at Nettuno, January 22–May 26*. Nettuno, Italy: Edizioni Abete, 1989.

Saltzman, Charles E. *Emigrant from Zamboanga*. Privately printed, 1992.

Scott, Hugh A. *The Blue and White Devils: A Personal Memoir and History of the Third Infantry Division in World War II*. Nashville, Tenn.: Battery Press, 1984.

Semmes, Harry H. *Portrait of Patton*. New York: Appleton-Century-Crofts, 1955.

Sheehan, Fred. *Anzio: Epic of Bravery*. Norman: University of Oklahoma Press, 1994.

Smith, Kenneth R. *Naples-Foggia*. Washington, D.C.: Center of Military History, n.d.

Smith, Richard Norton. *The Colonel: The Life and Legend of Robert R. McCormick, 1880–1955*. New York: Houghton Mifflin, 1997.

Starr, Lester G. *From Salerno to the Alps*. Washington, D.C.: Infantry Journal, 1948.

Stevenson, Eleanor, and Pete Martin. *I Knew Your Soldier*. New York: Penguin, 1945.

Taggart, Donald G., ed. *History of the Third Infantry Division in World War II*. Washington, D.C.: Infantry Journal, 1947.

Tolstoy, Leo. *War and Peace*. Chicago: University of Chicago Press, 1952.

Tregaskis, Richard. *Invasion Diary*. New York: Random House, 1944.

Trevelyan, Raleigh. *The Fortress*. London: Collins, 1956.

———. *Rome '44*. London: Coronet, 1983.

Truscott, Lucian K., Jr. *Command Missions*. New York: Dutton, 1990.

Truscott, Lucian K., IV. *Rules of the Road*. New York: Avalon, 1990.

U.S. Army. *Fifth Army History, Part IV: Cassino and Anzio*. Florence, Italy, 1945.

Valenti, Isadore. *Combat Medic*. Tanentum, Pa.: Word Association, 1998.

Vaughan-Thomas, Wynford. *Anzio*. New York: Holt, Rinehart & Winston, 1961.

Vandiver, Frank. *Illustrious Americans: John J. Pershing*. Morristown, N.J.: Silver Burdett, 1967.

Von Luck, Hans. *Panzer Commander*. New York: Praeger, 1989.

Wallace, Robert, et al. *The Italian Campaign*. Alexandria, Va.: Time-Life, 1978.

Wellard, James. *General George S. Patton: Man Under Mars*. New York: Dodd Mead, 1946.

White, Nathan W. *From Fedala to Berchtesgaden: A History of the Seventh United States Infantry in World War II*. Privately printed, 1947.

Wilmot, Chester. *The Struggle for Europe*. New York: Harper, 1952.

Wright, Mike. *What They Didn't Teach You About World War II*. Novato, Calif.: Presidio, 1998.

COLLECTIONS

Archives and Museum, The Citadel, Charleston, S.C. Mark Clark Papers, Fifth Army History: General Clark's diaries, memoranda, and correspondence.

Donovan Research Library, U.S. Army Infantry School, Fort Benning, Ga.: Advanced Officers Course Monographs.

Ernie Pyle State Historical Site, Dana, Ind.: Pyle's dispatches from Sicily.

George C. Marshall Foundation Library, Lexington, Va.: General Truscott's Correspondence, aides' diaries, orders, memoranda.

National Archives and Records Administration, College Park, Md. Operations reports, unit journals, and miscellaneous documents pertaining to the 7th, 15th, 39th and 60th Infantry Regiments, 3rd and 9th Infantry Divisions.

National Personnel Records Center (NPRC), St. Louis, Mo.: Morning reports, 39th Infantry Regiment.

U.S. Army Center of Military History, Washington, D.C.: Generals' biographies; unit histories.

U.S. Army Human Resources Command, Alexandria, Va.: Individual Deceased Personnel Files.

U.S. Army Military History Institute (USAMHI), Carlisle, Pa.: Senior Officer Oral Histories; personal memoirs; unit histories.

Special Collections and Archives, United States Military Academy Library (USMA), West Point, N.Y.: Unpublished manuscripts; Will Lang notebooks; officers' biographies, obituaries, memoirs.

MANUSCRIPTS

Anonymous. "Keeping Faith" (tribute to Colonel Harry Flint). USMA Library.

Cloer, Russell. "Infantry Replacement: The Story of My Three Years as an Infantry Officer in World War II." USAMHI.

Dickson, Benjamin. "A G-2 Journal: Algiers to the Elbe." USMA Library.

Kampstaffel Veterans. "Der Kampf um den Maknassy-Pass." USAMHI.

Lang, Rudolph. "Report of the Fighting of *Kampfgruppe Lang* in Tunisia." USAMHI.

Lusk, Edwin. "Personal Experience in the Battle of Maknassy in Tunisia." Unpublished.

O'Mohundro, Wiley H. "From Mules to Missiles." USAMHI.

Senior Officers Oral History Program Project 78–4: Gen. William C. Westmoreland Interview, 1978.

Thornton, Wilfred. "One Man's View of World War II." USAMHI.

NEWSPAPERS

Cartersville Tribune, November 13, 1944

Chicago Sunday Tribune, March 29, 1936

Cincinnati Enquirer, June 12, 1938; August 3, 1940

Cincinnati Times Star, June 29, 1944

Cleveland News, August 30, 1943; February 14 and June 27, 1944

Columbus Citizen, December 29, 1929; August 18, 1930; April 3 and June 26, 1944

Columbus Dispatch, June 12 and August 17, 1930; n. d., 1943; June 26, 1944

Danville Register, November 12, 1943

Jersey City Journal, November 13, 1934; June 26, 1944

Muskoka Sun, July 5 and 12, 1990

Newark Evening News, July 2 and September 30, 1943; June 26, 1944

New York Evening Post, August 25, 1930, July 3, 1934

New York Times, August 8, September 14 and 21, October 8, 1940; July 17, October 4 and 9, 1941; November 8, 1942; August 5 and November 14, 1943; June 26, 1944

Ohio State Journal, December 29, 1929; August 11 and November 12, 1943; May 24, June 3, 17 and 26, 1944

Philadelphia Inquirer, March 28, 1943

Stars and Stripes, Italian Edition, June 5 and 6, 1944

Syracuse Herald, May 5, 1930

PERIODICALS

The Chakett of Chi Phi, July 1944

Colliers, June 29, 1929

Journal of America's Military Past, Summer 1997

Life, September 15, 1941; June 14, 1943

Newsweek, October 25, 1943

Quarterly Bulletin, Northwestern University School of Medicine, Winter 1950; Summer 1953

Time, February 7 and 14, 1944

World War II, November 1996

VETERANS

These men, veterans of World War II who served in the Third and Ninth Infantry Divisions, have generously shared with me by letter, telephone, or email or in person their recollections of the war and of my father: Merwin (Whitey) Andell, Andrew Balaschak, John N. Boisky, Russell W. Cloer, Aus Wyett Colclasure, Anton Dietrich, Bill Dunn, Wilbert Goldsmith, Wallace B. Hawkins, Richard Kent, Albert Lubrano, Edwin Lusk, Lloyd B. Ramsey, Glenn Rathbun, Siegfried Reinheimer, George Byron Rose, Robert H. Rucker, Jerome Sapiro, Charles Scheffel, H. Price Tucker, Alfredo Vaiani, Isadore L. Valenti, Anthony Varone, William C. Westmoreland, Alphonse Zenka.

INDEX

AAAO, 106, 114, 124–25, 127

Ain-el-Turck, Algeria, 86, 93

Alban Hills, 165, 200, 210, 227

Alexander, Gen. Sir Harold R. L. G.,
    78, 81, 101, 103, 121, 129, 161–62,
    175, 193, 197–98, 205, 242

Allen, Dr. Harvey, 95, 159

Allen, Gen. Terry de la Mesa, x, 107–
    10, 139

Ambrose, Stephen, x

Anzio, ix, xi, 172, 181, 191, 193, 195–
    98, 200, 204, 212, 215, 217–18, 220,
    222, 227, 240, 245–46, 248–49

Arcenio, 14, 45, 112, 117–18, 158, 233

Aridor Company, 2, 20–21, 170

Armistice Day, 9, 73, 146

Baker, Bill, 6

Ballyho, 113

Barclay Hotel, 156, 174

Bates, Robert, 230

Beach, Mr. and Mrs. William N.
    (Uncle Billy), 18, 50, 117–18, 159,
    186, 222–23, 233, 235

Beatrix, Princess, 120

Beazley, Johnny, 53

Bellah, James Warner, 49–50, 77, 96

Bergdorf, Capt. Edward, 222

Berlin, Irving, 202, 249

Biddle, George, xi, 113, 133–43, 145,
    147, 148–49, 152, 158–59, 169–71,

174, 182, 191–93, 195, 210, 212, 219,
    241–44, 250

Bigwin Inn, 119–20, 242

Bizerte, Tunisia, 78, 83, 98, 103, 106,
    127, 180

Blackwood, Ned, 22, 218

Bond, Mr. and Mrs. Henry, 23

Bonesteel, Gen. Charles H., 184, 193,
    247

Bonham, Tiny, 53

Bonner, Barbara, 230

Bonner, Edith, 18, 19, 117, 118

Bonner, Paul, 118, 187

Bonura, Zeke, 96, 179

Borowy, Hank, 53

Boston Bees, 3, 4

Boyle, Hal, 105, 112

Bradley, Gen. Omar, 85, 106, 112, 114,
    115, 122, 130, 139, 239, 240, 242,
    243, 251

Brann, Gen. Donald, 162, 204, 207

Brenner, Olt. Harro, 83

Bridges, Tommy, 25

Brokaw, Tom, x

Brooklyn Dodgers, 4, 33, 107, 112, 132

Brooklyn, New York, 4, 19, 118, 233

Brooklyn, U.S.S., 59

Brooks School, 12

Brown, Capt. Gail, 88

Brown, Paul, 61

Browne, Gen. Beverly, 15

Bunnyhug, 197, 205
Burke-Wadsworth Bill, 7

Camilli, Dolph, 118
Camp A.P. Hill, 27, 29, 40, 55
Camp Avoca, 48–51, 58, 68, 74–75, 77, 89, 94, 129, 149–50, 156–60, 169, 190
Camp Claiborne, Louisiana, 39, 40
Camp Drake Replacement Depot, 231
Camp Forrest, Tennessee, 48, 68, 75, 244
Camp Pike, Arkansas, 12
Canal Winchester, Ohio, 223, 232
Cantigny, 32
Carleton, Col. Donald, 76
Carleton, Donald, 71
Casablanca, French Morocco, 58, 71, 238
Casablanca, 66
Caserta, Italy, 156, 181, 244
Casey, Hugh, 33
Cerami, Sicily, 108, 112
Chandler, Spud, 53, 118, 133
Churchill, Winston S., 7, 54, 58, 71, 129, 161, 197, 242, 245, 248
Cincinnati Reds, 3–6, 22, 24, 25, 28, 33, 42, 53, 77–79, 90, 91, 112, 117, 118, 132, 160, 185, 210, 211
Cincinnati, OH, 3–6, 21–25, 27, 36, 39, 51, 55, 60, 70, 89, 94, 151, 160, 188, 199, 215, 218
Cisterna, Italy, 164–68, 172, 197, 200–5
Clark, Gen. Mark Wayne, x, 24, 25, 40, 52, 58, 71, 121, 122, 129, 130, 139, 146–47, 150, 161–64, 172, 175, 181, 193, 198, 200–2, 204–5, 207, 209, 210, 212, 218, 222, 228, 245, 246, 248, 250, 251
Cloer, Russell, 220

Citizens Military Training Camp (CMTC), 15, 20, 23, 235
Cobb, Ted, 188, 190
Cohen, Dan, 5
Colli Laziali, 161, 162, 164, 207, 225
Columbus Academy, 57, 60, 233
Columbus, Ohio, xiii, 1–3, 7, 12, 18, 22–23, 26, 29, 39, 42–43, 45, 47–49, 55, 60, 67, 70, 89, 95, 96, 105, 113, 116, 118, 131, 136, 144–45, 152, 154, 158, 191–93, 196, 210, 212–13, 215, 224, 225, 226, 229, 230, 232, 233, 236
Columbus Red Birds, 89, 192, 213
Congressional Medal of Honor, x, 30, 52, 126, 141, 191
Connor, Albert, 180
Conway, Col. Theodore J., 95, 238
Cooper, Mort, 53, 132–33, 192
Cooper, Walker, 53
Cornell University, 16, 17, 20, 26, 37, 77, 135, 188, 190
Craig, Gen. Malin, 139
Crawford, Col. Joseph, 156, 177, 212, 219, 244, 245
Crosetti, Frank, 118
Crosley Field, 4, 21, 87, 89, 169, 185, 188
Cross-channel invasion, 24, 101, 121, 161

Danning, Harry, 5
Darby, Col. William, 104, 165, 189, 190, 191, 240, 245, 248
Dawley, Gen. Ernest J., 129
Dean, Dizzy, 4
De Rohan, Col. Frederick J., 24–25, 52, 54–55, 63–64, 80, 88, 113
Derringer, Paul, 24, 25
Dickey, Bill, 4, 53, 118, 133
Dilley, Maj. John, 96, 100, 137, 152, 184

DiMaggio, Joe, 28, 118
Dogface Soldier, The, 186, 187, 192, 199, 202, 206
Doolittle, Lt. Col. James, x
Downey, Morton, 151
Drum, Gen. Hugh, 8, 10, 27, 34, 36, 139

Eagles, Gen. William, 131, 247
Ebbets Field, 118
Eddy, Gen. Manton S., x, 40, 44–45, 51, 52, 54, 69, 73, 75, 95–98, 107, 109, 113, 114–15, 124, 127, 237
EFM, 142, 149, 158, 243
Eisenhower, Gen. Dwight D., x, 40, 58, 62, 78, 106, 121, 124, 127, 222
Exeter. *See* Phillips Exeter Academy

Far East Command, 231
Fayetteville, North Carolina, 53, 55, 67, 215
Fekete, Gene, 61
Fisher, Fred, 46, 48, 80, 184, 237
Fishwick, Dwight, 78, 86, 189
Fitzsimmons, Freddie, 33
Flint, Col. Harry A., 105–10, 124, 127, 131, 137, 192, 241, 250
Fort Benning, Georgia, x, 14, 19, 26, 28, 45, 48, 52, 55, 112, 126, 134, 184, 193, 230, 245, 247
Fort Bragg, North Carolina, 35, 51, 52, 54, 55, 56, 68
Fort Dix, New Jersey, 22–24, 26, 27, 28, 29, 36, 37, 40, 52, 55, 62, 121, 199, 210, 226, 231, 238
Fort Huachuca, Arizona, 106
Fort Knox, Kentucky, 7, 61, 230, 233
Fort Lewis, Washington, 40, 41, 44, 45, 73, 119, 130, 231
Fort Monroe, Virginia, 15, 20
Fort Riley, Kansas, 106

Fort Sheridan, Illinois, 11
Fort Wayne, Michigan, 11, 12, 44
French Morocco, ix, 58, 59, 60, 62, 64–66, 69, 70, 71, 78, 89, 94, 153, 243, 244

Gallipoli, 54, 129, 162
Gatch, Nancy, 89, 95, 98, 131, 140, 144, 151, 152, 194, 198
Geisel, Theodore, 17
Gela, Sicily, 101–2
Gervasi, Frank, 182, 237, 247
Goering, Hermann, 7, 24
Gordon, Joe, 119
Goumiers (Goums), 107, 120, 240–41
Great Gatsby, The, 117
Great Neck, New York, 112–14, 116–17, 118, 131, 150, 153, 158, 176, 211, 223, 232
Groody, Louise, 125–26, 179, 242
Gruenther, Gen. Alfred M., 182, 181, 209, 228, 251

Harley, Chic, 211
Harmon, Capt., 138–39, 143
Hartsville, South Carolina, 34–35, 118
Havens, Benny, 124, 131, 139, 192
Hawkins, Wallace, 84
Hayes, Woody, 233
Henrich, Tommy, 33, 53, 118
Henry Grady Hotel, 159, 245
Herman, Billy, 118
Henry, O., 211
Hershberger, Willard, 1–7, 51, 235
Hewitt, Adm. H. Kent, 58
Higbe, Kirby, 118
Hightower, Col. Louis V., 228, 251
Highway 6 (Via Casilina), 145, 197, 205, 208, 248
Highway 7 (Via Appia), 166, 197, 248

Hill, Sterling, 147, 150, 153, 154, 165, 198

Hines, Duncan, 29, 39, 42, 116, 237

Hitler, Adolph, 7, 28, 32, 22, 55, 65, 66, 71, 74, 82, 93, 101, 103, 125

Honolulu Military Academy, 13, 20

Hopp, Johnny, 53

Horvath, Les, 61

Hotel and Buick Fund, 115

Houston, Lin, 61

Howard, Aurelia Belle (Granny), 3, 7–8, 22, 26, 29, 41, 48, 51, 52, 55, 60, 86, 95, 101, 105, 142, 150, 152, 153, 178, 187, 191, 201–2, 211–15, 233

Howard, Homer, C., 1–3, 7–8, 22, 26, 29, 39, 41, 42, 48, 51–53, 55, 57, 60, 61, 74, 86, 100–1, 105, 112, 116, 150, 152–53, 155, 178, 197, 191, 201, 211–15, 232–33, 244

Howard, Nathaniel, 28, 100, 132, 159, 170–71, 177, 183, 216, 246

Howze, Col. Hamilton, 205, 207

Hubbell, Carl, 33

Huntsville, Ontario, 119

Hurdlebrink, Mike, 180

Ibold, Bill, 23, 94, 104, 127, 150, 156, 159, 188, 190, 219, 239

Indiantown Gap Military Reservation, 27, 40, 55

Iowa Seahawks, 61, 74

Irvin Cobb Hotel, 39, 237

Jackson, Andrew, 181

Jackson, Elbert McGran, 17

Jackson, Gen. T. J. (Stonewall), 57, 79

Jennings, Al, 211

Jobstown, New Jersey, 24, 39

Johnson, Col. Charles, 180

Johnson, S. K., 51

Jolson, Al, 125, 179

Juliana, Princess, 120

Jurgess, Billy, 118

Kammerer, Olivia, 68

Keller, Charlie, 53, 118

Kennedy, Mrs. Pat (Ione), 180, 196, 248

Kent, Capt. Richard, 55, 77, 182, 237

Kent, Mrs. Richard, 55, 237

Kent, Rockwell, 16

Kent School, 232

Kindlarski, Cpl. Jo, 138, 139–40, 171, 212, 219, 222

Kipling, Rudyard, 41–42

Kurowski, Whitey, 53

Lang, Col. Rudolph, 83. 239

Lang, Will, 165, 167–68, 170, 171, 175, 176, 178–79, 182, 188, 246

Lanham, Lt. Martin W., vi, 12–13

Lardner, John, 136, 151, 179, 243

Leatherlips, 211, 250

Licata, Sicily, 101

Liggett, Gen. Hunter, 139

Lincoln General Hospital, 30

Liri Valley, 161

Little Hut in Hoboken, A, 17, 236

Lombardi, Ernie, 4, 6, 118

Lubrano, Albert, 84

Lucas, Gen. John, 130, 161–63, 164, 165, 172

Lusk, Lt. Edwin, 56, 82, 92, 239

MacArthur, Gen. Douglas, x, 54, 139

MacDiarmid, Hugh, 23, 218

Mahoney, Skipper, 39

Maknassy, 80–85, 88, 93, 95, 98, 100, 126, 130, 222, 239

Malvergne, Rene, 65, 71

Mancuso, Gus, 118

Manhart, Col. Ashton, 212, 220–21, 250
Marion, Marty, 53
Marsala, Sicily, 105
Marshall, Gen. George C., x, 28, 52, 121, 127, 228, 243
Marshall, Lt. Jack A., 237
McCarley, Pete, 96, 125
McCormick, Frank, 5, 192
McCormick, Col. Robert, 31–32, 80, 237
McKay, Bonnie and Barry, 23
McKechnie, Bill, 5–6
McNair, Gen. Lesley J., x, 24–25, 28–29, 36, 52, 91, 97, 112, 125–26, 154, 159, 169, 172, 184, 188, 194, 224, 225, 228, 247, 250, 251
Medwick, Joe, 118
Melton, Cliff, 118
Memorial Day 1944, 207; 1945, 227
Messina, Sicily, 101, 103, 107, 111, 114, 115, 121–22
Mexican Border, x, 12, 14, 91, 247
Milder's, 5, 169
Military units
    Armies
        First, 8–9, 34–35
        First (British), 75
        Fifth, 121, 122, 124, 126, 127, 139, 146, 151, 155, 156, 161, 163–65, 168, 181, 193, 196, 197, 198, 202, 203, 209, 212, 218, 221, 239, 244, 245, 249
        Seventh, 101, 102–4, 106, 107, 116, 122, 197, 198, 205
        Eighth (British), 78, 101, 103, 121, 137, 196, 207
        Tenth (German), 197, 198, 201, 205
        Fourteenth (German), 175, 201
    Corps
        II, 78, 78–79, 81, 96, 106, 130, 204, 207
        VI, 129, 130, 164, 172, 173, 184, 188, 196, 197, 200, 203, 207, 209
        French Expeditionary, 207
    Divisions
        First, 12, 31, 32, 80, 107, 132, 133
        First Armored, 80–81, 83, 85, 210, 205, 251
        Third, x, 103, 114, 122, 126–27, 130, 132, 137, 145, 158, 161, 163–65, 166–67, 172, 175, 176, 178, 193, 195, 200–2, 204–7, 230, 231, 243
        Ninth, x, 51, 52, 54, 78, 96, 97, 98, 101, 104, 112, 122, 126, 152, 174
        Thirty-sixth, 122, 129, 130, 147, 163, 181, 200, 225
        Forty-fourth, 3, 8, 19–21, 23, 25, 29, 31, 33, 36, 74
        Forty-fifth, 101, 122, 195
        Eightieth, 45, 48, 68, 156–57, 244
        Eighty-second Airborne, 40, 102, 122
        Eighty-fifth, 207
        Eighty-eighth, 207
        Hermann Goering (German), 102, 165, 166, 206, 207, 225
        Tenth Panzer Grenadier (German), 83
        Fifteenth Panzer Grenadier (German), 105, 108, 111
        Twenty-sixth Panzer Grenadier (German), 166
    First Special Service Force, 200–1, 205, 207
    Regiments
        Combat Command C, 80–81, 83
        Fourth, 12
        Seventh (The Cotton Balers), 11, 44, 127, 165, 180, 181, 183, 186,

187, 188, 191, 193, 194, 201–5, 207–9, 212, 216, 218, 219, 224, 225, 246, 247, 248, 249

Fifteenth (The Can-Dos), 128–34, 138, 144, 146, 148, 151, 152, 163, 166, 168, 172, 176, 182, 191, 203, 205, 208, 219, 222, 243, 247, 249

Twenty-ninth, 19, 26

Thirty-ninth, 40, 52, 96, 98, 103, 104–13, 119, 212, 122, 127, 231, 240, 241, 242

Sixtieth, 52, 54, 56, 58, 62–64, 66, 68, 71, 73, 76, 77, 80, 81, 83, 84, 96, 113, 137, 152, 224, 238, 239

114th, 26, 30, 40, 44

317th, 51

329th, 12

Sixty-ninth Panzer Grenadier (German), 83

Twelfth General hospital, 86, 91, 124, 151, 158, 159

Miller, Eddie, 77

Miss Margaret's Rooming House, 33–36

Mission Inn, 43, 119, 186

Monroe, Col. Thomas A., 131, 243

Montgomery, Gen. Sir Bernard L., 101, 103

Moore, Col. Roy E., 175, 196, 247

Moore, Terry, 53

Morgan, J. P., 16

Mules, 113, 130, 138, 182, 247, 248

Mussolini, Benito, 142, 163

Mussolini Canal, 164, 195

Natchez Trace, 39

Nettuno, Italy, ix, 160, 163, 207, 230, 232

Newsom, Bobo, 24–25, 35, 115, 132

New York Yankees, 4, 28, 33, 53, 69, 118, 132–33, 141, 242

No, No, Nanette, 125, 242

Norfolk, Virginia, 56, 141, 154, 173, 213

Normandy, 122, 198, 212–13, 250

Oakdale, Louisiana, 39

O'Daniel, Gen. John W., 172, 175, 181, 193, 201, 203, 205, 208, 239, 246

Ohio Stadium, 61, 144, 155

Ohio State University, 2, 60–61, 70, 152, 155, 213, 232, 244

Olson, Capt. Arlo, 141

O'Mohundro, Col. Wiley H., 181, 191, 192, 194, 200, 201, 208, 216, 247, 248

Operations

Buffalo, 197–98, 200–1, 202, 205, 206

Crawdad, 197

Diadem, 196

Goalpost, 58, 64, 65, 68, 127, 238

Grasshopper, 197

Husky, 101

Shingle, 161–63, 198

Torch, 58, 101

Turtle, 197

Ott, Mel, 118

Owen, Mickey, 33, 118

Owens, Jesse, 211

Palermo, Sicily, 103, 104, 107, 111, 127, 128, 180

Palestrina, Italy, 208, 209, 217

Pardon My Sarong, 89

Parsons, Walter, 137, 152, 216, 219, 220

Patch, Gen. Joseph D., 48. 244

Patch, Mrs. Joseph D., 150, 159, 244

Patton, Gen. George S., x, 11, 40, 54, 55, 58, 71, 78, 85, 101–3, 106, 107,

114, 115, 122, 139, 162, 235, 237, 238, 240, 243, 250

Paul, Gabe, 5

Pearl Harbor, 36, 40, 98

Pershing, Gen. John J., 8, 12, 14, 235

Peterman, Ivan H. (Cy), 81

Philippine Islands, x, 12, 14, 43, 45, 233, 247

Phillips Exeter Academy, 14–15, 229, 230, 235, 251

Pine Bluffs, Wyoming, 46–47, 48, 80, 119, 185

Pine Camp, New York, 3, 22, 27, 34

"Pines, The," 193, 188, 193–94, 198, 202

Poinsett, Edgar, 25, 199

Polo Grounds, 118

Port Lyautey, French Morocco, 55, 58, 63, 64, 66, 67–68, 69, 71, 76, 171, 200, 224

Powell, Gen. Clifford R., 23–25, 29, 35

Pozzuoli, Italy, 163

Pride of the Yankees, 90, 142

Purple Heart, 196, 215, 225

Pyle, Ernie, 14, 84, 98, 110, 111, 113, 182, 235, 239, 240, 242

Ramsey, Maj. Lloyd B., 188, 190, 193, 198, 203–4, 248

Randazzo, Sicily, 113–14

Rathbun, Capt. Glenn, 193, 204, 209, 217, 220

Raye, Martha, 74–75, 179

Red Bird Stadium, 169, 213

Red Cross, x, 68, 95, 123, 124, 126, 149, 152, 154, 177

Redpath, Robert U., 77–78, 86, 182

Reece, Lt. Benny, 167, 178–80, 196, 218

Reece, Vera, 123–24

Ridgway, Gen. Matthew, 102, 115

Ritter, Col. William, 98, 104–7, 124, 126, 128, 129, 130, 131, 132, 140, 143, 151, 153, 176, 182

Road to Morocco, The, 66, 89

Rodt, Gen. Eberhard, 108, 111

Rome, Italy, ix, 121, 146, 161, 163, 164, 169, 175, 191, 193, 197, 198, 201, 203, 204–5, 209, 210, 212, 213, 214, 216, 218, 220, 222, 233

Rommel, Gen. Erwin, 60, 65, 68, 71, 77, 78, 80, 81, 83, 87

Roosevelt, Franklin D., 7, 8, 9, 22, 28, 32, 62, 71, 133

Roosevelt, Gen. Theodore, 107, 109, 113, 133

Roosevelt, President Theodore, 107

ROTC, 16, 16, 20, 193

Rowe, Schoolboy, 25

Roxbury School, 16

Rucker, Capt. Robert, 84, 92, 95

Ruffing, Red, 53

Russo, Marius, 33

Ruth, Babe, 15, 242

St. Louis Cardinals, 53, 54, 69, 90, 107, 132–33, 185, 192, 213

St. Regis Hotel, 186, 199

Saltzman, Col. Charles, 17, 94, 104, 126, 127, 144, 150, 151, 152, 156, 174, 184, 188, 189, 193, 219, 221, 239

Sapiro, Capt. Jerome, 127, 164, 180

Sarringhaus, Paul, 61

Schofield Barracks, T.H., x, 13, 36

Schwarzkopf, Col. H. Norman, 27, 40

Sebou River, 62, 63, 65

Shellabarger, Dr. Samuel, 226, 251

Sherry Netherland Hotel, 160, 174

Sicily, ix, 71, 78, 99–115, 116, 121, 122, 123, 128, 130, 146, 152, 165, 167, 187, 192, 198, 215, 225, 245

Silver Star, 65, 168, 169, 179, 183, 186, 194, 215, 225, 244
Sip, Mary Elizabeth, 11
Snyder, Col. Arthur, 209, 217, 220
Society Hill, South Carolina, 33–34, 36, 39, 52
Southworth, Billy, 53
Speaks, Oley, 211
Stack, Col. Robert I., 81
Stack, Lt. J. F., 92
Starr, Ray, 90
Station de Sened, Tunisia, 80–81
Stella the Belle of Fedala, 152
Susan B. Anthony, 56
Swain, Lt. Joseph, 110
Sweet Rosie O'Grady, 186–87

Teece, Col. Joseph, 96
Texas, U.S.S., 61–63
Throop, The Rev. Frank, 7
Thurber, James, 211
Toffey, Anne, ix–xiii
    the early years, 1, 3, 20
    army life on the move, 22–55
    letters from Dad, 67–201 *passim*
    aftermath, 211, 214, 222, 225–26, 229
    the later years, 230–34
Toffey, Helen Bonner (Deo), 20, 29, 37, 75, 75, 117, 118, 131, 140, 142, 152, 158, 172, 174, 188, 192–94, 215, 225, 226, 227, 233
Toffey, Helen Howard (Mom)
    meets and marries Dad, the early years, 16–21
    army life on the move, 23–55
    letters from Dad, 56–231 *passim*
    as widow, 214–28
    the later years, 228–34
Toffey, Irene, v, ix, xii, 232, 233
Toffey, John J., I, 11, 29–31

Toffey, Gen. John J. (Jack Senior), 9, 11, 12, 13, 14, 19, 20, 26, 43, 184, 226, 233, 235, 236, 247
Toffey, Lt. Col. John J., Jr. (Dad)
    youth, 11–16
    college, marriage, and civilian employment, 16–21
    stateside duty, 22–55
    first combat, 56–64
    wounded in Tunisia, 80–85
    recuperation, 86–98
    commands a regiment, 104–5
    59 days in the line, 129–48
    the beachhead, 161–96
    killed in action, 208–9, 217–18, 220
Toffey, John J., IV
    rationale, ix–xiii
    the early years, 1–10
    army life on the move; 22–55
    letters from Dad, 67–201 *passim*
    the later years, 228–34
Toffey, Molly, ix
Troina, Sicily, 108–10, 111, 112, 113, 114, 119, 212
Trout, Dizzy, 25
Troy, Hugh, 17
Truscott, Gen. Lucian K., Jr., x, 54, 56, 63, 64, 65, 76, 103, 107, 115, 127, 128, 138, 139, 162, 164, 165, 166, 168, 172–73, 175, 181, 197–99, 202, 204–5, 207, 224, 225, 227–28, 237, 239, 242, 243, 246, 247, 248, 249
Tullahoma, Tennessee, 48–51, 143
Tunisia, ix, 48–51, 143
Turner, Jim, 25
Turner, "Uncle Johnny," 15

Ulio, Gen. James A., 86, 97, 158, 215

Valenti, Sgt. Isadore, 220, 250
Valmontone, Italy, 197, 200, 204–8, 210, 212, 224

Vander Meer, Johnny, 4, 90
Vanderlip, Frank, 94
Volturno River, 131, 133, 136, 144, 146, 173, 182, 222, 243
Von Luck, Hans, 65

Walters, Bucky, 5, 6, 25, 27, 210, 211, 238
Walters, Lt., 27, 71, 238
Ward, Gen. Orlando, 81, 85
Welles, Gideon, 16
Welles, Sumner, 7
Wells College, 16, 17, 232, 236
Werber, Bill, 160
West, Dick, 6
Western Task Force, 61, 69
Westmoreland, Lt. Col. William, 109, 241

Westphal, Gen. Siegfried, 164
West Point (USMA), 11, 12, 17, 41, 117, 122, 225, 245
White, Robert, 93, 95, 130, 140, 142, 152, 199, 219, 238
Wigetman, Lt. Harold, 217
Wilce, Jack, 211
Willis, Bill, 61
Wilson, Jimmy, 6
Witek, Mickey, 118
Wrampelmeier, Mrs. and Mrs. Fred J., 23
Wyoming, Ohio, 2, 21, 46, 88
Wyoming (state), 46, 76, 80, 119, 185

Yankee Stadium, 192
Young, Pvt. Roger, x